The Tough & Tender Caregiver

A Handbook for the Well Spouse

David A. Travland, Ph. D.

and Rhonda Travland

www.SickPartner.com

www.CaregiverSurvival.org

Copyright © 2009 David A. Travland, Ph. D. and Rhonda Travland
All rights reserved.

ISBN: 1-4392-3485-X
ISBN-13: 9781439234853
Library of Congress Control Number: 2009903052

To order additional copies, please contact us.
BookSurge
www.booksurge.com
1-866-308-6235
orders@booksurge.com

Dedication

∂∽◦

To all Five of Our Children,

We hope that each of you will gain an understanding about us. Perhaps, you will achieve insight into our lives as we cared for your other parent. More importantly, we hope you never experience living as a well caregiver to your life partners. Chronic heartache and pain is something no parent wants for their children.
We want you to each enjoy a lifetime filled with love and happiness.

We love you all...

Table of Contents

❧❧

Acknowledgements

❧❧

A special thanks to the *Well Spouse Association* & its members for saving our lives, and to its President, Richard Anderson, for his encouragement.
We appreciate the kind words of our colleague, Terry Weaver, M.P.S., N.H.A., C.M.C., A.C.C.

Thank you to our former spouses for the on-the-job training. We could not have made a contribution to the lives of caregivers without you. We learned a great deal. We wanted nothing more than for you to receive the best care and find your own peace.

Finally, we appreciate the information and editorial assistance of Alan Gadney and Carolyn Porter as we embarked on this publishing journey.

Author Biographies

❧❧

David Travland, Ph.D.

Clinical psychologist and former well spouse. He earned his doctorate from the University of Iowa, including a clinical internship at Yale University. He had a thriving clinical practice and eventually became a pioneer in the business consulting industry. David has maintained a successful reputation as an organizational development business consultant for the past several decades in the Southeast.

❧❧

Rhonda Travland

Geriatric Consultant and former well spouse. She is a graduate from the University of South Florida with an undergraduate degree in gerontology specializing in long-term care administration. For over a decade, she was a licensed nursing home administrator and worked in various professional capacities in the industry. She is currently working on her master's degree in human services and will pursue a specialty in counseling.

❧❧

Together, Dr. David and Rhonda Travland started the Caregiver Survival Institute (CSI). CSI is an organization devoted to assisting caregivers with support and coaching services. Believing that caregivers, especially well spouses, are under-served by society, the medical community and social service organizations, the authors have devoted the remainders of their careers to working for recognition, education and financial support for family caregivers of all types. Caregiving for a loved one takes dedication and devotion. The price paid for caring is often personal bankruptcy, health declines and isolation. Their book offers real support and suggestions, something they had a hard time finding when they were full-time caregivers.

Caregiver Survival Questionnaire

DIRECTIONS: Read the statements and answer YES or NO. Add the total of your YES answers. Your total could be as small as 0, or as large as 22.

_____ As a caregiver, do you ever wake up in the morning and wish you had not?

_____ Are you afraid to admit you are beginning to dislike your ill spouse?

_____Sometimes do you get the urge to run away and never come back?

_____Do you sometimes wish you could become sick or injured so you would have to be hospitalized?

_____Do you often have trouble going to sleep at night?

_____Do you sometimes drink too much alcohol?

_____Do you sometimes yell at your ill spouse?

_____Do you feel that sometimes your ill spouse takes unfair advantage of you?

_____Do you notice that your ill spouse has become indifferent to your comfort?

_____Have your friends disappeared since you have become a caregiver?

_____Are you resentful that your sexual needs are not met?

_____Is your ill spouse jealous when you do something recreational?

_____Have you discovered that you no longer have much to talk about with your ill spouse?

_____Have your children and other relatives stopped visiting your home?

_____Are you eating too much, or too little?

_____Do you have a lot more headaches or other aches and pains lately?

_____Do you have fantasies about having an affair?

_____Do you find yourself depressed or in a bad mood these days?

_____Have you begun to neglect your personal hygiene?

_____Do you find yourself driving more carelessly than before you became a full time caregiver?

_____Are you a primary caregiver because of your wedding vows?

_____When you feel burned out do you feel guilty?

KEY:
0-5: Relatively low level of caregiver stress.
6-10: Moderate stress impact on caregiver, need relief soon.
11-15: Severe stress, immediate action recommended.

16-22: Catastrophic stress, need emergency relief, counseling, or specialized coaching.

Foreword

❧❦

By Richard Anderson, President, Well Spouse Association, April 4, 2009

Spousal caregiving differs from family caregiving in two main respects: sex and money. No other caregivers have intimacy thrown into the mix of the relationship with their loved one, producing deeper and more intense emotions. Secondly, spousal caregivers are far more likely to live in single-income families, since their spouses usually are not able to work, due to chronic illness and/or disability, and therefore often face greater financial hardship and stress than other family caregivers.

As a Well Spouse Association (WSA, http://wellspouse.org) member, and later President of the organization for four years, I have never seen spousal caregiving explored as thoroughly as in this book, *The Tough and Tender Caregiver,* by David and Rhonda Travland. The title refers to the two poles of spousal caregiving.

In places, the book reads like boot camp for spousal caregivers. Vignettes of the authors' experiences before they divorced their respective spouses paint vivid pictures of the "Caregiver Hell" that burnt-out and emotionally-raw spousal caregivers can easily fall into, especially if their ill spouses are negative or in denial about the "elephant in the room:" the chronic illness or disability.

Yet, there is also a tender side to the book—it is an instructive, not a bitter work. For many, caregiving for a spouse is a much more positive experience. It helps so much if both the well spouse and the ill spouse are positive about the illness, and the two partners can communicate. The authors take pains to detail how that communication can take place, and to explain how the relationship between the two can best work.

Along the caregiver journey for the spousal caregiver, losses in intimacy and sex are inevitable. Little or no sex is the unfortunate result for many, as fatigue often robs the ill spouse of their libido. Where other books tend to ignore or gloss over this issue the authors devote a whole chapter to it. They catalog all the possibilities and make it clear there are alternatives, but one thing is for sure, you cannot go back to the way things were before the illness came along.

The realism in *The Tough and Tender Caregiver* squarely puts the ball in the spousal caregivers' court; it's up to them to be proactive, make choices and adapt to the changing situation of the illness, in order to regain balance in their lives. The book reflects the WSA's two mottos, *You are not alone,* and *When one is sick, two need help,* and in the process brings aid to caregivers in their tough and tender lives.

The subtitle of *The Tough and Tender Caregiver* is *A Handbook for the Spousal Caregiver.* This is a book you really need to read in sections—take it up for a while, then put it down and reflect on what you just read, and how it relates to your life. Some, on first reading may find parts in it too strong, or feel a passage does not relate to their personal experience, but I would be willing to bet that if they come back to it later, they'll understand more fully how it all relates to their journey as a spousal caregiver, and find ways in which they could be more proactive about their own emotional and spiritual health, and become better caregivers for themselves, and for their ill spouses.

Introduction

☙❧

This book is a brutally honest call to action. Caregivers of permanently ill or disabled spouses or partners intuitively know they must take care of themselves or they are useless to their spouse who is ill. Unfortunately, the typical advice they receive about caregiving is as dangerous as it is ineffective. They are told to suck it up, hang in there, count your blessings, trust in God, and so forth. However, what they are really saying in ignorance is: *Your caregiving role is a life sentence. There is no light at the end of the tunnel. You are doomed.*

The authors know that this book will challenge conventional wisdoms and individual personal philosophies. It may even make some readers angry at first blush. That is not the purpose. The intention is to offer some realistic advice, suggestions and practical solutions.

Those who volunteer to care for a beloved spouse who has become chronically ill or disabled are heroes, indeed. They deserve the respect and gratitude of extended family and the community at large. However, the very admirable qualities that make them dedicated and self-sacrificing are the reasons they are vulnerable to burnout. They are compassionate to a fault. They give their all at their own expense. It is a crime that they receive ineffective and dangerous advice from those who really do not understand what this kind of caregiving is like. Spousal caregivers deserve better.

The term "spouse" is used throughout this book. The authors were spouses in traditional marriages, but the lessons apply to all permanent partnerships regardless of composition. They refer to "Caregiver Hell" throughout this book. That was their term for what their lives felt like on occasion during their endless days of caring for a sick spouse. It sounds like a harsh view, but caregiving can feel hellish particularly when help seems to be in short supply.

The authors want those dedicated and compassionate individuals to have access to the advice they really need. The knowledge contained in this book can assist a caregiver in making decisions that will benefit not only themselves, but their loved one as well. The ideas in this book may not be popular, nor supported by friends and extended family members. However, we are offering real options. For those readers experiencing Caregiver Hell, it is high time to be honest.

While reading these chapters, we implore the reader to answer these questions realistically. How much more are you willing to do? How much energy do you have left at the end of the day? Why are you sacrificing so much? Is martyrdom what you intended when this road into caregiving began?

Caregivers are supposed to suffer, right? Caregiving is a blessing, a calling. Sacrificing ourselves in the service of a loved one is like following in the footsteps of our most revered prophets. "Caring for loved ones pleases God" is a message we get from our society. It is noble to be a caregiver, so why should anyone complain?

The authors firmly agree with this spirit of caregiving; we did it. However, we would like to make caregiving a whole lot more pleasant and give it staying power. In retrospect, if we could do it over, we would have done it differently, and that is the point of this book. We will not deliver our best care if all we learn about spousal caregiving is:

- It is a blessing
- These duties are part of a Divine Plan
- We are selfish to think about our own needs as a caregiver

This self-sacrificing approach to caregiving is a form of slow suicide. There is no way you are pleasing God when you are yelling at your ill spouse, contemplating withholding medicine, or fantasizing about having an affair. Besides, most everyone understands what suicide means in his or her religious faith; it is not acceptable.

This philosophy of caregiving is similar to the concept of *Tough Love*. Giving in to children when they ask for something harmful to them is not a form of love. Love consists of telling them "No" firmly, and meaning it. Similarly, caregivers who sacrifice their health and thus harm their ill spouse are not displaying love. Telling the ill spouse, "No, I need some time to myself" is far more loving. Martyrdom is not an acceptable form of love. The authors believe that the only way we, as caregivers, can continue to play the role effectively is to stay healthy. A burned out caregiver is a sick caregiver. Without self-care, the caregiver will fail. In addition, it does not help to look for scapegoats, such as; "It is the fault of my spouse's illness that I cannot go out." "It is the disability that keeps me from living." "It is my wife's condition that keeps me exhausted." "My husband won't let anyone else provide his care, he needs me too much."

Furthermore, we have to understand that *we* are completely responsible for our situation, not our wife or husband, and not the disability. We have real choices, and to make them does not mean that we are bad, guilty or less devoted. We need to leave Caregiver Hell and ascend to the elite status of Tough & Tender Caregiver (TTC).

The reader must keep an open mind to consider the "radical" solutions in this book, or there is no help for you in sight. This book is not meant for the ill, dependent recipients of care; those people have a wealth of support systems. They have their doctors, case managers and social workers. Many ill spouses still have friends who visit and express interest in their status. The authors have witnessed sick spouses hold court when visitors come by, telling "enchanting" tales about the trials and tribulations of the disease process. A rare visitor bothers to feign interest in the caregiver by asking them, "How are you holding up?" "How can I help you?" "What do you need?"

This book can be construed as a "how to" book, but it is more. It is also a story about how two spousal caregivers survived in the face of excruciating circumstances. This book is a lifeline for those isolated caregivers who are currently living in unimaginable circumstances, and anticipating a shortened life span because of it. The authors had looked everywhere for definitive answers and found nothing to help them cope effectively with the emotional turmoil a well spouse experiences. Finally, in desperation, they decided to put their own lives first and let the chips fall where they may. It sounded selfish at the time, but they know it was the path to caregiver salvation. Perhaps the final irony of their "selfish" decision is that their ill spouses seem to be doing better, too. Everybody won because the authors became TTCs.

The authors acknowledge that their stories are one-sided; they reflect only the authors' perspective on how it felt to be the well spouse caregiver. There was no attempt made to write a caregiving book from the perspective of their ill spouses; nor was this book meant to be a memoir. The names of individuals in the examples and vignettes have been changed to protect identities. There are also some composite cases cited.

Chapter 1
THE BIRTH OF A NEW CAREGIVER PARADIGM

Our Perspective, Grief and Guilt Management

ॐॐ

Dr. David Travland's Perspective

"Full-time caregiver" became my only identity. After more than ten years, I was not happy about it. Knowing I was nearing my saturation point, I had to stop and reexamine how I got there. I went from independent professional man, productive husband, to part-time caregiver, then to full time nursing assistant. My occupation became nurse's aide without my consent. I was caring for a woman with more ailments than I could manage. Simply stated, she required total assistance.

I let life wash over me. "Full-time" duty coincided with an age that many years before had been designated by me as my "year of retirement." It was a goal I set to look forward to retirement financially secure, healthy and enjoying life. I could not have been more wrong about how my life was turning out.

For me to recapture some of the goals I had for myself and for my wife, I had to examine the decisions I made and what I really wanted going forward. I grew up in a family who did not show affection or support for one another. There was an expectation throughout the members of my family that one was to be independent, mind your own business and never complain. I knew early on that I was alone in the world. I needed to make my way to success without asking for help. My parents divorced when I was about nine, which left me to live full time with my mother and younger sister. In retrospect, as a psychologist, I am now able to understand that my mother was schizophrenic.

Because of the dysfunction in my home, I was starved for companionship and nurturing that could not be taken away from me. In an attempt to meet that need, I married too young to my first wife, Shelley. As much as I thought I love her, I did not possess all of the maturity a marriage required. I was too needy and a little self-centered. The marriage only lasted two difficult years, but I was heartbroken after the demise.

I drowned myself in school and found I was in need of permanent companionship. I was lonely. Kate was available, also recovering from a romance gone astray, and seemed like good wife material. I needed a friend and she was willing to work while I completed the last of my Ph. D. requirements. By most standards, the first 20 years of my marriage to her were uneventful. I was tolerant of her issues and I suppose she was tolerant of mine. I cannot recall a great deal of love or passion, but I was not going to fail at a marriage a second time. By the time I thought we may have been better off divorced, we were raising two children born nine months apart and I knew I was never going to have them raised in a broken home. I was aware that I was recommitting myself to my wedding vows if I stayed with Kate. I was not going to revisit the thoughts that a divorce was an option.

Kate's illnesses and disabilities began almost from the first year of our marriage. Over time, I just accepted ailments as normal. But, my zest for life was waning under the burden of her limitations. I hid my sadness and pain in activities outside of our home, but I never sought companionship in another woman. It took the form of classical music and motorcycle riding.

This book was conceived in pain over the state of my life in my mid-forties. I wrote the original draft of this book when Kate and I were entering our 20th year of marriage, a year I was beginning my orientation to full-time caregiver. The draft was, in retrospect, a quest for answers for my own personal misery. I focused on the lessons I was teaching my psychotherapy patients, thinking these lessons would bring me the same kind of relief they were experiencing. At the time, for some reason, I ignored my own advice, slipping into an *"Acceptable Resignation"* about my life. I retreated into my professional career and allowed my marriage to descend ever further into Caregiver Hell.

During the year of my awakening, I found it necessary to revisit the draft of this book in an effort to discover how my life had gotten so horribly off track. Rather than drive my Harley Davidson into a bridge abutment, I looked around for some kind of support system. In desperation, I stumbled upon the Well Spouse Association. I quickly discovered they had no support groups in my local area. I was so desperate for help I decided to start a group for my own sanity.

Rhonda came to the first group meeting. I listened to her story about being married to a man with premature dementia and who seemed abusive. She was so sad, so poised, so articulate, and so much in crisis that my heart went out to her immediately. I encouraged all participants to talk to each other outside of the support group setting. Since most of us had already been on the Online Well Spouse Forum, emailing each other would be of similar support.

That led to numerous emails between Rhonda and me for the next year. The more dialog I had with Rhonda, the more I realized I had made a mess of my life. Through getting to know her situation, I found the hope and inspiration to start to look backwards to where my life had gotten off track. In trying to help Rhonda, I realized that I had strayed from the sound principles I had worked so hard to write down earlier.

In order to get healthy myself, I had to re-visit these ideas. I was shocked at how many mistakes I had made in my personal life because I had ignored my own advice in so many areas. Rhonda and I both made a good-faith effort to apply the tools in this book to our own troubled marriages. Her efforts inside her marriage to Andy did not succeed in creating a new way of life because of her ex-husband's cognitive limitations and the toxic impact of their social support system.

My efforts led to a divorce because Kate and I had slipped into the habit of blaming me for her physical and emotional limitations. I blindly accepted all of it as my responsibility. She made it clear that she was not willing to participate in any of the required changes we needed to make together to repair our life. Kate did not want outside help to enter our home. I could not do the physical work any longer.

With spouses not able or willing to participate in making change, Rhonda and I, independently of each other, used the tools in this book to make decisions about our own lives. We had to untangle our old paradigms and learn to make the most of the only life we have. Ultimately, Rhonda and Andy were divorced, and I became divorced from Kate.

Rhonda and I are now happily married and believe making these powerful ideas available to everyone could help others find personal fulfillment. Divorce from an ill spouse is not the solution for everyone, but finding the right answers for all concerned parties can be found by following the pathway we outline. We continue to use the relationship strategies in our current marriage with great success. Our path may not be right for everyone, but it was an option that worked for us. There are no guarantees.

❧

Rhonda Travland's Perspective

In my desperate need to find help, I interacted with many people via online support groups. These dedicated people live all over the globe. The online connections became a much larger support system than was available to me locally. I began to depend on the chat rooms to survive my daily life. Being a caregiver to an ill spouse is an isolating experience, and I was not prepared. Upon realizing my life would never be better, I began to dislike every moment of it. When I sought the comfort of friends, they politely reprimanded me for not looking at a bigger picture, "He's not dead, count your blessings. It could be worse." Well-meaning friends and family gave me information on clinical trials, home remedies and names of other doctors. I had simply had enough. I once yelled to a friend, "I do not care if you read that Andy should stand in the corner on his head with a carrot in his ear to rid himself of this disease, I do not want to hear it anymore!"

I was fortunate enough to meet Dr. David Travland when I was at the lowest point in my life. He shared with me his expert advice and visions of how relationships really work. I was indeed blessed to see the information as a path to a happier life. Because of my joy, I wanted David to share the tools that he gave me with other people who are in pain. I wanted others to learn to make better decisions, and save themselves, as I was able to do.

Through understanding how relationships really work, I understood how I got into this situation. I finally understood how to get myself out of a destructive relationship. It was hurting my children, their ill father and me. While I know the words contained in this book are perfect for a suffering "Well" spouse, the lessons can easily be applied by anyone else who is dissatisfied because of the way their lives are unfolding. They will learn why they are finding limited happiness in life, and confused about their relationships. A reader will begin to see why situations seem to keep repeating themselves, and why nothing they do seems to make a difference.

David and I met because he started a local support group via The Well Spouse Association (WSA). Their online forum was something I had joined exactly two years before I met with David and other local well spouses. I was despondent over the numerous and unnamed chronic illnesses which had been plaguing my husband for at least a full decade. I was seeking answers and solace. I needed camaraderie, a place where I could vent about my horrible life and not be judged. David's help gave me permission to absolve myself of guilt, embrace my grief and begin to heal. While it seems unbelievable, even now, that an email to a stranger could change my life, it did.

While I was able to reclaim my life, I was also able to save my children from what would have been a horrible childhood. The unanticipated result for me is that my disabled spouse is now better, too. I fervently believe that making some tough and unpopular decisions about my marriage and my role as a primary caregiver also enhanced his quality of life. While our resolutions are not perfect, there is no denying the fact that each member of my family is now living a better, happier, more productive and peaceful life.

David and I, despite our respective professional training as a psychotherapist and a health care administrator, lost our way. Therefore, it made me wonder how many other people are suffering in their caregiving roles when they are without the small advantages we had in our areas of expertise. If we could feel lost, lonely and defeated when faced with challenges that we should have known how to handle, what chance do others have when faced with these stresses?

It took me years of pain before finding the Well Spouse Association and then only by chance. I searched the internet for information about other people who were living like us. It was hard to come by. David, as a caregiver, was so emotionally beaten by his role that he "forgot" how to survive and use his relationship tools. When Andy, my ex-husband, had unusual medical needs, was abusive, and required long-term care, I "forgot" how to use the health care system and how to survive. We learned how to do this again through the words contained in this book.

I knew David was saving my life long before our relationship developed romantically. Because of David's help and his wisdom regarding relationships, we have created a marriage, professional partnership and friendship, which are everything that I ever dreamed. While we now have the ideal partnership, we had to walk through fire to get here. Because we communicate exactly as recommended in these chapters, neither of us ever loses sight of our ultimate goal as individuals: happiness.

If this book can help just one other person or couple find true peace and happiness, then I will claim this book a success. David helped me change my thinking and accept responsibility for my life. I found relief from emotional pain, worry, hurt feelings, fear, physical illness and constant sadness. I had been praying for help years before I met David. My daily prayer was always the same and included words about how my family needed to be saved. I did not know how I could continue to live as I was. I needed help in every conceivable way a person could need help. I was in fear of losing my mind while trying to cope with the dark abyss in which I lived.

Eventually, my daily prayer was shortened to a few words. I would pray, "You know the prayer, you know what I need, please help me." I believe David's entry into my life was Divine intervention, which is another story entirely, yet brings me to a final point. This book neither requires nor negates religious beliefs. That is the beauty of understanding the philosophies in each chapter. When we understand the basis of our behavior and the rationale behind the decisions we make, we can then see the world with greater clarity, hence, find our own joy.

❧❧

Broadly defined, nearly every adult in this country is now, has been, or will be a caregiver of some sort during their lifetime. As adults we care for children, aging parents, sick neighbors, disabled siblings, and, perhaps most tragically, ill or disabled spouses or domestic partners. If it is a temporary situation, it is easier to be a caregiver. We are all going to be faced with taking care of someone with a broken leg, someone who needs surgery, someone who has a temporary disease, and so forth. It would be foolish indeed to single-handedly take on the responsibilities of caregiving assuming that this was going to be a permanent arrangement. Once an acute illness for a spouse appears to be becoming a chronic condition, all standing agreements and previous expectations need to be evaluated. The caregiver must ensure that their own needs as well as those of their life partner are going to be met before volatile emotions intrude. Failing to make this evaluation is the origin of burnout, anger, depression and longing for a different way of life, even hating the partner we once loved.

Caregivers must care for themselves first—a piece of advice heard all the time. The problem with the remark is that nobody offers the companion advice on how to do it. The authors know that caregivers must learn how to recognize their needs and get those needs met. If this is not a priority, then the person becomes useless as a caregiver. When caregivers' obligations to themselves are not acknowledged, everyone suffers. Of course, it applies to everyone in the caregivers' lives. They cannot be the best husband or wife, the best partner, the best mother, daughter, brother, teacher, lawyer, plumber, etc.

As caregivers, we cannot be happy if we buy into the clichés and deadly misconceptions that we hear constantly from society. These misconceptions are destructive and can cause a caregiver to act in ways that are counterproductive to their well-being. Buying into the maxims will block one's ability to become a tough and tender caregiver; a TTC.

DEADLY MISCONCEPTIONS ABOUT CAREGIVING
- Once you have made a commitment to care for a loved one, the commitment is forever.
- The needs of the dependent spouse are more important than the needs of the caregiver.
- The dependent person's needs and wants are equally important.
- It is always inappropriate to say "no" to requests of an ill spouse.
- For better or worse, in sickness and in health..." means exactly what it says.
- There is something noble about sacrificing your life for a spouse.
- Love is forever.
- God never gives you more than you can handle.

There is an important theme running through each of these clichés, social rules, myths, and proverbs. They represent a kind of propaganda initiated, perhaps, by insecure people who want ironclad guarantees, that if they become sick or disabled, their partner will be required by these social rules to stick around. The primary club they wield through these rules is Guilt, the tool used to bind them to their partner. If their caregivers so much as fantasize about walking away from their caregiving responsibilities, guilt will keep them there.

Caregivers often live by a set of rules that are based on these deadly misconceptions and other myths involving unrealistic social expectations. In the end, trying to live by these misconceptions empowers no one, and harms everyone. People who are not caregivers to a dependent spouse perpetuate societal expectations. They are not the ones who are beckoned into service with a bell or a yell. Some of us have even been sarcastically told, "Oh, don't be a martyr" when we dared to share information about our lives and frustrations in our attempt to educate others on what spousal caregiving entails. People are dismayed at the unpleasant details that are the daily reality for any caregiver.

This kind of disbelief is especially obvious from those who are most influenced by the unshakable belief that any marriage is forever, that "what God has wrought let no man put asunder." For non-caregivers with this opinion, it is unthinkable to question one's commitment to a spouse. These same people unfamiliar with spousal caregiving tend to personalize the situation by wondering what would happen to their own partners' resolve if they got sick. Sadly, the truth is that some spousal caregivers are forced to make choices they could never have anticipated until it is a personal journey.

Other examples of our ignorance of human affairs include the following Deadly Misconceptions:

- It is wrong to be selfish.
- Love means never having to say you're sorry.
- It is more blessed to give than receive.
- We are responsible for each other.
- Blood is thicker than water.
- Always tell the truth.
- People's personalities never change
- Somebody has to be in charge in a marriage.
- In a conflict, someone always gets hurt.
- If he really loved me, he would know what I need.
- Every dark cloud has a silver lining

For some caregivers, the only strength they hold onto is the Deadly Misconception: "God never gives you more than you can handle." While there is no intent to challenge belief systems, there is a deeper issue embedded in this kind of statement. The authors understand that your beliefs may be the only source of comfort you have. No matter what your religious beliefs happen to be, this statement amounts to a commentary on human resilience. It amounts to reassurance to caregivers that they will "make out just fine." Or, "I know you will bounce back," or "we all have these crosses to bear in life."

The truth is, for caregivers of chronically ill or disabled spouses, things are *not* going to be just fine. It does feel like life is too strenuous. There are financial hardships, intimacy problems, unmet needs, and a rising level of exasperation and anger that is real and potentially deadly. To be sure, there is a whole list of psychological needs that go unmet. To make matters even worse, caregivers in this situation are often so tired of medical waiting rooms that they will not see their own doctor when they should. It is not uncommon for the caregiver's physical health to deteriorate for this reason alone. There is no cure, and the exhausted caregiver is waiting for one of them to die for pain relief.

Unless the caregiver decides to make some radical changes in the nature of the caregiver relationship, there is no comfort in the saying "God is not going to give you more than you can handle." Before we can move forward in our understanding of how relationships work and how we got into caregiver hell, we need to understand more about the "two G's," guilt and grief.

THE GRIEVING PROCESS

వంశ

If you suppress grief too much, it can well redouble. -Moliere

వంశ

Understanding that grief is a legitimate emotion for the spousal caregiver can be a brand new concept. Well spouses are offered grief counseling if they are caring for a spouse with a terminal illness and death likely. It would not normally occur to anyone that those caring for the *chronically* ill or disabled are also struggling with grief. Grief does not begin with becoming the caregiver and end while coping with the death of a spouse. When our spouse is chronically ill or disabled, the grief is ever-present.

We see our responsibilities as infinite and consuming. There will be no remission. We know that the death of our ill spouse is not likely to be premature, and that the caregiving role is predicted to last the remainder of the spouse's life. While we do not wish our ill spouse to die, we just do not know how to make life feel better. We confuse grief with anger or depression, which are two components of grief. The feeling of grief ebbs and flows. It feels like a wound that never seems to heal. People who have lost a loved one speak of closure. Chronic long-term caregiving for a partner does not allow for closure. There is no way to "move on." There can be no moving on when the ill spouse is looking for constant assistance. It blocks the ability to plan for the future.

It is difficult to understand is that the grief felt by a well spouse is *unique*. Grief is not always about the ill partner. Rather, the grief is for us. It is about what *we* lost along the way. While a spouse of a terminally ill person will be similarly grieving for their loss, the grieving process is to be expected. Help is readily available. On the other hand, self-help venues do little to assist the well spouse of the chronically ill to identify and deal with the grief.

Many healthy well spouses feel like they are in constant mourning, yet there has been no death. The ill spouse is alive and in the same home. The grief is constantly present and the worst of it is that they wrestle with the dichotomy of mourning what they have lost in life versus not feeling the same emotions for their ill partner's losses. We begin to feel guilty for grieving our own loss. The well spouse internally concludes she is "just being selfish." The well spouse man with minor children in the home often feels like a single parent, yet there is another adult in the family the children call "mom."

For many caregivers, they are watching their life disappear and their best friend slowly become a dependent ward. For those spousal caregivers who did not have a great relationship before the disability arrived, the diminished life feels like a living prison sentence. Nevertheless, of course, it is not "acceptable" to speak of these things.

We may be grieving that our life, as we knew it, is gone. We are grieving that illness and disability came in and stole our hopes and dreams. It is heart wrenching to wake up one day and realize that the dreams you shared with your spouse are now unattainable. Living without hopes and dreams feels like a form of death because nothing about becoming a spousal caregiver is what we envisioned our future to look like—not ever. It feels like control of our future has been wrenched away from us.

Recognizing grief can stave off the next, and potentially more harmful, step in the progression: chronic depression. If the caregiver assumes these feelings are a form of depression rather than grief, it will not permit the well spouse the chance to acknowledge real losses. The healthiest approach is to recognize the grief and allow grieving to occur. This approach will help us regroup and make plans to live a healthier life as a caregiver. We will talk about tools to help us regain control of our future.

෧~෧

As is pertains to grief, Rhonda was stressed about Andy's unpredictable health status, his failure to be reliable for work and his erratic behavior. He was constantly at the emergency room and as a result, they were unable to meet all of their financial obligations. Rhonda's parents were helping to take care of the children almost daily and her dependence on them grew. The children had blurry lines about who were their parent figures.

During all of this turmoil, Rhonda's mom was diagnosed with an aggressive form of breast cancer and three extended family members died. While Rhonda did not feel like she was mourning the deaths, she did feel depressed. She described it as if she was walking around in a fog. She was living in the hospitals with Andy and could only think about one moment at a time. There was no planning, no dreaming, no freedom and no joy.

In retrospect, it was not "depression" that had consumed her, but "grief." She was grieving about her losses. She was filled with grief about her mother's health and her own inability to help her parents because Andy's issues dominated her time. Grief because her responsibilities increased as her parents had their own very serious health crisis, and she no longer had help. She was grieving for the future she would never have.

ॐॐ

Grieving that goes on for a long time can develop its own momentum. While it starts out as an involuntary emotional reaction to loss, or the prospect of loss, grief can become a voluntary state of mind. If the prospect of taking action to rebuild one's life seems too difficult, it often can be a form of self-indulgence to wallow in the grief. It can be a substitute for action, blocking efforts to rebuild a life that has become fragmented. It has a familiar feel to it that can seem seductively comforting. The longer this pattern continues, the harder it becomes to resume a normal life.

THE "MAKE 'EM FEEL GUILTY" STRATEGY

ॐॐ

"God may forgive your sins, but your nervous system won't." -
Alfred Korzybski

ॐॐ

When there is, a natural ending anticipated for caregiving, the well spouse can cling rather easily to the idea that this will soon be over and life will be back to normal. However, in a situation involving permanent impairment, illness, or disability, everything is much more difficult. Some the problems include:

- Financial hardship
- Absence of sexual intimacy
- Enforced togetherness
- Increasing inequity in the partnership exchange
- Rising levels of caregiver exasperation and anger

The concept of guilt in a caregiver's life is real and palpable on a routine basis. It is hard to admit we are unhappy, and we tell ourselves that we knew what we were doing when we chose to take on this role. It is becomes easier to believe that our dissatisfaction with the caregiver role means we are failing somehow rather than admit we hate the lifestyle. This self-proclaimed ineptness leaves many caregivers with guilty feelings that interfere with finding solutions to the real issue—the unhappiness. Hence, the caregiver often falls into a state of despair. To paraphrase O. Hobart Mowrer, "There ain't no such thing as *feeling* guilty, you are either guilty or you are not." So then, the question caregivers must ask themselves is of what are we guilty? Is it wanting a life where some of our needs are met, too? Guilt is deadly when allowed to settle into daily life unchallenged.

Being raised in the Catholic faith, Rhonda struggled daily with guilt. Serving herself in any fashion connoted a breach in her role as wife and mother. In a search for a cure for her husband ostensibly to save his life, she also wrestled with the guilt she felt over being angry that the life she dreamed of, the husband she wanted and the happiness she was chasing was apparently not going to be found. She felt selfish for wanting more, so she tried to assuage her guilt feelings by trying harder to be the perfect caregiver. Naturally, this made matters even worse. In her late twenties, she was consumed with guilt and unable to find a way to relieve it.

David asked Rhonda at a Well Spouse support group meeting, *"Just why do you feel so guilty?"* It sounds like such a simple question and yet was hard to answer. Rhonda felt guilty because she wanted something more for her life. She felt guilty because she was not delivering the kind of childhood she wanted for her kids. She felt guilty because Andy's illness was costing money that she did not have. As she borrowed from family and left necessary bills unpaid, she felt increasingly resentful. Ultimately, she admitted she felt guilty because she wanted out. Now the challenge was to find out exactly what 'out' meant to her. Did out mean death for one or both of them, did it mean a vacation or a divorce? For a well spouse, it means guilt over entertaining a violation of your marital vows as well. The journey to that answer was long and difficult for Rhonda.

Upon asking Rhonda and the rest of the group the question about guilt, David was now forced to examine his own unresolved guilt. Why did he feel guilty when he left Kate to go to the store? Why did he not want to take her everywhere he went? Before the illness crept into the marital dynamics, he claimed that he and Kate were the "best of friends," now he hated to be in the same room. Whenever he received a moment of freedom from his ill spouse, David ran out the door in a flash. Sadly, Kate would call within 30 minutes and want him to return immediately. If he did not return to her satisfaction, she would make threats regarding the mess she was going to make in her bed as punishment. The fact that David believed that he had to return home despite his fatigue was evidence that guilt was winning in a battle he had not known he was fighting. How dare he go out and leave her at home?

He had begun to believe that his momentary freedom from home was not deserved if Kate could not go. He would cut all social engagements short and return the instant his phone rang. Intellectually, he knew better, but the guilty feeling that he was failing her was something he could not shake. Our loved ones finely tune the "You owe me because I am not well" mantra and use it with great skill.

ॐ∽

Chapter 2
WHERE IS HAPPILY EVER AFTER?

Defining Our Needs, Being Proactive, Shaping Our Own Destiny

࿔࿓

"You have Alzheimer's"...and with that the door of hope which she propped open for so long slammed shut. Rhonda had been waiting for 10 years while she sought answers to her husband's strange behavior, searched for a cure, lived in a violent hell, and held out hope that she would find her husband again after 14 years of marriage. She wanted a happy family. Now it was all gone.

That is when her real nightmare began. Once she admitted that she had exhausted every avenue in the medical community of finding the man she married, she began to feel like she lost her own mental health. For so many of the preceding years, she kept telling herself that Andy was sick, but he could get well if they just could find out what was causing this strange behavior and wild temper. She thought the next doctor or the next test would give those answers and a cure. She argued with medical professionals, *"No, Andy is not depressed, he's not crazy, he is not full of heavy metal exposure, no he never broke his neck, no he is not drug seeking, no he does not have a history of cardiac problems, no he is not lazy, no he is not a hypochondriac, no, no, no, no, no, NO!"*

Revisiting all of this now, mentally healthy, Rhonda realizes how it looked and how she must have looked. Especially when one emergency room professional, caring for Andy, told her that perhaps, she was the one who needed the anti-anxiety medications and some professional help. Alas, the nurse was probably right, although Rhonda just did not realize it at the time. What the nurse got for her compassionate interest was a verbal lashing for *"All of their stupidity. Can't they see Andy is not a normal 37 year old? He needs help, not sarcasm."*

త్రీ

MARRIAGES & LIFELONG PARTNERSHIPS

To begin the process of pursuing happiness and making the caregiving relationship work, we must understand the very essence of relationships and spousal caregiving paradigms.

The authors have spent a great deal of time in the past few years talking, reading and researching the lives of caregivers. They have also examined their own lives and scrutinized their own histories for answers.

The two of them have sought reasons why they allowed their own individuality to be consumed with the role of caregiver to the point of self-destruction. They have called this obsession a "Caregiver Think Tank." Through participation in this "think tank", they have realized that once a person is caught in a caregiver net, it seems to become all-encompassing and all the exits are blocked.

Happiness becomes an impossible dream. "Caregiver" seems to become a brand new identity that is nearly impossible to shed. Once a caregiver, always a caregiver. Former well spouse individuals continue to feel like a caregiver after the role has ended. A former well spouse will grieve and attempt to heal, but the crucible in which they lived while being an active spousal caregiver is similar to surviving a trauma. This "trauma" continues to require interaction with others who understand what life was like for them as a caregiver. A former well spouse begins to interact with the "healthy" world with a different set of standards. The level of sacrifice and devotion is in direct proportion to feeling that you cannot interact with those uninitiated in spousal caregiving. The emotional pain cannot be resolved by befriending people who have lived in "normal" marriages. The well spouse has a keen sense of what anguish means. They have also become intolerant of men and women who complain about silly issues regarding their healthy spouses. Those people have no comprehension as to how lucky they are to have a well companion.

While the caregiver role comes in many different forms, there is nothing to compare to caring for an ill spouse. A sick child elicits unconditional devotion. Caregivers to sick children find it relatively easy to find emotional support from a spouse, a relative, other children and so forth. There is a built-in support system in that communion of heartache. Like every other caregiver role, parenting a sick child has its uniquely tough issues and is not to be minimized. The burden of worry, sadness, and financial stress is overwhelming.

When we care for an ill or elderly parent, the commitment to their care is tempered by circumstances. Caregivers may have their own family obligations, a career, or a spouse and these commitments cannot be ignored. Therein lies a built-in respite that limits commitment. While the adult-child-to-parent caregiving relationship is stressful and has unique stressors, it is more likely to be a part rather than full time. The limits are usually set in place automatically. The recipient ill parent is often aware of the burden they feel they are causing their child and allows for other substitute care providers a bit easier.

With a sick spouse, however, a person faces a road filled with challenges to their internal strength as well as their physical strength. Caring for an ill spouse can become a 24/7, all-consuming commitment. Caring for a spouse with a long-term chronic illness will test the most faithful, devoted of souls regardless of their system of beliefs. The well spouse realizes, like being slapped, that love is conditional and always was. The stress faced by well spouses raises all manner of taboo questions, and the quest for answers begins.

IS THIS GOING TO LAST FOREVER?

Let us deal with another Deadly Misconception, *"Once you have made a commitment to care for a loved one, the commitment is forever."* This is a completely unrealistic understanding of the nature of all relationships. Any relationship, especially with a life partner, is constantly changing as our needs change. Changes include our ability to give certain kinds of services to our spouse. With chronic illnesses, there is a change in our economic circumstances. The relationship is dynamic and change must be expected in any marriage, but even more predictable are the changes when a spouse is ill.

It is unrealistic to make any kind of lifelong commitment that you will continue to do one thing for another person forever. Everything changes, and we must have the ability to re-think and readdress what we want a relationship to look like. The caregiving relationship is no exception, and we have to be able to assess continuously the effectiveness of our caregiving. Looking at what we bring to the caregiving process and the effectiveness of the entire arrangement must be constantly evaluated lest we fall into a kind of a morass of automatic behavior that serves no one. The truth is the commitment to caregiving is not forever—no commitment is forever. All caregivers aspiring to be a TTC (Tough and Tender Caregiver) must understand this.

Any discussion of caregiving involves a universe of taboo questions, fuzzy answers, and challenges to so many of society's rules and customs that the entire concept of caregiving has become fraught with pain and controversy. The news flash is that *all* caregivers think thoughts they wish they could obliterate. The problem lies in not acknowledging that caregivers have limits, needs and only one life to live. Caregivers need to learn how to survive as individuals.

Human misery is all around us regardless of our caregiving status. We all know people who make the same mistakes repeatedly. They make terrible decisions about their lives. They take awful risks and end up losing health, property, self-respect or all three. They drive away the people who love them. They sacrifice themselves for hopeless causes. They enter into a succession of impractical relationships. They commit psychological and physical violence on their fellow man and themselves. As a result, they feel frustration, depression, anger, guilt, envy and despair. They often grasp at straws to find relief. They turn to astrology, fringe religions, faith healers and palm readers. They may look for chemical relief in alcohol, tranquillizers, or cocaine. These people may not even be caregivers. Take the troubles outlined above, multiply by ten, and you may come close to how bad the caregivers' mistakes can be when you consider stress and the absence of support systems.

శ్రీ

Both David and Rhonda did this. David found his rescue in drinking too much to blot out the calls for endless fetching for Kate during the nighttime. He drove his motorcycle with recklessness in a passive attempt to end his misery. "If I die, I die" became his guiding motto. Rhonda did this in eating in restaurants too often, consuming the wrong foods, spending money she did not have, choosing to immerse herself in entertainment activities rather than be responsible for her bills. She thought, "Who cares what happens, my life couldn't be worse than it is?" They took risks to numb emotional pain.

శ్రీ

WHAT ARE CAREGIVERS DOING WRONG?

Why do decisions go sour? Why are spousal caregivers unable to meet their needs or feel the joy that other people seem to garner? The list of what goes wrong is seemingly endless, but here are some examples of what is behind such bad decisions about relationships, regardless of caregiving status.

They...
- didn't understand the situation there were in
- misread the motives of others
- thought people would react differently than they did
- misunderstood the risks
- made no attempt to control what was happening
- did not think things through before taking action
- lacked the skill to make the right things happen
- allowed their emotions to overwhelm their judgment
- failed to communicate their intentions
- made promises they couldn't keep
- allowed their ego to interfere with negotiations.
- wouldn't listen to sound advice.

- wouldn't let others know what they really wanted.
- refused to confront someone
- ran away from the problem
- believed something unrealistic
- sought answers in the wrong places
- fell "in love" and threw caution to the winds
- put up with indignities
- refused to find out what other people wanted
- tried to exploit someone.

There is a theme that ties these classic mistakes together. These errors occurred because of *Ignorance*. These people did not understand reality. They thought the world was playing bridge, but it is really playing poker. They lacked knowledge and discipline. As a result, their decisions did not meet their needs.

☙❧

Rhonda certainly made these mistakes. She assumed her life would be better by chasing answers and trusting that family members cared about the downward trajectory of Andy's health. She believed family and friends when they said they wanted to help. She believed that the ideal relationship was still possible for her marriage. She had trouble seeing the reality of the situation.

Andy's illness had become an all-consuming aspect of daily life. He used the bad behavior to get what he wanted when he wanted it. His illness demanded a certain schedule, and he was impulsive without it. He was turning into a very large child, and Rhonda continued to maintain the traditional roles in front of the kids; "It is your father and you will respect him" kind of living. When Andy exploded, it was her eldest child who took care of the younger children and it only enhanced the disrespect. Rhonda had to focus on Andy to make him calm. It was a method to survive, but the children paid a price while Rhonda soothed Andy.

The cycle is the classic pattern of spousal abuse, but Rhonda did not recognize it as such at the time. She believed explaining away the behaviors as an illness would compensate for the hell in which they lived believing that a person never gives up on their life partner. She thought she would have time to explain to the children all of her motives and that the children would develop an appreciation for her devotion. After all, wasn't this setting a good example for the children about a devoted marriage?

ॐॐ

David, for his part, thought if he kept up the domestic duties and learned to be a better nursing assistant to Kate, she would finally reward him with praise. She would tell him that he was a good husband and had always been. This was something he never heard from her. David devoted his days to her care and had no real life of his own. He stopped playing golf, one of the reasons they had moved south. He stayed home because Kate could not move around the house without assistance. She refused to allow anyone else care for her so he could see a movie with a friend or attend a concert. He thought this request was because his care was so good and she was only comfortable with his abilities to meet her expectations. She needed him. He put her requests before his own well-being.

ॐॐ

We get just enough gratitude dangled in front of us to think we may be making a difference. That fuels the continuation of this charade. Two examples follow:

As the support group friendship developed, David told Rhonda a story about how he had recently given a lecture where Kate was in the audience. That same evening, he overheard Kate on the phone telling their grown daughter what a wonderful presentation David had given that day. However, she never told *him* how much she admired his work. He never heard that she thought he was a talented psychologist, but, now, she was telling their daughter. He longed for that recognition from the woman he had chosen to be his life-long partner. Overhearing the praise dangled in front of his nose was enough for David to continue care giving. In retelling the story to Rhonda, it was clear to her that he was feeling pretty good that Kate must really have cared for him all these years and knowing it now it seemed to justify the rest of the hard work that caregiving brought into his life.

꙳

Andy's sister, Mary, asked Rhonda what she could do to help with the caregiving situation. Mary had been very vocal about knowing her purpose in life, now; it was to help Rhonda help her brother. Being self-employed and limited with time, Rhonda finally asked Mary to take Andy to the store for groceries. Andy would like the change of pace and Rhonda never liked going to the store after work with three kids in tow. Besides, Andy would be too stimulated with the whole event if the children went along and that is why she hated the duty of grocery shopping. Mary agreed, stating she was glad to be able to help. Rhonda gave her three hundred dollars and a shopping list.

Mary and Andy had a day filled with activity outside of the house. The two of them brought back a freezer filled with food but nothing on Rhonda's original list. They purchased groceries that appealed to Mary. The purchases were what made Mary feel good, what she perceived to be a better value, not what Andy's family liked. Her "help" was a sham. Rhonda misread the motives of her sister-in-law. It was clear the offer to help came with strings attached and an expectation of compliance. However, when you are a desperate caregiver, you will take help no matter the price if it means a few moments of solace.

꙳

Both David and Rhonda gave up their identities and performed in a manner dictated by others. Their preferences were obscured by the desire to maintain the sense of duty they felt for their ill spouses. Neither of them considers this strength of character, nor do they relish the title of martyr. They consider the actions in hindsight to be, frankly, stupid. Succumbing to the pressures of the ill spouse left both families in dangerous waters. The demands made on them by their ill spouses and from other interested parties were often at odds with their ill spouses' health care needs. Giving in to the demands was an unhealthy surrender.

ॐॐ

TTC; THE PURSUIT OF HAPPINESS

One defining idea emerged from this "Think Tank," the concept of *sacrifice*. Neither of the authors, as caregivers, thought that assuming the caregiver role involved nearly fatal sacrifices. Caregiving became a way of life. They were clueless about the toll it was taking. Both of them allowed life to become devoid of all pleasure. Many caregivers do this and find themselves one day wondering how it all happened.

How does it happen? It is sometimes called the *boiled frog syndrome*. As cold-blooded creatures, frogs adapt to temperature changes automatically. As this metaphor goes, place a frog in a pot of cold water, put the pot on the stove, and without alarming the frog, the temperature gradually rises to the point that the frog is boiled to death. As caregivers, the authors were not aware that their needs were being gradually shelved to the point that only the care recipient benefited, not the caregiver.

On-line forums, such as Well Spouse Association, were initially the only places the authors could express their socially unacceptable thoughts. It appeared then, and now, that only caregivers would recognize, accept, and understand these desperate pleas and angry expressions of frustration. Caregivers to sick spouses start to wonder how long they can live this way and how to stop what can feel like madness. Well spouses wonder how long they can deliver constant care, wonder if they are ever going to have fun again, wonder if they can remain celibate and true to their vows. They feel internal pressures building to say, aloud, that they have had enough of the doctor

appointments, the hospital visits, wiping behinds, distributing medicines, dressing wounds, and that they cannot take it anymore. Then,
of course, they wonder if that means they are a bad person.

For those caring for a spouse, they never dreamed when they
got married that they would look at the person who once was "the
love of my life" and think, "Did I ever love them?" When they find
themselves in this untenable situation, the well spouse reviews wedding vows with a new sense of questioning. "How devoted was I, what
did it all mean and can I do it anymore?" "Would my spouse be doing
the same for me if I were the one who was ill? Would I even expect
them to?"

The help offered by David's relationship concepts gave the
Well Spouse support group members the *permission* and the *right* they
were seeking to put their needs first. What followed over a period of
months was a healing process.

The Tough and Tender Caregiver is firmly in touch with reality. TTCs understand their environment, and how to be comfortable
in it. They know what they need, what is available and how to get
it. Because conditions change, TTCs realize they must be constantly
open to new learning in order to stay in touch with reality. They are
always prepared to give up what they believe and substitute something new.

In their pursuit of happiness, TTCs use this knowledge of
changing reality to make good decisions about their lives. Their decisions reflect their knowledge of themselves, their understanding of
human affairs, and the skills available to them. As a result, the outcomes of their decisions meet their needs. The results of their decisions make them comfortable in their environment. In other words,
TTCs know what decisions will make them happy, and those are the
decisions they make. They understand that they must take the right
kind of action in order to get their needs met. If they are successful,
they will be happy.

Nobody is a TTC all the time. We all have certain gaps in our
knowledge. Sometimes we do not control our emotions as well as
we should. Situations change and we do not notice right away. We

thought we knew how to do something, and find we really did not. Even when things turn out well for us, the way we got there might not have been pretty. There were false starts, mid-course corrections, the need to back up and re-think something. Happiness continues to be something to which we aspire. As we become older, we should become happier; our batting average should improve. We should make fewer mistakes, and those we make should be less important.

THE QUALITY OF THE PRE-ILLNESS RELATIONSHIP

The caregiver and spouse (if possible) must openly examine the pre-illness relationship when faced with the prospect of life-long caregiving. Knowing the dynamics of the existing relationship and then understanding where the relationship is headed because of the disability can help to avoid problems with issues like burnout and frustration. The authors firmly believe that the ability to sustain the role of well spouse for a lengthy period without experiencing detrimental side effects is directly related to the quality of the pre-illness relationship. Another factor is also tied to the amount of time the relationship has been a functioning union.

Spousal caregivers who have been in close, supportive, loving relationships for many years demonstrate an ability to accept life in this role a little differently than the people who have not had the same benefits. For partners who were already experiencing marital woes and hardships as the disability was diagnosed, the role of primary caregiver became another issue to handle in a tumultuous relationship. This is not to say that any caregiver regards their marriage vows any less seriously, but it is one of many indicators as to the level of stress or complete acceptance a spousal caregiver may feel.

It is plausible that a person could care for sick or disabled spouses for long periods without losing their own identity as an individual. What is not known for any caregiver is the *length* of time that a caregiver can hold out before reaching their "tipping point" and having to make major adjustments to the caregiving relationship. This length of time appears to be a direct function of the kind of relationship that existed in the marriage *before* the disabling injury or illness invaded.

If the relationship lacked quality before the beginning of caregiving, the tipping point may come rapidly. For those relationships, it may mean that the unhappiness is felt early for the caregiver, and forbidden thoughts like escape fantasies become more and more intrusive. If the quality of the relationship prior to the illness or injury was excellent, it is theoretically possible to provide care for a longer period without reaching that tipping point. In such cases, there would likely already be contingency plans in existence.

The problem with many of these long-term caregiver situations is that the relationship was not wonderful beforehand. It was not the kind of relationship where the partners were extremely attentive to each other's needs in the first place. The illness or injury simply made a bad relationship rapidly worse. If the relationship has been a good one—even a reasonably good one—then implementing the lessons in this book should be relatively easy. The oriented ill partner is likely attuned to the fact that the needs of the caregiver are not being met. They should be open to negotiation about modifications in the standing agreements that govern their relationship. Making modifications to ease the burden on the caregiver is easier in these situations because a level of trust already exists; the ill spouse is not likely to be concerned that their needs will be ignored.

The caregivers who will have the toughest time making these adjustments will be those whose pre-illness marriages were unpleasant, adversarial or merely tolerable. In these situations, it is much more likely the caregiver will encounter hostile resistance from the ill spouse. This means the caregiver will actually have to impose solutions on the disabled partner. Their imposition will be met with resistance and possibly verbal abuse. So, caregivers in unsatisfactory relationships should be warned not to expect cooperation.

A well spouse's life will be vastly improved and, ironically, so will the lives of their ill spouses when they impose their will on the world for getting their needs met. When there is no structure, anxiety ensues. The dependent ill spouse of a dysfunctional pre-illness relationship may panic when the well spouse begins to show signs of independence after long standing martyrdom. Implementing structure and boundaries into the life style routine can alleviate the panic.

Structure and clear expectations will represent a process that the partners can count on for getting each of their needs met.

The healthy pre-illness relationship can also benefit from structure, but the protests from the ill spouse will not be as strong. The partners instinctively know their needs will not pre-empt their partners' needs. We see the same types of panic in minor children who have no structure in the home or who have been abandoned. They need to know who is in charge and how their needs will be met because they understand they are ill equipped to meet their own needs independently.

STARTING WITH THE BASICS
THE FROG POND

In order to move toward the happiness ideal, it is necessary to build on certain fundamental assumptions that the TTC *instinctively* understands. The human being is an organism living in an environment, much like a frog living in his environment, the frog pond.

The frog has certain basic needs that must be met. He needs food, water to keep his skin from drying out, temperature control, oxygen and so forth. Even though the frog is a simple organism, he also has certain comfort needs. He prefers certain water temperatures to others, loves to sit in the sun, and can relax better if he is out of sight of the lunker bass that chases him periodically.

Because of these needs, the frog is automatically in conflict with the pond. To meet his needs, he must make changes in his environment. The environment is not thrilled, but will begrudgingly go along with the program. For example, when the frog is hungry he sets about to change the pond by reducing its bug population. The pond allows the bug population to be reduced. So what?

The 'so what' is that the pond is very indifferent to the needs of the frog. The frog could be starving, floating on his back, begging for food, and the pond would not deliver a single dead bug into the frog's mouth. The pond does not care if the frog's needs are met or not. This means that the frog must accept total and complete responsibility for getting his needs met. The frog must personally impose his will on the pond by chasing bugs, carving out a hiding place in the reeds, swallowing water, breathing air and climbing on lily pads. If the frog will not take action, his needs will not be met. Moreover, the pond will not care.

In like fashion, we human beings have a set of needs, physical needs (oxygen, food, temperature control, etc.) and psychological needs. Until modern times, people could not worry much about psychological needs. They were too busy worrying about survival. However, progress, at least in the Western world, has provided us with an opportunity to focus a lot of attention on the issue of *happiness*. It would be a shame to settle for what our ancestors *had* to settle.

As with the frog, these needs put us in conflict with our environment. By eating a steak, we reduce the cow population of the planet. By walking into our bank, we signal the teller to stop doing one thing and do another. By driving our car, we pour hydrocarbons into the atmosphere, deplete petroleum deposits underground, and smash insects on our windshield. Our environment does not care.

Our physical and social environment is indifferent to our needs. Certainly, the physical environment cannot care, but the people do not really care either. This is a controversial point to be expanded later, but for now we must recognize that people are so preoccupied with getting their own needs met that they have precious little energy left for us. People will allow us to influence what they do, but only if the price is right. They have to get something in exchange. Again, much more will be said about this later in the book. This places all of us in the position of the frog. *We must impose our will on the world to get our needs met.* Unless we shape and mold our environment to suit us, we will not be happy.

This is not the way things should be. Friends, relatives, neighbors, coworkers and in-laws should all gather around and offer to help. The skeptic asks, wouldn't it be a horrible world if everyone ran around doing whatever they wanted without regard for their fellow man? That is true. It depends on how far-sighted we are and how much we understand. There are many bodies of moral and spiritual thought from which we could draw reasons to place limits on man's freedom indiscriminately to shape the world to his own liking. These moral arguments really are not necessary, however.

TTCs have a clear picture of what their needs are, and a keen vision of whether they can be met in the end. They know their needs cannot be met without the cooperation of other people. They know that we have to attend to the interests of other people to get what we need from them. We have to give to get back. We have to invest to be entitled to a return on our investment. This idea about how the world works is call Enlightened Self Interest. These are examples of the kinds of psychological needs that can only be met via our relationships with others:

- Acceptance
- Achievement
- Affiliation
- Autonomy
- Challenge
- Competence
- Control
- Dominance
- Excitement
- Financial security
- Growth
- Heterosexuality
- Integrity
- Intimacy
- Introspection
- Mentor (to be a)
- Nurture others
- Order/structure
- Power
- Privacy
- Respect

Caregivers must be able to tune in to what their needs are, such as needs for adult conversation, intimacy, emotional support and so forth. Caregivers, because of guilt based on the Deadly Misconceptions, frequently ignore their needs, and by doing so, make it virtually impossible for those needs to be met.

WHY DON'T PEOPLE KNOW WHAT THEY NEED?

Surely everyone knows what they need, right? Well, not exactly. For one thing, over the full range of psychological needs, some make louder noises than others do when they are not met. For example, our need for companionship is powerful in that loneliness (i.e., an unmet companionship need) is a painful experience. When people need to be with other people, they are usually acutely aware of it.

Other needs are more subtle. For example, the need for privacy has a very soft signal. It often does not kick up the kind of fuss it should, particularly with people who have a keen sense of obligation to family, friends, children or colleagues. They respond to the needs of others automatically, shoving under a rug their need for time to themselves. In these circumstances, if this need were not being met, it is unlikely to be noticed until the deficit is acute and results in a louder signal. Routinely, a person would have to concentrate, to dredge up this need signal, in order to pay much attention to it in the decision process.

To gain insight in how to become a TTC, general knowledge about signals will help us recognized soft or subtle signals as early in the sequence as possible. The example below exemplifies how people get so busy and stressed that missing soft signals such as the need for privacy is easily done. Listening to our internal signals should become a way of life for all of us, regardless of caregiver status.

Rhonda was acting a single mother most of her marriage, but toward the end there was no concern for her privacy needs. She worked all day in the contracting company that required constant supervision of employees and work sites. In the afternoon, she picked up all the children from school and tended to their extra curricular activities. When she arrived home in the evenings, the typical family routine ensued; dinner, baths, homework, housework, bill paying, etc. All three of the children required her attention and Andy required a certain amount of non-typical attention (medication review, evaluation of daily events, etc). She claimed that her real work began when she got home at night. By the time, everyone was settled for the evening, usually around midnight, that was the only time she could carve out for herself.

Unfortunately, because she was up and going again at 5 a.m., after midnight was an unrealistic time to devote much attention to herself. She gave up trying. This resignation over time became a free-for-all by family members on all matters where privacy or alone time should have been strictly enforced.

Andy was unreliable as a parental figure; he was never able to watch the children. Because of his volatile temper, the children preferred not to ask him for help or engage him in any manner. Therefore, the children would open the door when she was in the bathroom. They would ask her questions while she was in the shower. They would sleep in her bedroom. She could not have a telephone conversation without the children wanting to know who was on the phone and what they wanted.

She was so filled with empathy for the children's concerns and fears regarding their father that she would often sleep on the sofa to hear them if they needed her in the night. She would rationalize that what they asked for from her was more important than doing something for herself. Essentially, anything that Rhonda attempted to engage in for her own well-being was fair game for intrusion by family members. There were no boundaries and there was no privacy for Rhonda. She assumed that living in two worlds for other people was what her life had become—one for Andy and his needs, one for the children to give them a sense of normal. These worlds were adversaries, but she thought it would only last until all the children were grown, then she could get some rest.

However, the stress began to undermine her strength. In a state of complete exasperation, Rhonda said at the support group meeting she felt like she was being eaten by piranhas. David inquired as to why was she simply not locking the bathroom door? Why was she not shutting her bedroom door when she wanted to talk on the phone? Why was she not insisting that she have "Mom Time" to be left alone to decompress at a reasonable hour every day? Rhonda's response was simple, "they needed her all the time." She could not see a way of meeting everyone's needs including her own. Feeling a sense of duty to family, her own needs took a back seat. One might call this, "Compassion Run Amok".

≈≈

It all sounds so easy to say, "lock the door," but when we cannot "hear" our internal signal saying "you need privacy, tell the kids to wait 30 minutes," there is no fix.

≈≈

David was similarly attuned to his obligations to Kate because of her total care. She could not stand up, so she could not transfer from the bed to the potty chair, or to the wheel chair. A hydraulic lift was needed for each move, and she outweighed David by nearly 250 pounds, so wheeling her across carpet once airborne was all he could do. His responsibility was total and complete. She wanted/needed him to be physically present 24 hours a day, 7 days a week. It is no wonder he lost track of what he needed for himself.

≈≈

Personality is another issue affecting how well we know what we need. Some people are naturally more introspective than others. At one end of the continuum are those who spend a lot of time thinking about themselves, their needs and desires, their fantasies, their resentments and so forth. They are naturally more attuned to their inner life. Psychological research on cognitive styles has identified people with so-called "internal locus of control" who pay more attention to internal than external signals when deciding how to behave.

At the other end of the continuum are the "external locus of control" people who are heavily influenced by events around them. They have trouble zeroing in on events within themselves, such as their psychological needs. An extreme example of external locus of control is the kitten captivated by the ball of yarn. It is as if the yarn reaches out and grabs control of the kitten; hence, external locus of control. Children do something similar with a shiny new toy.

Different life experiences often make an impact on how attuned individuals are to their psychological needs. A person raised in poverty might have been so concerned about getting physical needs met that there was little time for thinking about psychological needs. People raised in very large families often had access to a very small proportion of family resources with which to pursue need satisfaction. Battered children are punished for attempting to satisfy their own needs, so they may suppress awareness of many psychological needs to reduce their frustration.

Signal blockage can occur when some unrelated internal signal, usually an emotion, overpowers need signals. An insecure man is afraid his wife will have an affair and begins to check on her. He calls her office constantly, follows her to her bridge match, reads her mail, and constantly checks the contents of her purse. This behavior interferes with the stability of the marriage. His emotion (fear) blocks his awareness of his need (for intimacy).

To complicate matters, many psychological needs cannot be met immediately, but instead require planning and a long-term perspective, such as the need to nurture children as a parent. Such signals lack immediacy compared with impulses (e.g., to eat a dish of ice cream). Thus, need signals are often a lot weaker than other internal signals and have a tough time competing for our attention in the personal decision process.

IMPLICATIONS OF NOT KNOWING OUR NEEDS

Any time our need signals are not available, because either they are suppressed or too weak, our decisions will be based on other signals, both internal and external.

Personal decisions must often be made at the time needs are already being met. Nevertheless, these needs must be allowed to influence the decision process. This is ordinarily done by anticipating how events could eliminate need satisfaction, thereby creating loud signals.

A married man who is reasonably happy has many of his psychological needs met (e.g, orderliness, intimacy, heterosexuality, financial security). An attractive young female associate who appears romantically interested in him might trigger a decision about what he should do. His current internal signals might not prevent his decision to have an affair. After all, the needs satisfied by his marriage are silent because they are being met.

In order to make a decision to resist the temptation, the man would have to anticipate what his signal pattern would look like if his source of need satisfaction (i.e, his marriage) were damaged or destroyed. He could then compare the benefits of the affair (immediate gratification of sexual desires, inflated ego) against the costs of the affair (unmet needs for orderliness, intimacy, financial security). It should be obvious that even if all these data are present, the man could still choose to have the affair if he decided the benefits were worth the cost. Naturally, this decision would be more likely if the marriage lacked quality. In short, people who are not aware of what they need are likely to make bad decisions (i.e., decisions that do not meet their needs).

For the caregiver, a situation might play itself out like this: The caregiver is invited to a party by friends. The ill spouse for a variety of reasons cannot attend the event, and makes it clear that they are not happy about being unable to attend. The ill spouse requests that the caregiver not go either, stating it would be "unfair" to leave them with an aide. In this situation, the caregiver must weight their need for socializing against the conflicting request of the ill spouse. Does the caregiver attend the party and suffer the wrath of the ill spouse? It might actually be worth it to attend the party and send an important message to the ill spouse about the urgency of the caregiver's needs.

GETTING IN TOUCH WITH WHAT WE NEED

It is amazingly difficult to define what we need. In psychotherapy, the question is asked of clients in a variety of ways. What do you need? What do you want? What are you after? What's in this for you? When clients were asked questions like these a large proportion would respond with a blank look and say, "I'm not sure."

Sometimes psychotherapy clients directed to come up with a list of what they need are able to come up with a good first list. For some people, it seems helpful to sit with pen in hand, but this does not always work. It is sometimes useful to start with a list of needs.

One important tool for defining what we need might be called the *similarity assumption*. We need pretty much the same things as other people in our general circumstance (i.e., age, gender). When it comes to fundamental psychological needs, we are all pretty much alike. Different individuals place different priorities among the needs, and certainly some are better equipped than others to act on those needs. Personality and style differences will lead to differences in how those needs can be satisfied.

The similarity assumption allows us to obtain guidance about our own needs by getting information from others about what they need. This can be done directly by asking, or indirectly by listening or watching people carefully. Gathering information from others about what they need will also reassure us that our needs are not strange, weird, oddball, or something of which to be ashamed. This can increase our willingness to make use of need signals in our personal decisions.

THE TTC

A large percentage of the TTC's needs fall in the interpersonal realm. For any human, other people are needed for our needs to be met. Our needs for companionship, sexual contact, nurturance, and respect, to name a few, all require the cooperation of others. Therefore, TTCs are keenly aware of how any of their actions will affect other people, which is the TTC's source of goodies. Long-term self-interest keeps the TTC from hurting other people. This is all included in the concept of Enlightened Self Interest. If TTCs are efficient at serving their own needs, everybody wins.

In order to become a TTC in this life, to find our slice of personal fulfillment, we first have to understand as much as possible about how the world really works. If we seek to have a happy and successful life by believing a false set of rules, our decisions and actions will lead to continuous frustration, and we will never escape Caregiver

Hell. While this is true for average people in their ordinary lives, it is especially true for a spousal caregiver. Caregivers need education to understand the keys to obtain fulfillment and happiness.

Chapter 3
RELATIONSHIP REALITY

Learning How Relationship Really Work

∂◦◦

When the subject of caring for our spouse comes up in a casual conversation with the average non-caregiver, who has little or no experience in the matter, they will react in certain predictable ways. They might say how lucky the disabled person is to have us in their life. What a noble calling to be privileged to care for someone who needs us. How wonderful it must be to know that someone depends on us for everything. The well-meaning friend or neighbor might make commentary about how the enforced togetherness is an opportunity for us to re-discover the original love that brought us together.

They even try to make it sound romantic, or gallant, and all-in-all a positive experience. Initially, perhaps out of fear, a new spousal caregiver wants to believe it and will try to make the best of it. When Rhonda's husband was diagnosed with dementia, they jokingly said life would be like the movie "50 First Dates." Caregivers new to the task might be a little flattered by the praise acknowledging their duty and hearing the words of admiration. However, it does not take long to realize there is nothing attractive about the role of caregiver, especially when caring for an ill spouse.

The more seasoned caregiver may get some mild enjoyment from this kind of reaction from others because it may be the only praise, thanks and attention they get for months on end. When you talk candidly with an experienced caregiver for a permanently disabled spouse, where there is no end in sight, what you hear is an entirely different story.

You will hear about:
- Ungrateful recipients of care
- Verbal Abuse
- Physical violence
- Financial stress
- Unmet caregiver needs
- Absence of sexual intimacy
- Forbidden escape fantasies
- Forbidden urges to withhold needed medicine to end it all
- Depression and thoughts of suicide

There are newspaper stories of murder-suicide and abuse tied to untenable caregiving situations. Caregivers find themselves at their wits end, not knowing what to do. These stories have nothing to do with a romantic unbreakable marital bond that resulted in a loving euthanasia-type wish on the part of the dependent spouse. Rather, these are stories of caregivers who snap under the pressure, and strike out at the source of their frustration. The authors want to head off those horrific endings by educating caregivers about real, practical solutions described in this book.

While those stories seem extreme, anyone who has been a caregiver can understand how it happens. We read stories about a caregiver who is charged with murder because they say they were only following the wishes of their loved one. Yet, for many caregivers, we wonder if that was the real story. Was it a gift the ill person was trying to give their well caregiver, or was it the caregiver's blind exhaustion, or rage?

One of the most dangerous byproducts of spousal caregiving is *burnout*. Often caregivers set themselves up to burn out by ignoring the early warning symptoms, such as fatigue, irritability, insomnia, changes in eating patterns, and so forth. These symptoms usually exist because the caregiver is not conscious of the actual emotional reactions that are raging beneath the surface. This defense mechanism, designed to protect the individual from pain, is called *denial*.

It is common for spousal caregivers, particularly those new to caregiving, to deny to themselves how disruptive the illness or injury is to their personal lives. They often tell themselves that things will be just fine, that this is just part of marriage, and that there is nothing that can be done anyway so complaining about it will just make matters worse. This is not to say there is no value in denial as a defense mechanism. After all, it does defend us from some emotional pain. Denial can work as a temporary bandage. We know of caregivers who describe their life as if they are emotionally fortified by this type of denial. They state that if any event threatens to peel a layer of defense away, they sense there will be no stopping the flood of emotions from becoming unmanageable. They fear they will no longer be able to function on a daily basis if they admit they are sad, grieving or generally unhappy.

In the end a true understanding of what the turmoil looks like and its origins is far more valuable to the caregiver; it sets the stage for remedial action. Without this insight about the actual nature of the turmoil and the damage it can do if unchecked, the caregiver may be in for burnout and all the dysfunctional damage that it can do to the caregiver and to the ill spouse as well. In most cases, it if far more helpful to put the denial aside and take an honest look at the damage that self-denial is having on both parties.

The authors believe that the ultimate key element in surviving caregiving, particularly spousal caregiving, is a comprehensive understanding of how relationships work; *not* how they are *supposed* to work, but how they *really* work. Unfortunately, what is available now in books, blogs or advice columns has absolutely nothing to do with the realities of caregiving, especially as it pertains to caring for a spouse. If you look for help for caregivers, it focuses on how to *be* a good caregiver.

The only advice out there to help caregivers survive includes information like: smell the flowers, go into nature, go to church, use relaxation techniques, write, etc. You can find idealistic information about implementing organization in the home, keeping a journal of thoughts and feelings, and communing with nature. The advice is not only naïve, but harmful. It implies strongly that caregivers in crisis should just suck it up, hang in there, make the best of it, and so forth.

It is said in the health care world that caregivers are the backbone of the health care system. However, it is a sad statement when caregivers, particularly well partners, do not have any resources, reliable information, or appropriate assistance to help them provide care in their home. On very bad days, that kind of advice about journaling or smelling the flowers seems like "fluff." Some of that fluff is helpful and is not being negated here, but it is only helpful in very limited ways. Until now, via the publication of this book, it has not been considered appropriate or acceptable to discuss the ugliness of caregiving formally and comprehensively. It is difficult, at best, to have an open dialogue with our spouse, family and friends about how we are at our wits end.

The fact is that no effort to find a long-term substitute activity or words of sympathy will ever bring enough relief to the caregiver. The only source of relief for the caregiver of a chronically ill or disabled spouse is to *make changes*. This often-bad situation cries out for some form of true resolution. The caregiver *must take action*. Going only half-way or compromise solutions will not work.

TWO APPLICATIONS FOR RELATIONSHIP MANAGEMENT TOOLS

The caregiver has two separate and distinct interpersonal challenges that require a finely tuned sophistication about relationships. First, the caregiver will need to be proactive in evaluating the exact nature of the *current caregiving relationship*. In what ways is it different from the pre-illness relationship? What impact has there been on the capability of the ill spouse to attend to and meet the caregiver's needs? How willing is the ill spouse to make changes that will improve the caregiver's quality of life?

This analysis will require the caregiver to comprehend some of the relationship tools described in this chapter, such as the Internal Ledger, Equity, Exchange of Social Credits, Sending Bills, Return on Investment, Accountability, Confrontation, Negotiation Tactics, and The Big Club Theory. Much of this evaluation can be accomplished jointly with the ill spouse, and should be in order to get maximum support for the modifications required.

Many of these concepts will be considered radical by some spousal caregivers. The authors believe that if they do not make perfect sense at first, go to another chapter or put the book aside for a while, and try again later. These ideas about relationships apply to everyone even though few people have talked or written about them. They represent the actual mechanics of relationships and will make anyone's interactions with others more productive and satisfying.

Second, creating the optimum balance between Tough and Tender will require outside assistance. Those individuals or family members who have the ability to lighten the burden of caregiving may not necessarily be eager to help, nor are they easy to communicate with about the caregiver's daily challenges. There are some harsh realities to be faced by the spousal caregiver, and they must be thoroughly understood if the caregiver has any chance at all of exercising control over these forces to benefit the caregiving relationship.

These realities include:
- Friends and relatives will not do what they promise to do
- Other caregivers will be threatened by your respite opportunities,
- Your spouse's family resents you taking time off
- Unscreened nurses aides will steal from your home

An effort has been made in this chapter to include as many caregiver examples as possible, but there are at least as many examples out of the business world, child rearing, marriage counseling, and so forth designed to most clearly teach how these relationship mechanics actually work. The intention here is to help individuals understand the entire compass of many types of relationships and subsequent interactions. For the caregiver, this insight can assist in making choices and using relationship dynamics for their own best interest in maintaining a fulfilled life as a TTC.

THE SPECIAL CASE OF DEMENTIA OR OTHER COGNITIVE IMPAIRMENT

For those of us who live with a partner who has some form of cognitive impairment, there are even fewer reliable sources to devour in a quest to educate ourselves on how to live with this person and retain some normal life. With younger people being diagnosed with dementia, traumatic brain injuries (TBIs), and other diseases that leave our loved one with an altered mental status, all the socially acceptable resolutions seem unrealistic.

The ideas in this book will challenge your current plans and your visions for the future. You may find a foundation on which to make some important life decisions; hopefully, guilt free. Ill spouses would need all their mental faculties to understand how to negotiate, what agreements mean, what it means to be held accountable, and so forth. Caregivers need to be able to evaluate what techniques can be applied and which ones will not work.

At one end of the continuum of mental acuity, we have normal people who have all of their mental faculties intact. At the other end are people who have none left. Regardless of where on the continuum the ill spouse functions, the authors implore the well spouse to examine honestly, what the pre-illness marriage was like when reading the section on how relationships really work. Is the marriage you had the one that you are sacrificing your life for now? Is it worth it? Would your spouse have wanted you to live the life style that you currently living? What calls to action laid out in this book can be utilized for the caregivers to make decisions based on these sound principles?

POISONOUS MESSAGES ABOUT RELATIONSHIP MANAGEMENT

Engineering an escape from "Caregiver Hell" is not easy. The authors do not literally mean leaving your incapacitated spouse, *but* it can mean exactly that for some worn out, hope-depleted caregivers. The intention is to assist caregivers in finding a better way to live through learning just how spousal caregivers ended up living unfulfilled lives. There are so many traps to avoid. There is so much misinformation floating around that leads us astray. Our biggest problem is ignorance, and it is not really our fault. Our culture tells us how we are supposed to view relationships in general, especially marriage and other domestic partnerships.

- Absence makes the heart grow fonder
- Love means never having to say you're sorry
- You can't teach an old dog new tricks
- Do unto others as you would have them do onto you
- A good man is hard to find
- It takes two to Tango
- Know what side your bread is buttered on
- Love is blind
- Let bygones be bygones
- Forgive and forget
- A man's home is his castle
- Money can't buy happiness

These ideas are poison for any relationship. They contaminate our thinking and force us to compare our lives to societal ideals. They make our relationships dysfunctional. In fact, most of them are so far out in left field that it is amazing that we fall for them generation after generation.

"Love means never having to say you're sorry" keeps issues from being resolved in a long-term relationship. If a partner is not sorry for rude or destructive behavior, the spouse on the receiving end will not *"forgive and forget."* On the contrary, the receiver will tuck that slight away, shove it under the carpet, and never, ever forget it. Over time, the couple comes to live in a house with a *"lumpy carpet."* Every time they take a step, they trip over an unresolved issue. The odds that this marriage will survive are slim indeed. *"Let bygones be bygones"* because *"A man's home is his castle,"* connotes the same message. *"Love is blind,"* implores us to ignore *our* needs and become a servant to the indiscretions of our loved one.

These messages also exude the hidden meaning that we shoulder some of the responsibility in the dynamic of the relationship when there is conflict. This is true, until there is a disability or illness. Then everything change. The Marriage Contract is Broken and sadly it is not attributable to any person or intentional action. When the marriage contract is broken in marriage where both parties are healthy, resolutions seem clearer.

THE MARRIAGE CONTRACT IS BROKEN & I DIDN'T DO IT!

Marriage is like a corporation. The partners are the board of directors. Each partner owns fifty percent of the voting stock in the marital corporation. When the marriage hums along properly, there is an ongoing exchange process in the relationship. She does for him (invests) and he does for her (gives her a return on her investment). They exchange "Social Credits" on an equitable basis. For example, when he wants to spend money in a certain way, he has to decide if that decision falls in his job description. If she has been using her voting stock in making financial decisions during the marriage, then she will be automatically consulted. Major decisions in the marital corporation are made by consensus.

None of the insights offered regarding voting rights, etc., pertain to legal definitions of marriage, nor do they imply real property ownership. The example also does not account for past roles within the marriage. This "marital corporation" is used to exemplify how marriages routinely work and how they work when a chronic, life-changing event occurs. We caregivers get into "caregiver hell" when we do not acknowledge the functional changes in our marriages and act accordingly.

When one of the partners becomes permanently physically disabled, they are no longer capable of holding up their end of the marriage corporation. This does not mean they lose their voting stock, only that their equal ownership of the stock changes. Their ability to offer their spouse an adequate return on investment becomes severely limited. The relationship from that point on lacks Equity; which means the voting stock is also unequal. The shares of ownership should be distributed to match the amount of partner investment.

For example, the well spouse is performing daily care for the ill spouse, accomplishing household chores, and making financial decisions about how money is spent for care and other domestic needs. Perhaps, the new voting stock is a 70/30 split where the well spouse retains a commensurate amount of voting power based on investment. Therefore, the original marital (corporate) contract becomes null and void. The voting stock, by default, is now transferred to the caregiver, and the caregiver is now the majority stockholder in charge of the marriage in the new corporation.

Because the original contract is no longer in effect, all bets are off. This requires a new contract to be negotiated between the partners. The only exception to this scenario is when the couple is dealing with dementia or any other disability where an altered mental status is involved. Then, the well spouse has complete control of the marital corporation. This healthy spouse must be able to make decisions for both parties that serve the best interest of *both* of them.

Unfortunately, in most spousal caregiver situations, the caregiver and the disabled partner both assume the original terms of the "well" agreement are still in effect. The disabled partner says, "Jump" and the caregiver says "how high" because they are still operating with the idea all life is unchanged. To acknowledge that this is not the cruise either of them signed up for is unthinkable. After all, they said vows, didn't they? Did they not promise to love, honor and obey in sickness and health?

There is very little about caregiving for a chronically ill or disabled spouse in this chapter. The reason for this is that spousal caregivers must first understand the mechanics of relationships. The caregiver will not find the courage or skill to prepare and execute an action plan unless they have a thorough understanding of relationship reality. The ideas in this chapter are unique because, as a society, we are not accustomed to looking at the reality of relationships. The only way the caregiver can prepare for these ideas is to resolve to keep an open mind. The true test of the validity of the ideas is whether they work for the reader. The reader should try them on for size.

RELATIONSHIPS 101

Getting our needs met is the challenge we face. Once we get beyond the basic physical needs, most of our needs involve people in one way or another. Our interpersonal needs are the most pressing of all for most of us. When these needs are not met, we are in pain, the pain of loneliness, rejection, conflict, anger, or perhaps worst of all, indifference.

We see it most vividly in our intimate relationships. Intimacy can be ecstasy when it goes well and agony when it does not. When a young couple in their 20s spends a weekend at a resort, playing tennis, sharing beautiful scenery and fine food, and making love long into the night, the world looks heavenly. But, if later that same couple fights because she did not handle an obnoxious drunk to meet his specifications; the world becomes hell on earth.

Other family relationships create similar variations. The teenager who achieves special recognition for excellence in school makes parents proud enough to pop their buttons. But, adolescents involved in drugs, vandalism and sexual activities can make parents prematurely gray. Parents visiting their grown children can make themselves welcome with their tolerance of a life style different from their own, or make their visit as memorable as toothache.

On the job, we must interact constantly with other people. Business and industry exists to serve people, so "customer relations" is always a bread and butter issue. Irate customers handled well become regulars, but will go elsewhere if not satisfied. The business will suffer the consequences of poor relationships. In the "professions," such as law, medicine, and dentistry, interpersonal skills (bedside manner) can make the difference between distinguished service and a practice that limps along. People-skills are often considered "soft" skills. People with sharp minds study engineering or medicine.

Some consider knowledge of how people tick. Since people are so unpredictable, how can anyone pretend to study behavior scientifically? Professionals in the behavioral sciences, like psychology, probably bring some of this on themselves by pretending to know more than they do at times and some of them are truly weird. However, the main culprit is the social tradition that puts interpersonal skills near the bottom of our collective educational agenda.

Since we acquire such "people" skills haphazardly, our knowledge of the principles, which govern relationships, is full of holes. Without a workable fund of knowledge, we fall prey to our emotions. Because we feel compassion for someone, we may leap in and try to help, only to bungle the whole deal by depriving them of the strength they would have gained by handling it themselves. Our unschooled instincts often allow us to be swept up in other people's agendas, accommodating to their wishes much like we obeyed our parents as we were growing up. This is a problem when their objectives interfere with our own, or when we are asked to give up something with little in return.

It is not uncommon for caregivers new to their role to be so compassionate that they actually set the stage for unnecessary problems later in the caregiving relationship. For example, they may take over completely and do more for the ill spouse than is necessary. This can deprive the ill spouse of a sense of accomplishment in performing some of their own self-care. It can undermine the ill spouse's self-esteem in the process. It can also send the wrong message about the willingness of the caregivers to submerge themselves totally into giving care, a pattern that might be tough to break later as the needs of the ill partner increase correspondingly to the caregiver's feelings of burnout. Essentially, it is necessary to pace the use of caregiver resources.

Shaky knowledge of relationships can cause us to use ineffective strategies for managing a broad spectrum of situations. We may try to confront someone constructively, and only succeed in alienating him or her. We may attempt to give someone feedback they badly need, only to lose a friend. In giving someone advice, we get our feelings hurt when they ignore it. In trying to build a relationship, we either go too fast and scare them away or too slow and bore them to crossword puzzles.

THE NEED FOR BASIC RELATIONSHIP THEORY

There is nothing more practical than a good theory. A good theory put man on the moon, allowed for the creation of the internal combustion engine, polio vaccine, computers, thermal underwear, and baked Alaska. A theory is a set of conceptual cubbyholes that allows us to organize the past and predict the future.

A good relationship theory helps us make sense of what is going on in our interactions with others, and to predict accurately that if we do X, they will do Y. The ability to make accurate predictions gives us the power to control the direction of relationships. The alternative to good theory is bad theory; that is what we learn from our friends when we are young. Bad theory leads to bad predictions, which leads to disappointment, confusion, unmet needs and finally unhappiness.

A good relationship theory is invaluable to the spousal caregiver. The theory allows caregivers to predict with some accuracy how grateful ill spouses are for special consideration, and how to parlay that into concessions by the ill spouse. That is, capitalizing on the exchange process becomes a way of "buying" respite time for the caregiver. It allows caregivers to understand the value of those moments of genuine sharing that the ill spouse can actually handle, and how it contributes to the overall quality of the caregiving relationship. It helps caregivers become better listeners because they can look for those little indicators, or "tells" that help provide a roadmap for successful negotiation of critical issues.

The first step is a theory of how relationships develop, beginning with how they get started and continuing through the initial stages of creating a workable, mutually beneficial contract.

Step 1—Knowing What We Need

Relationships that work serve the needs of both parties. The computer salesperson initiates a relationship with the owner of a retail chain. The motive of the salesperson centers on the commission to be received on the sale of equipment. The owner of the business is open to new ways to simplify her life or she would not agree to see the salesperson. Both parties start out looking at the prospective relationship from their own perspective. What's in this for me? It must be assumed that both parties start the relationship knowing exactly what they need from the other person. Nobody thinks of this as a silly or preposterous idea. After all, business is business. You scratch my back and I'll scratch yours.

To take this simple idea a step farther, we also intuitively know that if the salesperson for some reason did not know what he needed, his relationships with prospective customers would never get off the ground. He would not even bother to call on the executive, let alone attempt to serve her needs. The need for a sales commission is a beacon in the night, guiding and motivating the salesman's efforts. It makes him goal-directed and persistent. The relationship is a means for him to get something he needs. His needs are the engine, pulling the relationship caboose.

The same can be said of the executive. If she did not think the relationship with the salesperson would serve her business needs, she would not give him the time of day. Self-interest drives her decision to meet with him. If she did not understand her business needs, her business would quickly go down the tubes. Nothing strange about this, we stated, "business is business," but what about all our other relationships? Are we not after something for ourselves? Of course, we are. We enter all relationships looking for what we want.

The plain truth is that we are all far more concerned with what we receive than what we give in relationships. For a variety of reasons, our interpersonal needs are often poorly defined. In fact, it would make a fascinating parlor game to ask each member of couples at a party to state exactly what they were hoping to get for themselves when they entered the relationship. The game would quickly send the guests home and give the host a reputation for meddling. Their discomfort lies in people's poor understanding of how personal relationships serve them. Even the very idea of entering a relationship for oneself can be seen as crass and "selfish." The romantic ideal of trying to make others happy is deeply ingrained in our culture.

The first step in creating a relationship that has vitality and staying power is to understand our own needs. Relationships are potent, all-purpose tools for helping us shape our future. Our interactions with others are the hammer, nails and lumber we use to build a house, but without a blueprint, our efforts could very well resemble the aftermath of an earthquake. Our goals, dreams, aspirations and hopes provide guidance for relationships. If we do not know where we are going, how can we hope to nudge gently a relationship in a direction that serves us?

The most efficient way of defining our needs is the creation of a mission statement, described in later chapters. This can serve as foundation for building solid relationships in every realm of our lives. Even a primitive, first draft of a mission statement is better than being the willing victim of everyone else's needs.

This is a real danger for caregivers. The entire landscape in caregiver land is dominated by the needs of the ill spouse. Often the arrangement of space is geared to the needs of the ill spouse. That may include a hospital bed, stacked up medical equipment, a wheelchair, or shelves of medical supplies. There may be ramps instead of steps. At times, the house may reek of foul odors. Then there are the doctor's appointments. The entire household schedule is likely to be controlled by the needs of the ill spouse.

In short, everywhere the caregiver turns there is evidence of the needs of the ill partner. It is not surprising that often these needs swamp the boat, crowding out any consideration of the caregiver's needs.

It is often useful for caregivers to remember what needs were being met by their spouse at the beginning of their relationship. This can help counteract the tidal wave of information about the ill spouse's needs, and help to re-connect with what might be currently missing in the caregiver's life.

Step 2—Remembering Our Interdependence

There is a danger to beginning a relationship by thinking only about what we need. We might forget where our bread is buttered. Most of us rely on others for meeting even our most basic physical needs. We do not grow our own vegetables, slaughter our own hogs, make our own shoes, build our own shelter, weave and sew our own clothes, or set our own broken bones. We are highly specialized and interdependent in modem civilization. We must rely on others to get our needs met.

While we enter relationships for ourselves, we must not cut off our supply of goodies by exploiting their source. Our benefactors must get their needs met too. Those who take unfair advantage of others sometimes make spectacular gains in the short run. The thief is temporarily ahead of the game with his ill-gotten gains. However, they stand to lose in the end. Exploitative people are sued, imprisoned or shunned. Their short-term gains are often small comfort in the end.

Therefore, we must enter relationships with a determination to make both parties winners. In order for us to get what we need over the long haul from any relationship, the other person must be served. There is no free lunch. We must always pay for what we get from others. Even if another person wears a "kick me" sign and bends over, we are best served by helping them up and removing the sign. We take advantage of others only at our own peril. Remember, the TTC knows they need other people to get their needs met.

Once the caregiving process has begun, remembering our interdependence has more relevance to constructing, or tweaking, our support system. Those who provide relief to the caregiver, whether it be mowing the lawn, fixing a meal, or sitting with the ill spouse to provide some respite time, the person helping out will have some kind of expectation in return. The "repayment" may be nothing more than a demonstration of gratitude by the well spouse. Helpers are often motivated by feeling they have contributed something meaningful to someone else.

Step 3—Selection

When we meet someone for the first time, we must decide whether to pursue a relationship with them. This is not solely about a romantic relationship. This is about any introduction, business or personal. If the meeting takes place in a business setting, both parties routinely assess whether the other person can contribute something to their business interests. Does the other person know people I need to know? Is this person's company in need of products I sell? Does this person have knowledge I need to help me? If there is no affirmative answer to questions like these on both sides, the "meeting stage" of this potential relationship will be short-lived.

For the well spouse, the selection of their life partner, now their ill spouse, was certainly based on the perception that the partnership was mutual. Assuming the relationship was working well, then the caregiving arrangement should be relatively easy to work out. Where the partnership was working very well before the illness or injury, the principles in this book are relatively easy to implement. Only if the relationship was not good will it be necessary to execute more in-depth solutions.

The meeting stage is handled differently for most personal relationships, platonic and otherwise. We do not consciously and deliberately ask whether this new person can make a contribution to our lives. Rather, we zero in on short-term and temporary characteristics of the person. Are they physically attractive? Do they appear to like us? Do they make me laugh? Do they smile? We look for "chemistry" or "good vibes."

In the end, most of our personal relationships serve us because we gradually rid ourselves of those people who contribute nothing to our sense of well-being. Some people stay in our circle far too long, long enough to take advantage of us or, at least, waste our precious time. Most of us do a terrible job of initial screening. We let people in who have nothing to contribute to the relationship.

In selecting someone with whom to have a relationship, there is one quality that everyone should have; *personal integrity*. Someone with personal integrity always does what they say they will do. No games. No excuses. No baloney. No B.S. If the person promises something, we can put it in the bank, because we know it will be done. This is an important quality because all relationships are based on a variety of agreements, and someone who breaks agreements will not hold up their end of the deal. This is particularly critical in dating and mate selection. It is equally important for a caregiver who is developing reliable resources for help with the ill spouse.

An important tip-off is how someone handles scheduling commitments. If someone promises to meet us at 8 o'clock and consistently does not show up until 8:45, we should run from the developing relationship. If they are willing to break small contracts like time commitments, they are very likely to break other, more important contracts. Such people are certainly not partner material in any endeavor. In a good pre-illness partnership, it is highly likely that the relationship was characterized by personal integrity.

The Likability Trap

Losers, hangers-on, con men, and other unsavory people who lack personal integrity understand humans love to be liked. The need to be liked by others appears to be universal. For people who are inclined to take advantage of us, all they have to do is appear to like us, and we will be tempted to enclose them in our circle The term Con Man is short for Confidence Man and originates from their ability to seduce us into taking them into our confidence, to trust them.

This becomes a particularly important issue for caregivers. There are unscrupulous people who recognize that households with an ill or disabled person are relatively easy targets. Caregivers are often so desperate for help that they jump at any offer that appears to make their lives easier. They fall prey to those who ingratiate themselves to the caregiver, and when trust is established, they help themselves to valuables in the caregiver's home. Freelance nurse's aides are ordinarily hired without proper background checks. They typically have free access to the ill spouse's home with little or no supervision. It is more expensive to hire an aide through an agency, but usually safer for caregivers, who are unlikely to have experience supervising people or performing background checks.

As further evidence that long-term spousal caregivers tend to fall into the likability trap more easily than others is the fact that many of us were natural nurturers. We were primary caregivers as parents. We are typically the professionals in the healthcare fields. We are teachers, professors or counselors. Because of our occupations, we believe that we should handle caregiver responsibilities better than others. We receive our motivation from the sense of fulfillment. Con men can notice this vulnerability when we are under pressure from caregiving duties. There are some ways to spot people with integrity problems.

- They arrive late to meetings
- The "forget" to bring you something they promised
- They make excuses for why they didn't email you directions
- They "forgot" their wallet
- They borrow cab fare

There are artificial integrity problems that are easy to handle if understood. Patients with dementia often have trouble with memory; forgetting is real and is only technically an integrity problem. Ill spouses with severe physical limitations or chronic pain also seem to "forget" easily. Well spouses are only minimally inconvenienced by these problems if they have sufficient insight to not take it personally.

Step 4—Diagnosis

Diagnosis is a lot harder than selection. In Step 3 the focus of our attention is on us. Hard as that may be, it is considerably easier than figuring out what someone else needs. Self-interest is part of our biological heritage and is more "natural" than an interest in others. Our task is complicated by people's natural defenses. They are likely to display a mask of who they want us to think they are, concealing what they need. Especially in the meeting stage, people often confine their remarks to superficial chitchat.

This means "Person A" will have to make a conscious and deliberate effort to find out about B's needs. Questioning and listening are again the main tools. Questions, such as the following are helpful for initial "getting to know you" meetings. What do you do with your spare time? What are your hobbies? What business are you in? How has the economy affected your business? Where do you live? How long have you lived there? Where did you come from? What do you like best about living out there? How old are your children? What school do they attend? How do they like it?

Questions like these uncover needs only indirectly, but this is the only socially acceptable way that is practical. A more direct approach would be considered prying, and the defensive barriers would slam shut. It should also be noted that Step 3 and Step 4 are usually handled simultaneously. Questions are then perceived as a natural part of socializing, not the third degree.

In a marriage involving caregiving, more direct assessment is required and needs cannot be met in the absence of pure honesty. Diagnosis in the context of caregiving would often focus on an assessment of the ill spouse's needs, and how they are separate from the ill spouse's wants. It also must focus attention on which of the ill spouse's actual needs can only be met by the caregiver, and those can be met by anyone who happens to be available. This diagnostic process could be crucial to creating an effective action plan that will allow the caregiver to achieve a better balance between satisfying the needs of both the caregiver and the ill spouse.

Diagnosis not only sets the stage for a truly reciprocal relationship, but it helps eliminate *"Coin of the Realm"* problems. Misunderstandings occur when one person metaphorically wants to be paid in U.S. currency, but is instead paid in Japanese yen. This is seen most dramatically in certain troubled marriages.

The wife goes in first for counseling, as is typical, and complains that many of her needs are not being met. Reluctantly, the husband agrees to attend a session. He arrives late and is angry. He tells the counselor he has been a model husband. His wife has a new car, diamond jewelry, a beautiful home in the suburbs, two wonderful children, and a closet full of designer clothes. What else could she possibly want?

The counselor then tactfully suggests maybe she would like some more of his time, communication about issues she is interested in, emotional support, tenderness, and maybe some romance. Things like that which he may have forgotten. He has been giving her what he finds convenient to give, rather than what she really needs. He never thought about diagnosing what she really needed. He was displaying all the sensitivity of Charlie the Tuna, but there was a problem at her end, too. She believed in the Great American Myth: *If he really loved me, he would know what I need.* The Myth has another, even deadlier variation: *If I have to tell him what I need, it won't count when I get it—he's got to think of it all by himself.*

This pattern leads to frustration and unmet needs on both sides. He does not bother to find out what she needs from him. Instead he gives her what he has available, thus feeling he has done his part for the marital corporation. She refuses to tell him his investments are off target, forcing him to read her mind. Therefore, she withholds affection, and he views her as ungrateful. She gets little understanding and he gets little affection. Nobody gets what they need and they are both to blame. What a mess this can become.

The caregiver who wants closeness and intimacy comparable to what was available before the illness or disability will probably not be able to attain it. Furthermore, what the ill spouse has to offer will not compensate for what is now missing from the relationship. Only through an in-depth diagnostic process will the caregiver uncover an appropriate 'coin of the realm' to keep the ledger from becoming unbearably unbalanced.

Step 5—Investment

Through the first four steps, person A now knows there is potential for a viable relationship with person B. The next step is to "launch" the relationship by making an investment in the relationship. Since A has gone to the trouble to find out what B needs, the initial investment can be made with the accuracy of a rifle. People who do not go through the diagnosis step are forced to use a scattergun, hoping some of the shot pellets will be on target. What gets invested depends entirely on what person A learned during diagnosis. We call such investments "social credits." These credits include investments such as: helping person B solve a problem, doing B a favor, lending B something useful, giving B new information, introducing B to someone, running an errand for B, or even sharing a good joke.

Investing the right amount is also important. Investing too much initially can make people suspicious. A suitor brings a gold bracelet as a gift on the first date. A salesperson offers a golf outing before the first order is written. These investments are too great and will probably backfire. But an investment can also be too small. If person B receives too little, it may not look like an investment, and lead to no movement whatever.

It is possible for a spousal caregiver to decide it is their duty to invest at a greater rate than their partner could invest at the onset of a disabling disease process or sudden disability. The common perception is that the ill spouse would do the same if the situation were reversed. Perhaps, for the caregiver to the chronically ill, the well spouse even mistakenly perceived that this unbalanced investment would only be during a "recovery" period, then all would return to normal. It becomes hard to determine when a well spouse moves from a mindset of "this is temporary" to "uh oh, this is permanent." Over-investment can become a habit that is difficult to break later.

Step 6—Send Bills

Since we will not get repaid by doing or saying nothing, we must request repayment by sending a bill. Ordinarily, this consists of simple requests like the following: "Could I borrow your recording of Beethoven's fourth piano concerto for about a week so I can burn a CD?" "I'd like to use your snow blower this afternoon." "Would it be possible for you to help me think through my insurance dilemma? I need about 30 minutes of your time." "Would you be willing to call George Allen for me and let him know what business I will be in?"

When sending a bill, we must be specific. Vague hints will not work. We must tell the other person what we want, how much we want, when we want it, what style is to be used, and so forth. If necessary, we must use a paint-by-the-numbers approach. Beware of the Great American Myth ("if I have to tell her, it won't count when I get it") because it undercuts the value of sending of bills.

What if the bill isn't paid? There are two main possibilities. Either something went wrong with the whole transaction, or person B is simply not interested in a relationship with person A. Before concluding the relationship cannot proceed, it is important to take two more steps. Recheck the initial investment. Did we accurately diagnose what B needs? Did we make B aware of our investment? Did we send a bill for something B can actually deliver? Send a past due bill. Either make the same request again, or at some later time ask for an equivalent favor or service.

If person B is still not willing to pay up, it is pointless to continue. This does not mean person B is a jerk. It may merely mean B is not currently in the market for another relationship at the moment. Person B may have another supplier of what we were willing to invest. Person A should assume a "no fault" stance about the whole episode, and go elsewhere.

Because there is always a possibility our bill will not be paid, it is extremely important to remember the most important rule of playing poker: never bet more than you can afford to lose. That is, in starting to develop a relationship with someone, we must start small so we never get burned.

Can we send bills to an ill spouse? Because of the limitations of the ill spouse to hold up their end of the relationship, it might seem like a pointless exercise to send an invoice to an ill spouse. It is certainly the case that caregiving puts rather severe limitations on what can be accomplished by sending routine bills. On the other hand, if the caregiver has gone to the trouble, as advocated in Step 4, Diagnosis, the caregiver should have a pretty clear idea of what can reasonably be expected back form the ill spouse. At the very least, the ill spouse can:

- Minimize complaining or judging the well partner's delivery of care
- Show sincere gratitude routinely
- Make only reasonable requests of the caregiver
- Cheerfully accept alternative sources of care during respite outings

Step 7—Return on Investment (ROI)

If all goes well in the preceding steps when building a mutually satisfying relationship, there is a good chance person B will recognize the wisdom of a reciprocal exchange process, and honor person A's request. Once the bill is paid, a condition of equity exists. The relationship has stability and is not a source of stress to either party. Many relationships never get past this infancy stage. Even if both parties are satisfied with the first exchange, neither of them may ever get around to initiating another such interchange. From that point on, they define each other as "acquaintances," nodding acknowledgement as they pass on the street, or chatting briefly about mutual acquaintances if time permits.

This is something that a well spouse will experience when interviewing people to help with caregiving to find relief from primary duties. We may interview a person who came highly recommended from a trusted friend. During the interview process, we realize that it is not going to work out. We may not want interactions to continue and we left the relationship in the infancy stage, but we are connected as acquaintances because of our mutual friend.

The most common reason such relationships go nowhere is because of limited time available for relationship maintenance. Every relationship we encourage means a commitment of time to keep the flame alive. Thus, we are constantly setting priorities among the people we know. Some relationships last until another, more useful one is created. The circle of people we relate to is in constant flux, changing composition from week to week, month to month. Some of us wonder what happened to someone we once viewed as a dear friend. We recall nothing specific about a demise of the relationship, but we may not have spoken for years. Basically, the friendship evolved as far as either party cared to nurture it. Our ROI was mutually disproportionate to the effort it required.

A well spouse will often wonder where their friends went after the onset of the illness or disability. A couple of possibilities can occur. First, the assistance that the ill spouse required may have seemed overwhelming to friends. They exit the relationship in fear that they will be called upon for assistance. The ROI, for those friends, was going to be far less than investment was worth.

Secondly, if the caregiver's ledger is unbalanced because of the limitations of the ill spouse, we feel owed. It is possible that to balance the ledger, we have unknowingly sought ROI from our friends. They may have even tried to compensate us, but it is *never* enough. The friends will seek an exit from the relationship lest *they* begin to feel owed.

Step 8—Building a Stronger Relationship

If a relationship looks particularly useful after the initial exchange, it might be desirable to escalate to a higher level. This person might be especially attractive because what they can contribute is in short supply, or they need something we have wanted to give someone. Many times such a relationship "clicks" in that certain intangibles are exchanged that neither party bothers to define consciously, such as a particular form of humor, a quality of warmth, or a stimulating communication style.

A poignant example would be particularly true for members of a support group similar to those sponsored by the Well Spouse Association. Through support systems of this type, members are able to have their battered self-esteem soothed. Spousal caregivers find the acceptance and the past-due acknowledgement that they are seeking. Well spouses need to know that what care they provide is valuable, necessary and appreciated. Well Spouse members offer the emotional connections that become cravings when caregiving morphs into tangible loneliness. This may be the reason many "former" well spouses continue to rely on the support group.

In other types of relationships, the initial level of exchange should be repeated several times. The parties borrow small items from each other, take each other to lunch, invite each other fishing, help with special transportation needs, and so forth. Every effort must be made to keep the exchanges roughly equitable. Obviously, no relationship has exact equity at every moment of its existence. Once an investment is made, the relationship is out of balance. If an acceptable ROI requires two installments, equity is of course not achieved after the first payment. In order to ride out the periods of technical inequity, both parties must develop trust that when they make an investment, it will be repaid. By exchanging social credits for a while at the initial investment level, both parties have an opportunity to check out the trustworthiness of the other.

When confidence has reached a high enough level, it is time for one party to make an investment which is clearly worth more than the value of previous exchanges. To exemplify this interchange in everyday life, Jane might ask Betty's family to join them at the beach for a long weekend. This is a critical stage of the relationship. Betty has the option of accepting or rejecting the invitation. The meaning of a rejection is not always clear.

Betty might have conflicting plans and is unable to accept. Jane has no foolproof way to determine whether the conflict is real or an excuse not to go. Sometimes the way Betty refuses contains clues. If Betty seems genuinely remorseful for the missed opportunity, the relationship might still have the potential to grow. However, if the refusal is perfunctory, the friendship may have reached its upper limit.

A refusal can only be clarified with time. If Betty later offers an investment at a higher level, Jane knows the initial refusal represented a genuine conflict. Alternatively, if Jane tries again at the higher level, and the second offer is accepted, then the friendship still has greater potential. On the other hand, Betty clearly has the right to stop any increase in the level of exchange. She could have been completely satisfied with all previous exchanges and still limit the friendship to the existing level. For example, she might have too many other commitments to devote any more time to Jane. This does not mean Betty wishes to end all further transactions. It just means enough is enough.

Unfortunately, communicating this complex message is tricky at best. Jane could easily feel rebuffed and exit completely from the relationship. Our society does not teach us to talk comfortably about levels of exchange in a relationship. Recent psychological research has demonstrated that couples treat the quality and future of their relationship as a taboo subject. In all likelihood, it would never occur to Betty to say, "Jane, I have very much enjoyed our friendship, and I want us to continue exactly as before. I have run out of time for this relationship. I cannot devote any more time to it. I do hope you understand how much it means to me in its present form. Let's have lunch tomorrow." For most of us, this would be speaking the unspeakable. Nevertheless, this is the only hope Betty has for continuing at the present exchange level if Jane has been dead set on escalation.

On the other side, it is presumptuous of Jane to assume that a higher level would be seen as desirable by Betty. Sometimes we are trapped into believing other people feel the way we do, or that others would be fools to pass up the opportunity to have a stronger relationship with us. Both of these assumptions represent a form of arrogance. It would be far better if Jane could keep her ego in check and prepare herself for limits placed on the upward spiral. This is hard to pull off because our needs for acceptance and intimacy are so incredibly powerful that we often take others' limits as rejection. The well spouse, when feeling owed, is vulnerable to misreading other people and is especially hurt when limits are set by others.

LIMITING INVESTMENTS

Limiting the growth of a relationship is probably the most troublesome action for a person to take in any relationship. The Deadly Misconceptions, in general, are the driving force behind this tough directive. We are indoctrinated that it is better to give than to receive and that there is something noble about sacrifice. We are told when we marry that we have become "one" and it is reinforced when we are reminded of our vows. When building a platonic relationship with an individual we want in our intimate circle, we tend to give without conscious tally in the internal ledger because we expect the ROI will be a lasting friendship. As stated earlier, it is of the utmost importance not to give more than we can afford to lose.

Another Deadly Misconception is "love is forever." This is an idealistic notion. The truth is that love is a byproduct of a good contractual relationship. Love tends to flounder when our partner becomes too ill or incapable of delivering their end of the contract. If the original relationship contract becomes null and void because one party cannot deliver what they promised when the contracts were being negotiated, then how is it rational to assume that the byproduct of a good contract, mature adult love, could still exist in that form? Realistically, when the contract becomes void the love is certainly altered, and may, in fact, disappear. Often the love changes to resemble the love of a parent for a child. The fondness and friendship may continue, but the mature adult love is unlikely to remain. Nothing is permanent and love is not forever.

This does not mean that a well spouse should stop investing in the relationship. Rather, the well spouse should limit the investment to better match the anticipated ROI. In other words, stop sacrificing to the point of feeling owed. What are the expectations of the marital contract now that there is an illness or disability involved?

Feelings of warmth and trust for another person are certainly necessary ingredients of any long-term intimate relationship. When we were courting (our now ill spouse) these evolved naturally, as interactions panned out at one level and moved to higher levels with more intimate exchanges. However, we have suggested that mature adult love is a byproduct of an equitable contract, that agreements are the engine with love the caboose. It is because of the complex feelings involved on both sides that we must handle our ill spouse with the utmost delicacy during the re-negotiation process. The intention of the well spouse to limit higher levels of investment into the relationship with the ill spouse must be handled diplomatically. We need to be able to communicate that this new marital contract is the only way we can continue to deliver care without becoming burned out.

EXPLOITATIVE RELATIONSHIPS

On the other hand, accepting investment at a higher level with no intention of reciprocity is a form of exploitation. Well spouses may feel like they are being exploited when there is no show of gratitude. Yet, spousal caregivers continue to believe that love means never having to say you are sorry, or restated, love means never having to say thank you. Several variations of this pattern are common.

1. Take It and Run

In this pattern, one party takes from the other with full knowledge that the relationship is going nowhere.

෧෧

Kate accepted jewelry from David, and politely keeps putting him off when he sent half-hearted bills. She threw him enough tidbits of gratitude to encourage him to keep investing, but when he finally said it was not enough, she filed for divorce.

෧෧

2. *Quest for Acceptance*

This situation begins with one party so eager to be accepted by someone, anyone, that they bend themselves into a pretzel on the other's behalf.

❧❦

Rhonda was so needy that she interpreted politeness from Mary as an invitation to invest more into a friendship foundation for Kate long-term benefit. She threw all her resources into the relationship, participating in events Mary planned, spending money she did not have just to be involved in Andy's family. For their part, Andy's family felt a bit sorry for Rhonda. They tried to make her feel involved.

It honestly never occurred to them that their acceptance was terribly misleading and was building an emotional trap for Rhonda that would ultimately snap shut. Finally, when Rhonda inevitably asked for a commitment, tried to make her case for Andy's irrational behaviors and begged for understanding, the entire family shot her down in flames. Rhonda was the one with the problem, they proclaimed. The investment was for naught.

❧❦

3. *Misrepresentation of Needs*

This particularly destructive form of the pattern begins when one party deliberately pretends to be someone they are not. A women married to a man with destructive qualities is asked this question by the counselor; "How much of this did you know before you married him?" The typical answer is, "None of it!"

❧❦

Mark put the rush on Arlene. He went all out to please her. They went to the restaurants she preferred, her movies, her music, and so on. Her wish was his command. He jumped in to fulfill her desires, however small. Of course, Arlene was flattered, and ultimately swept off her feet. Mark's strategy was almost evil. He deliberately withheld from Arlene what he wanted in return.

He pretended to want very little from her so she would make a long-term commitment. Once they were married, he changed overnight. All of a sudden, she was swamped with his demands, many of which interfered with her ability to meet her needs. He demanded absolute obedience and full control of the finances. Had she known this side of his personality, she would never have married him. He knew this, which is precisely why he wore a mask throughout courtship. Now she felt trapped in a horrible marriage. This situation is intolerable when the additional problem of illness or disability encroaches into the existing dysfunctional marriage. Are we still bound to our wedding vows? The whole marriage has been a sham. How devoted are we now and should we sacrifice the remainder of our lives?

∾∾

From these examples, it should be clear that accepting higher levels of investment without a clear and mutual agreement about reciprocity is dangerous indeed. Every effort must be made to prevent one-sided relationships from getting started or being perpetuated, especially when an illness or disability is involved. Recognition of these developing tendencies may be something the spousal relationship has never before experienced, but with the emerging imbalance of the internal ledger, the relationship becomes dysfunction. This is an area where knowledge is power. Awareness of the mechanics of relationship development should help prevent misunderstandings and keep those that occur from contaminating all other exchanges, a necessary component when renegotiating the marriage contract.

RECIPROCITY AT A HIGHER LEVEL

Accepting an investment at a higher level is akin to a non-verbal contractual agreement. To accept a "payment" at a new level conveys a willingness to be sent a bill for the more expensive investment, and to pay up. Complications can arise, of course, if we are offered something we really need or desire, even though its value exceeds any previous transactions.

Without realizing the implications, we might impulsively accept. Then when the bill is sent, we might be shocked at its magnitude. Such misunderstandings are common in a corporate environment, in business transactions and in courtship. This is why it is so important to understand ramifications of the more expensive investment into the relationship before accepting it. There needs to be special caution for the spousal caregiver in this arrangement, both as the giver and as the receiver. Well spouse caregivers are often so needy for relief that any contribution into a relationship is taken without regard for the anticipated repayment.

❧❦

Rhonda's cousins spontaneously offered to keep the three children for a weekend, making the offer ostensibly because they figured Rhonda was exhausted. She gladly accepted the offer, and used the weekend to catch up on her sleep. What she did not realize is that her cousins intended to take their own four children and Rhonda's three children to an expensive amusement park. Along with two days worth of admission, and food for two days for the entire group, they ran up a bill of nearly a thousand dollars. When they brought the children home, they presented Rhonda with a detailed invoice and expected her company to pay for the entire outing. Rhonda ran her own service business and it was always in deep financial straits for a variety of reasons. But, her cousins were jealous of her business, and they saw this as a way to profit at Rhonda's expense. It was difficult for Rhonda to smell a rat because she was in such dire need of what they offered.

❧❦

Conversely, because spousal caregivers are constantly carrying around an unbalanced ledger when something is asked of us, no matter how small, we may comply with the requested investment. However, we feel like the investment was such an upset to our routine that we sometimes require a repayment that far exceeds the investment. We may even seek the payment from other sources.

If the higher investment level is accepted and returned, a higher exchange level has been established between the parties. Now the principle that governed the initial exchange applies; exchanges on this new plateau must be repeated until a new degree of trust is established. The entire process must be repeated at each new step up the intimacy ladder until one or both parties are unwilling to go further. For a well spousal caregiver, if trust is not established and payments are not mutual, it magnifies the sense of feeling owed. Ironically, for many well spouses accepting without repaying is a common scenario because we continually feel owed. This is perhaps a reason that we tend to lose our friends and support systems.

INTERNAL LEDGERS & FEELING "OWED" SPOUSAL CAREGIVERS

While simply being a caregiver is tough enough, there is something that is even more insidious that needs to be discussed. It is in the context of the ill effects of the caregiver relationship. The brain of any human being has a mind of its own, so to speak. When we feel owed, we are in a state of chronic deficit and that deficit puts us in a state of constant anger.

Feeling owed is a deadly affliction because we may seek to be repaid anywhere we can find what we need, whether or not that source is appropriate. Therefore, we walk around constantly looking for the world to be kind to us, to be charitable, to give us strokes, congratulations, sympathy, or whatever it is we feel we can get from these people. When this is combined with our anger, it is potentially harmful. The collision of our anger and feeling owed sets the stage for a lot of dysfunctional behavior. In extreme situations, caregivers consider suicide. More commonly though, they vent in the car in the form of road rage and they scream at inanimate objects. They refuse to complete tasks because every day merges into the next and diminishes any sense of urgency.

Caregivers, when angry and feeling owed, withhold services to their ill spouse and to other people who count on them. Sometimes the distraught caregiver will consider withholding medication from the ill spouse. Owed caregivers will often take out their frustrations on innocent service-oriented businesses and their employees. The caregiver complains constantly and is never satisfied with the service or the merchandise. The people trying to serve us are yelled at and verbally assaulted. There is a feeling that we can say anything we please because we do not know these people and we get out our anger before we return home to our burdens.

INTERNAL LEDGER & FEELING "OWED" EVERYONE

For anyone in any sort of relationship, once we have invested in a relationship, we expect something in return. It is not that asking for something back is optional; it is not that casual. We are all carrying around an Internal Ledger that keeps track of what we invest and what we get back. It keeps track whether we want it to or not, like an automatic computer. Our internal ledger is silent when there is equity between what we invest and what we receive. That is, when the subjective value of investment roughly equals return on investment, a kind of stability exists, and the ledger is quiet. The moment an investment is given, or received, an alarm goes off signaling a departure from equity.

For example, a shopper leaving a department store is about to push through the outer doors, when she becomes aware of a man, arms full of packages, about to leave the store behind her. Being polite, she holds the door for him. Now she has made a small investment in the relationship and her ledger is unbalanced. She expects something in return. Not much, because it will not take much to restore her ledger to balance. All he has to do is smile, nod, or better yet, say "thank you." However, suppose the man does not acknowledge the service she performed in any way whatever. Her alarm goes off. She is not despondent or depressed, but she is irked. Her investment went for naught. She very likely utters "Jerk!" to herself.

In another example, a motorist is backed up in traffic at a red light when he spots another driver emerging from a driveway on his right, wanting to enter traffic. Being polite, the motorist signals the other driver to move in ahead of him as traffic begins to move. He has made an investment, and his internal ledger is slightly out of balance. All he wants is some kind of non-verbal acknowledgement that a service has been performed. Again, assume the driver ignores the favor and drives off, nose in the air. The motorist is clearly irritated that his politeness was ignored, and feels like issuing some kind of non-verbal rejoinder. His alarm has gone off because his internal ledger is unbalanced.

There would be nothing controversial about this observation of the human condition except for the message most of us receive growing up: *it is wrong to keep track.* Most of us consider it somehow uncivilized to keep a running tally. With this concept, we envision ourselves wearing a green eyeshade and thick glasses, pouring over ledgers in a dingy back office. The truth is we keep track whether we think it right or not. We do not have a choice.

If our conditioning was especially successful, we may be able to tone down the alarms, or figure out some other way to ignore them. We might even successfully convince ourselves we do not actually keep track, which, of course, is a form of self-deception. Even if we suppress what is going on in our heads, we will be affected because unbalanced ledgers create stress. Stress that is not dealt with constructively hangs around and affects our behavior or our physical condition in indirect ways. We call it burnout. Dr. Travland's experiences with clients in psychotherapy and marriage counseling uniformly demonstrated the predictability of stress related illnesses, unbalanced ledgers and feeling owed. His conclusion is the heart of this section, feeling owed because of an unbalanced relationship is a major cause of the "stress" in many if not most stress-related illnesses.

How can we keep our ledgers balanced? Can we not rely on the good will of others to realize they *owe* us? Will they not simply give us what we are owed? Unfortunately, when we rely on others to give voluntarily and spontaneously to us an adequate return on our investment we will usually feel cheated.

There are three main reasons for this. First, an individual's needs and wants are more pressing than the needs and wants of others. We are, by nature, much more attentive to what we are owed by others than what we owe them. This is precisely the reason that following blindly the "Deadly Misconceptions" as if they were solid truths, leads people to unhappiness, inaction, denial or the inability to accept responsibility for their own life.

For example, if we get a physical examination and our doctor has failed to send us a bill, what are the odds that we will rush to the phone after 30 days or so, and find out what we owe so we can pay it? The odds are slim, not because we mind paying the bill, but because we are likely to forget about it. In Western society, the responsibility for repayment rests with the investor. If an accountant runs up a $1200 bill for tax services to a corporation, fails to send a bill for services rendered, the accountant will not be paid. The corporation will assume it is up the accountant to be paid. We likewise assume it is up to our doctor to get paid.

In ordinary interactions with others, we cannot be adequately repaid unless the other person makes an effort to diagnose what we need. Any attempt to repay us without diagnosis would involve a scattergun approach, which will be wide of the mark. The odds are overwhelmingly against our getting a reasonable return on our investments in relationships if we simply ignore this approach to repayment. So, what do we need to do? People who are owed—an unbalanced ledger with an over due account—sometimes try to recoup their loss by investing even more into the relationship. For instance, an airline passenger tries to make friends with the person sitting next to him, but is rebuffed. Later, as the flight attendant pushes the cart down the aisle, the passenger offers to buy his neighbor a drink. One problem with this strategy is that the drink may yield no more warmth than the initial attempt. The drink would then represent throwing good social credits after bad.

The more important problem with this strategy is that it *devalues* what we invest. By giving disproportionately to what we receive, we come to believe what we give others is not worth as much, pound for pound, as what we receive. Over time, we begin to operate on an erroneous system of internal currency. Our self-esteem begins to suffer. We think that what we offer no longer matters to anyone. That is a stiff penalty for being a nice person.

For the caregiver to a chronically ill or disabled spouse, devalued currency is a huge problem. Caregivers give and give, and the return they get back from the ill spouse is only a small fraction of what the caregiver's investment was "worth." It is inevitable that this imbalance works on the self-perception of the caregiver. The value of what the caregiver invests is degraded automatically because an equivalent return is not forthcoming, thus adding to the frustrations which are intrinsic to caregiving. It creates damaged self-esteem which is often experienced as a sense of worthlessness or inadequacy, and accompanied by depression. Then caregivers begin to feel owed.

The authors believe that the concept of feeling owed is the center of any caregiving relationship dynamic. Caregivers are compassionate and accepted their roles willingly. However, there is usually no way to anticipate the unbalanced ledger issue. When a caregiver begins to feel owed, they dismiss the feelings by telling themselves they are just being selfish. Thoughts of anger feel taboo. We remind ourselves that it is not our spouse's fault that we ended up as full-time caregivers. After all, nobody chooses an illness or disability. However, failure to admit that we feel owed will still seep through in unconscious ways.

჻

The Brown Stamp Example of Feeling Owed

It is an ill-conceived strategy to ignore imbalances. Write them off and forget about it. *Turn the other cheek.* At very limited times, this is a prudent course of action, but as a policy, it can be disastrous. This can be considered a Brown Stamp Strategy. Every time we fail to be repaid, it is like pasting another stamp in our brown stamp book. All is well until we paste in the last stamp. Then we cash in the whole book at once. For example, everyone knew Ralph was obnoxious, but Ben was nice to him anyhow. Every time Ralph rubbed Ben the wrong way, Ben did not react, but he did paste another brown stamp in his book. Then one day Ralph did it again, Ben pasted in his last stamp, and exploded in an angry rage. Ben's reaction was out of proportion to Ralph's behavior, or perceived infraction. It carried the steam of all the accumulated resentments Ben had stored away.

჻

For a well spouse, the accumulation of brown stamps leads to a variety of possible consequences within the caregiving relationship. Caregivers give so much on a daily basis, but the ill partner has limited ability to give back, to redress the unbalanced internal ledger. Nevertheless, we feel owed. These resentments, which have been tucked away, ignored or unmanaged, accumulate and a variety of consequences can occur. Some are extreme, but they occur.

- Subtle sarcasm, little jabs toward the ill spouse
- Name calling, general verbal abuse
- Passive aggressive retaliation against the ill spouse, such as "forgetting" to do a favor
- Cashing the whole Brown Stamp Book in at once; physical violence, melt down
- Not keeping the ill partner informed about daily activities
- Making the ill spouse feel like a burden, making them pay for the debt they have accumulated

Caregivers must avoid accumulating too many "brown stamps" and limit the investment in the ill spouse to those needs that can *only* be fulfilled by the caregiver. This also means distinguishing carefully between needs and wants. The typical ill spouse is not likely to make that distinction, so this awareness must come from the caregiver. Needs must be met, but not wants.

STRUCTURE & INTRUSIONS

One way to counteract the chronic and debilitating stress from the perpetual imbalance in the relationship is to rely on a carefully orchestrated structure. Caregivers need to perform certain household duties at certain times, such as shopping, meal preparation, medical procedures, and so forth. This carefully scripted activity becomes one of the only ways caregivers have any chance of carving out any time for themselves. It is also a way of blocking out awareness of the bleakness of the caregiver's situation, making life ever so slightly more livable.

Well-meaning neighbors, friends, or extended family members may wish to visit, often under the flag of wanting to 'help out.' Much of the time such visits feel like intrusions. Caregivers are already stretched thin, and playing host threatens to topple their house of cards. Everything out of the ordinary requires triage for the overextended caregiver. Outsiders are often dumbfounded by the caregiver's lukewarm receptivity to such visits, not realizing such visits are a threat to the caregiver's finely tuned arrangement.

කර්ග

David's niece Tiffany, who lived out of state, emailed a request that she be allowed to stay for a week or two with David and Kate. A decade earlier, Tiffany had stayed with them for about a week and it was mostly a pleasant experience. However, in recent years, David's caregiving responsibilities had become especially burdensome, and he found Tiffany's request to be insensitive and intrusive. David wrote her back and informed her she would not be welcome, that there would be no time available to entertain her.

Tiffany took offense, and many years later still has no understanding that her wish to visit felt to David like an assault on the carefully constructed routine which was keeping chaos at bay. He was under siege at the time, and her request was a threat, a potential tipping point.

Rhonda wanted nobody to visit her home during her years of coping with the demands of a sick husband. Out of town guests were referred to hotels. If they bothered to come to town, they were ignored except for perfunctory visits in the park or a shopping mall. Rhonda could not handle the intrusions. She tried to hide the chaos from outsiders lest they inquire as to what was wrong. She felt as if she was barely clinging to sanity.

කර්ග

THE TIPPING POINT

When this accumulated frustration, anger, or even rage, boils under the surface; the caregiver becomes a stick of dynamite with a short fuse. Normally they can keep things under control for quite some time in the absence of acute provocation. However, they inevitably encounter a situation with their spouse that is absolutely and positively the last straw. We call this a "tipping point." It symbolizes everything that has been happening. That is when the fuse is lit and the dynamite explodes. Tipping points occur in varies types of scenarios. It is simply when an individual has had enough of a repetitive situation. However, tipping points in caregiving can be volatile. The authors urge the well spouse caregivers to examine the concepts of feeling owed along with the following examples of unresolved less-than-satisfying situations. This may help the owed caregiver avoid becoming a "stick of dynamite."

Rhonda's tipping point occurred when her damaged husband erupted in a fit of anger and smashed his hand into the side of her van in an attempt to hit her. It was so violent and destructive that the passenger's door eventually had to be replaced. At the moment this occurred, she left him sitting outside and calmly called his relatives. She told them to come get him or she was calling the police. She explained that they had been through this before and it was too much. Andy would never be able to live with her and the children again. Rhonda had reached her tipping point. The violent episodes were endless; she could no longer tolerate fear as a way of life for her and her three children.

David's tipping point occurred when Kate, with oxygen tank, a urinary catheter and a wound vacuum, demanded that he shuttle her to a flea market. This flea market was dirty and the parking lot was not paved. At the end of that trip, he was exhausted, embarrassed and humiliated. Not only was he spent and angry, but he realized finally that her demands were not in her best interest, no matter what she dictated. She had an open wound in that dirt parking lot. How would she ever get better if he kept succumbing to inane demands, he thought. David immediately began the process of figuring out a way to get more help for proper treatment and perhaps recapture some of her independence. They both needed outside resources to survive. The endless demands without a support system had forced him to take definitive action. Fortunately, Kate's physicians agreed with the need for closer medical supervision.

⇛⇦

THE TOUGH & TENDER CAREGIVER

The TTC understands and acts upon the following basic principles governing the establishment and development of relationships.

- Non-caregivers are very naïve about caregiving realities
- Most advice given to spousal caregivers is geared to coping, not fixing
- Much of what society teaches us about relationships is misleading
- Caregiving involves a new shareholder distribution of voting stock
- TTCs must understand what they need from others to have good relationships
- Needs of the ill spouse are so pervasive TTCs may lose track of what they need
- TTCs can only get what they need by paying attention to what others need
- Successful relationship require integrity at both ends, doing what we promise
- The TTC's internal ledger keeps track of investments and return on investment
- Investing without first diagnosing the other person's needs is pointless
- Investing without an adequate return leads caregivers to feeling "owed"

- Failure to take action when the ledger is unbalanced leads to collecting Brown Stamps, which get cashed in all at once when a Tipping Point is reached
- TTCs understand that to get a return on investment, they must send invoices

Much of our success in life depends on our ability to manage our relationships with people in an effective manner. A realistic relationship theory helps us predict and control the direction and outcome of relationships. In order to develop a meaningful relationship, we must start with a clear definition of our own needs. Getting our needs met in a relationship depends on our willingness to help our counterparts get their needs met. We must carefully select people with whom to have a relationship. They must (a) have something we need, and (b) need something we have. Successful relationships require personal integrity at both ends; both parties must always do what they promise, no exceptions. Relationships are initiated with investments that are (a) large enough to be noticed, (b) small enough to make little difference if they are not returned, and (c) targeted exactly at what the other person needs.

Whenever we make an investment in a relationship, our "internal ledger" leads us to expect an equivalent return on investment. Over time, relationships must be characterized by equity if they are to survive; that is, investments on both ends must be approximately equal. After we invest in a relationship, we will be disappointed if we expect the recipient to volunteer to repay us. We must send bills specifying what we want, when, and how. If someone refuses to give us an adequate return on our initial investment, it is pointless to pursue it further.

Relationships must be consolidated at their initial level before proceeding to the next higher level. This builds trust that all investments will be returned. Before accepting any investment offered by another, we must be prepared to receive an equivalent bill and pay it.

We must base long-term relationships on the quality of the exchange process in addition to our feelings for someone. The TTC understands that caregiving relationships are inherently unequal, and that "feeling owed" is normal. TTCs know they must monitor their internal ledger constantly and take immediate action if they approach a Tipping Point from chronic imbalance.

Chapter 4
MAKING & ENFORCING AGREEMENTS

Creating a Better Understanding

๛

Caregivers now understand how the internal ledger operates to keep track of investments in relationships, and how they have to send invoices to obtain an adequate return on their investment. Now we will take the next step, which is to understand what partnership agreements look like, the different types of agreements, and the mechanics of how such agreements are negotiated.

The subject of accountability must also be understood. People do not automatically live up to their promises, so a workable partnership contract must contain provisions for enforcement. This chapter is designed to give the caregiver additional fundamental philosophy about how to manage relationships.

The TTC will require a sophisticated understanding of the mechanics of relationships to make practical adjustments in the caregiving relationship. There are pressures all around the caregiver to do things wrong. The relationship tools in this chapter can serve as arguments to help TTCs stand their ground in the face of this onslaught.

As with the earlier chapter on relationship management, some of the examples used to explain concepts have little to do directly with caregiving. Ultimately becoming a TTC will depend on relationship sophistication, and general examples will help explain the concepts. We will start with an analysis of relationship myths to be overcome.

RELATIONSHIP MYTHOLOGY

We learn many rules of thumb about how to relate to other people. Some of these make sense and hold up over time. Others are unrealistic, counterproductive or just plain silly. This motivates most of us to find out how we can relate smoothly to others. Unfortunately, much of that guidance leads us astray. Some of the more common myths are discussed below.

Myth: Intimate relationships operate by a different set of rules.

This is seen dramatically with professional men who handle their subordinates tactfully, walk on eggshells with customers, and exercise diplomacy throughout the workday. Then they walk in the front door of their homes at night with no diplomacy whatever. When asked about it, they point out they have had to control their reactions all day at work, and there has to be one place where they can truly be themselves. After all, *"a man's home is his castle"* perpetuates this myth.

The answer is they can be themselves when alone in the car or in the bathroom. When they are in the presence of another human being, the relationship requires management. Furthermore, the most important relationships to manage delicately are the ones at home. Unfortunately, many of us take liberties with our spouses, believing that this relationship operates according to a different set of principles.

The rules that govern relationships between adults are pretty much the same across the board. We may exchange social credits at a higher level in some relationships, but the need for equity is the same, the internal ledger operates the same, and the need to send bills is no different. It is ironic that many people are highly skilled at work, and then fail to use those same skills with the family.

Handling an ill spouse will require even more delicacy and interpersonal skill. A disabled spouse is likely to be frustrated by their own limitations, which could make anyone cranky at times. The TTC will have trouble keeping this in mind when, as a caregiver, the internal ledger is perpetually out of balance. We all want gratitude when we invest under normal conditions, but in a caregiving situation, crankiness and lack of gratitude can be devastating. It is possible to prevent these situations from getting out of hand by viewing these frustrating situations as occasions to renegotiate standing agreements and include accountability provisions. This will require an understanding of relationship rules.

Myth: People who care about us will live up to their agreements

Everyone knows that unscrupulous business people do not always live up to their agreements, and that nations break their word to other nations. However, we are taught that we can always depend on real friends, relatives, and certainly spouses. Unfortunately, this ideal is not an accurate picture of reality. The truth is that we all have a tendency to drift in the direction of self-indulgence unless someone is willing to jerk our chain at times. Our long-term interests give us weaker internal signals than our short-term impulses. All of us at one time or another are sucked into short-term gratification, and some people make it a policy. Alcoholics and drug addicts are notorious for making empty promises, often in good faith, to mend their ways.

We are taught by society and family that our relationships with family members are different from other relationships. This is an old story. Family member rescues family member, time after time, until a total break splits the family like a lightning bolt. The problem is mythology: *"blood is thicker than water."* Another version, *"love conquers all,"* discourages us from making restitution when we have defaulted on an agreement with a loved one. The assumption seems to be that automatic forgiveness is part of the package. But, making amends is no less necessary here than with any relationship.

To counter this mythology, we should stay in touch with the reality that all agreements with anyone should be treated in a business-like way. Everyone is capable of drifting toward short term, self-centered behavior. Failure to monitor and control agreements can often encourage this drift. If people know follow-up will occur, they are much more likely to do what they promised.

In the special case of caregiving relationships, ill spouses will tend to be preoccupied with their own needs, which is normal. They will forget commitments, but the TTC will have established a reputation for follow-up on agreements, including what they commit to do and what they expect in return. Another issue common to the caregiving scenario is relatives who make commitments to help in a variety of ways, but who default unexpectedly. Because the well spouse can make use of "good will" from relatives and friends, it is important to keep expectations relatively low so disappointments can be held in check. If there is a default, then the well spouse will usually get more at a later time from the culprit because of their guilt feelings. There is nothing wrong in this scenario. We are all interdependent and we need to capitalize of this type of event especially as a spousal caregiver who is usually in a position to accept any offers of help. Mobilizing support systems normally requires dispensing more gratitude than seems deserved at times or taking because the giver is filled with guilt. This is considered relationship management.

ALL RELATIONSHIPS ARE CONTRACTS

Now we know that all relationships are best understood as contracts. Even though people seldom define what they have with each other as a contract, the relationship nonetheless satisfies that definition. This is akin to the marital board of directors discussed in the previous chapter. In a business or legal sense, a contract is a formal agreement, usually between two parties, specifying what each will do for the other. Such bargains also contain stated or implied penalties for failure of either party to live up to the contractual provisions. Even simple agreements are contracts.

As a reminder, if we agree to meet someone at six for dinner, the other person has every right to expect us to show up. The unstated penalty is that they will be mad at us if we do not show. We enter into a contract with our automobile mechanic; he fixes our car and we pay a reasonable fee. If we do not pay, he might take us to court. If he does not repair the car, we will require him to do it again, or we might call the Better Business Bureau. Sometimes contracts are very subtle. When a group is sharing expenses and someone does not pay their appropriate portion, the others develop hard feelings. Even though our relationship with our minor children is somewhat one-sided due to our parental obligations, contracts still exist. They have privileges in exchange for expected behaviors; an unspoken contract.

The potential for disruptions and emotional pain is greatest, however, when we view our most important relationship, marriage, in unrealistic terms. These relationship contracts have provisions can be brought to the surface with a little effort, including *penalty* clauses. The remainder of this discussion will focus on marriage (or marriage-like living arrangements) because of the range and scope of interpersonal needs at stake. The principles discussed below apply equally to all relationships, although the main focus will be on partnerships involving long-term caregiving. Understanding the following information can assist the well spouse in making decisions about the state of the marital relationship and how to go about creating a new contract with their ill spouse.

Master Agreements

All long-term relationships are governed by a Master Agreement that consists of hundreds of standing agreements, supplemented by thousands of one-time agreements. The longer a relationship exists, the more agreements are contained in the Master Agreement.

By viewing marriage as a contract governed by a Master Agreement, we are less likely to rely on mythology to keep the relationship vital and alive. Instead of assuming our partner will approve, we check it out. Instead of fuming when we disagree, we challenge what was said and look for compromise. Instead of blaming our partner for misunderstandings, we look for defects in the agreement. The marriage becomes problem/solution-oriented rather than my fault/your fault finger pointing. This allows transactions, even on important issues, to take place calmly and rationally.

This is particularly crucial in caregiving arrangements. Caregiving is emotionally charged on both sides. The ill spouse cannot be satisfied to have lost the ability to function independently, and the caregiver is in a perpetual state of rolling grief over the loss of companionship and, often, intimacy. This crucible of high voltage emotion is fertile ground for poor and incomplete communication, which in turn fuels negative energy in the relationship.

If the pre-illness Master Agreement has not been replaced by a new one, moments of tranquility may be difficult to come by. Therefore, it is critical that a new Master Agreement be negotiated as soon as it becomes obvious that caregiving is a large part of the relationship. Denying that anything has changed will insidiously breed disaster for both partners. Byproducts of an effective Master Agreement are mutual advocacy and mutual respect. Mature love between adults cannot exist without them.

The opposite of love is not hate. The opposite of love is *indifference*. When the Master Agreement breaks down because of one spouse's long-term illness or disability, the byproduct of that broken agreement can become indifference. Indifference erodes respect and mature adult love fades away.

The impact of indifference on the quality of care delivered by a caregiver will be adverse. Indifferent caregivers are not passionate about the health of their charges. They do what is necessary, but going the extra mile would be considered optional, a gift. This does not mean indifference is an excuse to flee, to walk away from caregiving duties. It merely means indifference carries a risk to the ill spouse, and countermeasures should be considered.

The well spouse caregiver has to pay close attention to his or her own needs and execute a plan for getting a substantial percentage of those needs met; sooner rather than later. *Indifference ignored is indifference amplified, which is harmful to all concerned.*

One-Time Agreements in Marriage

One-time agreements generally involve small issues. A one-time-agreement applies only to one situation. "I'll meet you at the library at one o'clock." Thereafter, no agreement exists. They include things like taking out the garbage, picking up the kids at school, paying a bill, time of arrival, saving some hot water for your partner, washing socks, calling the plumber, and so forth. In the total, cosmic scheme of things, it makes little difference if these agreements are kept or not. But the quality of marriage is predicated on a collection of small issues. Agreements like these make a big difference in our perception of how devoted, reliable and trustworthy our spouse is to the "health" of the marriage.

When these agreements are honored, we reinforce the overall trust we have in each other. It is a matter of confidence that our mate will do what is promised. All agreements, even small ones, must be treated as a sacred trust. Breaking them should be viewed as a serious breach of confidence. Without mutual credibility, agreements are impossible. Without agreements, relationships are impossible. If this has been a long-standing way of life, breaking agreements, then how will a stressful caregiving role work out long term? Without attention to the integrity of such agreements, caregiving can become ensnared in bickering and pointless misunderstandings that detract from the rewards still available in the relationship. It is never too late to make changes in the way a well spouse interacts with an ill spouse.

Standing Agreements in Marriage

As important as one-time agreements are to the vitality of a marriage, standing agreements are even more critical. Because standing agreements cover a "family" of related and recurring situations, the breakdown of standing agreements can lead to constant conflict and tension. Even one poor standing agreement can disrupt a marriage enough to threaten its future. A standing agreement is tied to recurring situations. A good standing agreement is valid for years without the need for updating or revision.

For example, Peter and Maggie gave birth to their first child six months ago. Maggie was determined to win a prize for the world's greatest mother, and devoted nearly all her waking hours to childcare. This was not exactly the life Peter wanted. He felt lonely and neglected, but also felt his wife walked on the side of the angels. How could he be so cruel as to suggest she work on being a worse mother? He tried to broach the subject delicately, but she became so defensive that he quickly backed off.

Unless a new agreement about child rearing can be worked out, this marriage is headed for deep trouble. Where do standing agreements come from? They come from negotiation. What triggers negotiation? Confrontation. Why is confrontation necessary? It is because of conflict.

As a society, we tend to view conflict as something to avoid. We think conflict is destructive, and are so spooked by it we frequently pretend there is no conflict just so we do not have to face it. Yet, conflict contains the seeds of new agreements. When we become aware of a conflict with our spouse, it would be more appropriate to get excited, to salivate at the prospect of creating a new agreement. Conflict should be viewed in positive, not negative terms.

&~&

Joe had been Emily's caregiver for several months. She spent much of her time in bed because of difficulty walking and chronic pain. Her constant companion was the laptop she kept on her stomach, which she used to surf the internet. Early on, she began to download games to amuse herself, often charging the games to the family credit card. When Joe paid the credit card bill in the second month after she became disabled, he discovered she had run up a bill for $360 in a month for online fun and games. This was money that was not in their budget, particularly because of all the extra expense of her care, and the fact that she was now unemployed.

Joe showed her the bill, explained the financial strain they were facing and asked Emily to refrain from purchasing games online. She agreed that they could not afford to continue spending money this way. Joe agreed to spend time with her in the evenings playing cribbage and other card games, and watching television with her. They agreed that this would help with the boredom, and Joe assumed they had a new standing agreement that they both would honor.

&~&

Our work is not over when we have negotiated an agreement. We must monitor the agreement to make sure it handles the issues.

We continually ask, is it a useful and workable agreement? We must also monitor it to make sure the other party holds up their end of the deal. If not, we must be prepared to hold them accountable. Agreements without a system of accountability will nearly always be broken, sooner or later.

In summary, there is a sequence of events that leads to standing agreements which accomplish their purpose:
1. Conflict
2. Confrontation
3. Negotiation
4. Monitoring
5. Accountability

৵৽

David assumed he had a long-standing agreement with Kate to live a frugal lifestyle. The rules were that the family would live on no more than half of what David was able to earn, but Kate found a way around this agreement. Every year, like clockwork, Kate would express bitter dissatisfaction with the current family car.

Being of rather large girth, she would claim that she had some trouble with comfort in their existing family car. She complained continuously about her discomfort until David would finally relent and trade for a new car. This would always bust the budget, but Kate argued this was for medical reasons, and the rules should not apply. Wanting to be the good husband and believing fervently in his vow 'til death do we part,' and wanting to keep the peace, he went along with the program and therefore was a co-conspirator in breaking a standing agreement.

৵৽

CONFLICT
Conflict should not be confused with disagreement. When two people hold different opinions about something, they can easily agree

to disagree without hard feelings. Everyone is entitled to their own opinion. Even if some anger rises in a disagreement, it is usually easy to rise above it in a working contract. Conflict exists when two parties have *incompatible objectives.*

For example, if Tom and June each want to park their car in the same empty parking space, their objectives are incompatible. If Tom parks there, June cannot, and vice versa. Conflict represents a win-lose situation; if one party wins, the other automatically loses. Nations often have conflict. If Israel and Egypt each claim the same piece of land as their own, they have incompatible objectives.

Disagreements can be converted to conflicts if one person is determined to impose their views on the other. In some marriages, disagreement is viewed as a threat. Usually the threatened spouse is insecure about their own opinions, and the contrary opinion by the spouse rocks the boat. Any attempt to impose opinions on another is a Type II Boundary Error, discussed in detail in Chapter 7.

The first step in making constructive use of conflict is awareness. We must know a conflict exists to make good use of it. The existence of conflict is not as straightforward as it would seem. Many, perhaps most of us have learned to view conflict in such negative terms that whenever we can pretend there is no conflict, we will do it. We might ignore the objectives of the other person, or we might simply suppress awareness of our own, conflicting objective to maintain peace. Maintaining "peace at any price" becomes a way of life for some spousal caregivers. We mistakenly tell ourselves that this is necessary because our partner is not able to hold up their end of an agreement. We discount their potential and their value in the process. Inadvertently, we create a more unmanageable contract as a result.

❧

David did some consulting work for a group of medical doctors. Practicing the same medical specialty, they had banded together for economic reasons; efficiencies of scale, and sharing administrative costs would improve their net pay. These are the same reasons people practice in groups in other professions as well. Since their capital and risks were pooled, they had to reach decisions on a consensus basis, which required everyone to level with the group about their concerns. Unfortunately, all members of the group, who were given personality tests, came up as strongly non-confrontational. Therefore, nobody leveled with the group, real concerns were never discussed and the medical group began to fail financially. The inability to confront and handle conflict cost the group tens of thousands of dollars a month.

෧ ෨

It is nearly always in our best interests, in the end, to become aware of conflict as early as possible. The next step is to decide what to do about it. There are a few typical options:

- Confront the other person, which then should lead to negotiation
- Surface the conflicting objectives, but immediately concede the conflict in favor of the other person, hoping to win sympathy points.
- Say nothing

Which option we choose depends primarily on two variables, (a) the total situation and (b) the relative importance each side places on their own objectives.

Conflicts must be viewed in their complete context. If our spouse is having a rough time for other reasons, this is no time to surface a conflict. Another good reason to sit on a conflict is that we may have recently mishandled a conflict, and feelings are running raw at the moment. Our spouse could be under many temporary pressures and would not be receptive to more stress at this time.

On the other hand, with enough determination, we can always find some excuse to suppress conflict. If we keep putting it off and our resentment is building, it is likely we are using excuses rather than legitimate reasons not to confront our spouse. Of course, no decision is a decision.

How to assess conflict to benefit the contract

An assessment of the relative importance of objectives is a powerful tool for handling conflict productively. For convenience, the importance of an objective can be rated on an eleven-point scale. Let zero represent absolutely no importance, while at the other end, ten represents a critical objective. If my spouse has an objective in conflict with mine, and I know in advance mine is of no importance to me (i.e., a zero rating), there is no point in surfacing it at all. Nothing would be gained. Forget it.

Suppose my objective is of some importance to me, say a three or four on the scale. Now what? I might pursue negotiations if my spouse's objective is of roughly equal value. On the other hand, if I am up against a seven or eight on the value scale, it might make more sense to back off. Before deciding, it is essential to find out the importance of my spouse's objective. For example, we might ask, "Honey, I know you want us to go to the party tonight. How important is it to you that we go?"

Listening to the reasons behind their objective (to go to the party) should allow us to rate its importance. If the rating is seven or eight, our best strategy is to give in and go. But, if a lower rating is involved, confrontation followed by negotiation might be more effective. In other words, with a lower rating, now is the time to confront the spouse and explain why we do not want to attend. For the caregiver, it may be we are too tired to get out of the house or our spouse is not in any condition to go. Leaving the house for the party will create unnecessary issues to handle and we normally would give in to the request. With this assessment tool regarding conflict, caregivers can assess where to eliminate pressures in their daily life.

Concessions should probably be made in a three versus eight score. My objective's importance rating is a three and the rating is eight for my spouse's objective. Concessions should not be made without letting the spouse know a concession has been made. We have too much stake in our objective to give in quietly. If we do, we will feel resentment for the other person, which is destructive. It is another pathway to feeling owed. But more importantly, a larger kind of equity is at stake here. The Master Agreement must include a provision for an exchange of such concessions. That is, I will give in this time, but I expect you to give in when our situation is reversed. Unless the other person knows a concession has been made, there is no motivation for them to look for ways to "pay us back." Even our ill spouse can accommodate this reciprocity.

If our objective is important to us, and their objectives equally important is to them (e.g., seven versus sever), it is clearly in everybody's best interests to surface the conflict quickly. Failure to confront under these conditions can be disastrous. Issues are not resolved, and resentments build quickly. A rule of thumb may be helpful. In a long-term relationship, all-important conflicts should be converted to agreements. The number of times an important topic should be a source of conflict is *once*. If an important conflict surfaces more than once, we have made a mistake.

CONFRONTATION

Once a decision has been made to confront one's partner about a conflict, the method is critical. Making agreement totally impossible with poor confrontation technique is as easy as falling off a log. All we have to do is follow our emotions into the confrontation. Irritation nearly always accompanies conflict, but sounding irritated is a turn-off. It immediately makes other people defensive. Defensive people retreat behind their position and fortify it. Right or wrong, their fortified opposition makes negotiations all but impossible. Therefore, our first challenge is to control our feelings. If our emotions are running hot, we need to delay confrontation until we cool off.

Continued from the earlier example in the agreement section, when next month's credit card bill arrived, Joe was shocked to learn there was another $250 on the card for online games. He was instantly furious, stormed into Emily's bedroom and confronted her with the bill. Emily was anything but contrite. She attacked him for his lack of sensitivity, accused him of not understanding how boring it was to spend all day in bed. What was she supposed to do, die of boredom?

When Joe came into the room to confront Emily, he was angry. That was probably a mistake. He immediately put her on the defensive, she counter-attacked, and nothing was going to be accomplished. So, restating the first rule of confrontation, cool off emotionally before confronting the person. Figure out a way to keep the other person from becoming defensive.

The second step in confrontation is to consider the emotional status of our partner. Emotional arousal interferes with listening, so a delay might be appropriate as an investment in being heard objectively. Other factors make timing important. It will be hard to confront an issue successfully at 2 A.M., or when there is insufficient time for exploring the topic at hand. Conversation is tougher when either party is tired, or under a lot of stress, or under other artificial influences like medications.

Perhaps, the most important issue is diplomacy. While it is important to contain our irritation, we must go further by sugarcoating everything. Confrontation should be handled lovingly, containing generous doses of emotional support and understanding. We should let our partner know we think their position is understandable, that were we in their shoes we would in all probability take the same position. This is called *empathy*. For the well spouse, this is tough because our empathy reserves have been used and they have not been restored in quite some time. We know we have empathy or we would not still be doing this job, but using empathy in confrontation with our ill spouse has likely not been used as a tool to get what we need in a very long time, if ever.

Once the style is polished and the timing is right, the next challenge is the content. The first priority in examining content is clarity of definition. We should carefully define what our interests are in this situation. This is not the time to propose compromises. Compromises come as a result of negotiation. Rather, it is important that our partner get a glimpse of what has motivated us into confrontation. We must own up to what we want rather than imply that we are really trying to meet the partner's interests. It is far more useful to come right out with "This is what I am interested in." Diplomacy is one thing, misrepresentation another. This is no time for games. Besides, our ill partners usually see through the "I am only interested in what is best for you."

❧❦

How *should* Joe have handled the confrontation with Emily? A better approach would have been for Joe to cool down first, then approach Emily as follows: "Emily, I thought we had an agreement about purchasing online games. What happened?" Then allow Emily to explain that she could not resist the temptation, that she is sorry, and will not do it again. Follow-up the excuse with, "But Emily, that's what you said last time. What is different now?" Then, Emily explains that she seems to lose control of her actions and does not know why. "Is that likely to happen again?" She does not know is her answer.

෴

NEGOTIATION

Once a conflict has been surfaced through confrontation, the next step is to work out an acceptable resolution. If both parties' interests are to be protected, this must be done through negotiation. Before beginning the negotiation process, several characteristics of good negotiation must be understood. Collectively, these features constitute a specific point of view about negotiation which both parties should adopt before negotiations begin. There are steps involved in negotiation.

1. *The problem is the issue, not the other person*
While the other person has a point of view in conflict with ours, it does not make them our enemy. We must attack the issue, not the other person. It is easy to violate this principle when our emotions run high. When the other person's point of view is blocking satisfaction of our needs, it is easy to attack the person, accuse them of being selfish, enjoying frustrating us, or we try to undermine their credibility by pointing out their past mistakes.

෴

Emily has stated she does not know if she can control buying and downloading games. So, Joe continues: "OK, we cannot afford for this to continue. For two months in a row, we have had to rob our savings to pay for your online games. I need your help to solve this problem. What do you propose?"

❧❧

When Kate kept insisting that the only caregiving she would accept was from David, he was tempted to tell her how self-centered she was, that she could only think about her own needs, and to who cares little about everyone else. But, in a rare moment of clarity, he realized that she would immediately become defensive and nothing would be accomplished other than David discharging some of his pent-up anger in her direction.

Instead, he devised a way of approaching the subject right after she had eaten, when she was generally most receptive, and opened the discussion by saying, "Kate, I am having a problem staying focused on your needs the way I should. I think this is my problem and I would like your help in resolving it. The core of the problem is that I have not had enough respite time. I need some time away from my caregiving duties in order to clear my head and be the best possible caregiver for you. What do you think we can do about this?"

❧❧

2. Stick to the topic
The quickest way for negotiations to break down is to allow the conversation to stray from the main topic. Resolving an important issue is hard enough without contamination by unrelated subjects.

❧❧

Emily: "I am really hungry. Could I have some kind of snack?" Joe: "Emily, we are not going to get this online game situation resolved unless we come up with some ideas. What do you propose?" Emily: "I'm really tired. I need a nap."

❧❧

3. *Neither side has a pipeline to truth*

When we make a statement during negotiations, it represents how we perceive the world, not how the world really is. We are all trapped in our own way of looking at things. We can keep this idea alive with certain precautions. When we make a statement, we can preface it with, "This is the way I see it." rather than, "The truth is...." This represents a tip of the hat to our own possible fallibility, and makes our statement seem less threatening and more subject to modification. It also helps to use relative rather than absolute language. Use the words 'often' instead of 'always,' 'difficult' instead of 'impossible,' 'pleasant' instead of 'wonderful,' and so forth.

Another precaution is to remember that the other person is as trapped in their perceptions as we are in ours. When their statements sound like pronouncements from Mount Olympus, we must either have the self-discipline to discount the tone of the statement, or gently let them know how it sounded and ask them to rephrase it.

ॐॐ

For example, Joe might say, "Gee, when you said you needed a nap, it sounded like you were not willing to continue this discussion. I am certain you did not mean that. Perhaps you could clarify your willingness to work on this problem."

ॐॐ

4. *Listen*

This is the hardest part of negotiation. We have a natural tendency to reject information that differs from our beliefs. We also focus on that part of the other person's statement that we feel is clearly vulnerable, and begin constructing a reply in our heads rather than listening. It takes a conscious and deliberate act of will to hang in there with what's being said rather than mentally countering each point along the way.

Failure to listen is usually obvious to the other person, either through non-verbal signals (wandering eye contact, fidgety impatience for the other to finish) or because the response is off target.

People have a right and a strong desire to be heard, and they strongly resent not being heard. Conversely, listening attentively during negotiations will be seen as an act of caring and concern. This will help create an atmosphere of compromise and make agreement much easier.

❧❧

Joe: "OK, here's what I understand you to say. You are wondering if we could modify our television cable contract to include movie channels so that you can watch movies during the day. Is that what you are proposing?"

❧❧

5. Both sides must win

We enter relationships to get our own needs met. Yet, we must pay for what we get by helping our partner get what they need. The trick is to get what we need at an acceptable price. This principle applies on a smaller scale to negotiation. Neither party should set a goal of getting everything they want. If that was possible, there would have been no conflict. A more realistic goal of negotiation is that both sides get a portion of what they want. That means both sides must also be prepared to give up something they wanted as an investment in the long-term health of the relationship.

❧❧

Joe: "If we change our cable contract to include movie channels, how will I know you have stopped charging online fees to the credit card?"

❧❧

6. Hang in there

It takes time to arrive at a sound agreement. If a solution is not found in the first 15 minutes, or even the first hour, it does not mean further negotiations are hopeless. Even if neither party can think of anything constructive to add to what has been said, agreement is still possible. Men schooled in the tradition of "A man's home is his castle" often use an impasse like this as an excuse to "take charge" and simply impose their own "solution." They argue (and often truly believe) that in any kind of relationship, *somebody* has to be in charge. Not so. Between equals, the only kind of decision with staying power is that achieved through consensus; that is, both parties shape, mold, and support the ultimate outcome. If negotiations bog down, we must take a break and try again later in the day, tomorrow, or next week. The secret is to keep trying. We must not give up.

This is especially true for the couple where one has a disability or illness. In this scenario, the voting stock for the marital board of directors may be distributed unevenly for a particular issue. This could make consensus technically unnecessary for that specific issue. However "involvement leads to commitment," as managers know. Therefore, involving the ill spouse in discussions still has payoff because agreements work better if there is at least the appearance of consensus. A TTC will know how to use these tools for harmony.

❧

Joe: "Apparently you have run out of ideas for now. I will check with you again in the morning and see if you can come up with a way for us to eliminate these charges for the last time. I love you. Good night."

❧

MONITORING AGREEMENTS

Agreements without some way of verifying that both sides are living up to their promises are likely to be worthless. The issue of on-site inspection kept USA/USSR arms control negotiations bogged down for years. A supervisor must be able to keep track of employees' production to keep work flowing smoothly.

In complex agreements, monitoring procedures become part of the negotiation.

A person hiring a lawyer might ask, "How will I know you are actually spending the hours you bill me for?" Construction contracts may require weekly or monthly reports by the builder comparing progress with schedule. In long standing personal relationships, agreements are usually monitored informally through ongoing communication. When a situation is unusually difficult, or where there is a history of broken agreements, it may be necessary to make monitoring procedures more formal. Excessively zealous monitoring can easily be misunderstood. This is the case with couples where one is insecure and they check their partner's cell phone calls and emails. For well and ill spouses alike, this surfaces rather frequently when communication has broken down, fear of abandonment rises and the feeling of being taken for granted impedes resolution.

In routine and sensible monitoring of agreements, out-and-out violations will be obvious. This should lead to accountability procedures, as described below. Clear violations are less frequent than subtle indicators that the agreement is making the other person uncomfortable. The person may complain about certain provisions of the agreement, or complain indirectly with sarcasm. Sometimes the discomfort takes the form of slight variations designed to make inroads and erode the integrity of the original agreement. For example, if a couple has agreed not to spend more than $50 without consulting the spouse, he might spend $60 without explanation. This is a tip off that the agreement is breaking down.

Whenever monitoring uncovers these small signs that something is amiss, the issue should be surfaced immediately. "We had an agreement not to spend more than $50 without consulting each other. I notice you spent $60 on a new drill without telling me. What's happening to our agreement?" Surfacing the discrepancy clearly communicates an intention to enforce the original agreement. This should be followed by an offer to reopen negotiations on the subject. It may not be necessary to amend the original agreement, but the offer smacks of good faith and a cooperative attitude.

⭑⭑

Joe has an automatic way of monitoring his new agreement with Emily about not spending money buying online games. He should also arrange periodic conversations with her about how her new cable service is working and how well movies are keeping her from becoming bored.

తలుs

FEAR OF CONSEQUENCES
THE BIG CLUB THEORY

Holding people accountability for living up to their agreements requires that they be mentally alert and have the ability to concentrate and remember. Ill spouses with cognitive impairments, such as Alzheimer's or Traumatic Brain Injury, may not be able to participate in the type of accountability exercises described below. However, ill spouses without cognitive impairment should be able to respond to these techniques like any other spouse.

Fear of consequences is a powerful force in human affairs. Decisions that are more personal are based on fear rather than on anticipation of rewards. We stop our cars at red lights out of sheer, stark terror, not because we are afraid of getting a ticket, but the fear of being broadsided by another car. Students do not try to get good grades because of rewards, but because the consequences of not getting the good grades is intolerable. Guidance counselors who instruct parents to offer rewards for good grades could not be further off the mark. In an affluent society, one reward blends imperceptibly into another. Rewards just do not work reliably. Threats work.

In a relationship, particularly a marriage, the key lies in one's willingness to administer penalties. If we are absolutely convinced our partner will use a penalty at slightest, yet appropriate, provocation, then we seldom give them a reason to do so. In marriage, this is graphically illustrated by the "Big Club Theory". This is strictly a metaphor; violence is completely out of the question. The theory begins with the observation that we enter long-term relationships because of our own needs. We are responsible for monitoring the relationship on a frequent basis to determine if our needs are being met. Assume this is something we do on a daily basis. The question we must ask is, "Am I getting what I need from this relationship per our agreement?"

If the answer is 'yes,' we can relax. However, if the answer is 'no,' we must march over to our closet where we have a set of twelve imaginary "clubs", beginning with a little tiny one and ending with the twelfth club, four feet long with knobs on it, like a cave man's club. We grab the smallest club, walk over to our spouse, bonk them on the head (symbolically, of course) to get their attention, and say something like, "There is something I bargained for in this relationship that I'm not getting. How about we get a sitter tonight, we'll go to dinner and talk it through?" If our partner responds, "Gee, honey, I didn't know you were feeling that way. Sure, let's resolve it." We smile, put the club back, and look forward to the discussion. We face this situation with a cooperative partner. The first club represents our initial attempt to get our partner either to live up to the agreement, or sit down in good faith to renegotiate. However, partners do not always cooperate.

If our partner replies, "Don't bug me. I've got too many things going on right now in my life to worry about your needs," we trudge back to the closet, put the smallest club away, snatch up the next larger club, go back to our spouse, administer the larger attention-getter, and say something like, "Excuse me, I don't believe you understood the importance of what I just said. We need to talk."

In like fashion, we must keep working our way through the larger and larger clubs until our spouse's attention has been obtained. The largest club of all, the ugly one, represents our ultimate commitment to ourselves. That is to say, if we have worked our way in good faith through the other eleven clubs and still cannot get results to get our partner into the confrontation stage discussed in the previous chapter, then we must go elsewhere to get our needs met.

At first hearing, this seems harsh and crass. Our cultural heritage makes little provision for viewing marriage as a contract which can be legitimately dissolved. According to our traditions, marriage is a sacred trust based on true love. Most of us embark on a quest for someone who will love us unconditionally. Unfortunately, the only legitimate kind of unconditional love is that experienced by a mother for her infant. All other forms of love have strings attached. We are even misled by the marriage ceremony. We know that the marriage is legally a contract because divorces are available and must be dissolved in a court of law. So then, the transition to viewing daily as a contract should not be a difficult leap.

Viewing marriage as a contract represents what marriage is really all about. If we could actually convince our spouse that under no circumstances would we ever consider leaving the relationship, our partner would gradually stop paying attention to our needs. The existence of the twelfth club builds a little insecurity into the marriage, forcing the channels of communication wide open. The Big Club theory simply means that when we speak, our partner listens. It must be emphasized that in a marriage, there is a matched set of clubs on the other side of the closet as well. The secret to a good marriage is that both partners know how to use the "clubs" with equal skill.

ACCOUNTABILITY & WITHHOLDING

Accountability

The language describing the accountability principles in this chapter were conceived during thirty years of private practice as a shorthand way of simplifying complicated ideas. These principles work remarkably well in keeping relationships healthy, and in repairing broken relationships. The ill spouse, assuming they are not significantly cognitively impaired, is capable of entering into agreements, be they standing or one-time agreements. And, compassion aside, agreements still need to be honored by both parties if the caregiving arrangement is to have staying power.

Getting the ill partner's attention would depend on how accessible the partner would be to such interactions. With some illnesses and disability, the capacity of the partner to concentrate would fluctuate moment to moment, so the timing of attention getting would be an issue. Partners may be in pain, or have other physical symptoms that would render them somewhat inaccessible. The well spouse would just have to continue to monitor the situation for the right time to bring up certain issues, but using the "Big Club Theory" to open communication is just as valid when used under the proper circumstances.

Withholding

Of note, withholding services from an ill spouse is a little tricky because one must begin with a clear distinction between *Wants* and *Needs*. One can certainly throw wants into the negotiable bucket, but needs are normally off limits. One could not very well threaten to withhold food or medications from an ill spouse, for example.

So, the biggest club represents withdrawal from the relationship. What about the smaller clubs? The smallest club or two represent confrontation about the issue at hand. The clubs are words, polite at first, and more firm if the second club is necessary. Clubs number three through eleven symbolize action beyond mere words, action in the form of withholding of services normally part of our contractual obligation to our partner.

What can be withheld? The answer depends on the contract. To be effective, that which is withheld must be considered important by the partner. It could be anything from affection, washing his clothes, rubbing her back, smiling, meal preparation, running errands, even sex. Of course, if a failed agreement was important enough to consider such drastic measures, sex would be affected by this stage anyhow. When a spouse is ill, sexual activity may have been altered for other reasons, too.

You may ask, isn't this simply another name for retaliation? Aren't we just lowering ourselves to counter their unresponsiveness with withholding? The difference between accountability and retaliation is quite simple. The goal of *retaliation* is to *hurt* the other person, whereas *withholding* something of value from the other person in response to a broken agreement is designed to *repair* a relationship. *Retaliation is an act of hostility, but accountability is an act of love.*

Marriages without an effective accountability system rapidly become cesspools of resentment and hostility, threatening the future of the relationship. Again, the concept of "feeling owed" begins to wear on the caregiver if the ill spouse is not responding to the clubs. Penalties involving withholding are designed to get the attention of our partner, to let them know that we have credibility. Penalties are a way of upping the ante when our quiet voice goes unheeded. Penalties encourage movement into the negotiation phase when momentum has ground the marriage to a halt. Penalties are a signal: "Hey, listen up! My needs are important, too."

If a woman is not willing to hold her husband accountable for living up to his side of their agreements, he gradually loses respect for her. He begins to see her as "less equal." This undermines his respect. Like a scavenger, it eats away at the good parts of the marriage, and has the potential to destroy it. If he does not respect her ability to enforce agreements or to vote her stock in the marital corporation, he will develop a disrespect for her opinions, her comfort, her relatives, her space, her possessions, and her freedom.

ॐॐ

Rhonda tried for many years to achieve an equal balance with Andy. However, over the years, she was freely given all of the marital stock. Andy never cared what their bank balance looked like. He did not care about the details of the children's lives and he never uttered a word when she proposed moving into other homes, buying cars or switching the children's schools. Any big decision was made solely by Rhonda, right or wrong, there never a discussion. After many years of living like this, her respect for Andy had diminished greatly. By the time Andy received the devastating diagnosis of dementia, she had lost all respect for him and his opinions. She felt guilty for feeling this way, but the damage was done. Nothing could repair it and with the diagnosis, there was the proof that she did not need to attempt to consult him anymore.

Now, she felt only profound sadness and viewed Andy "damaged." Through careful introspection did she realize her indifference toward him was doing neither of them any good. Something had to change for the well-being of both of them. They both needed to thrive and pretending they had a marriage was stressful for everyone.

ॐॐ

The authors define marriage as a contractual agreement with the following characteristics:

- Both partners own 50 percent of the voting stock in the marital corporation
- Both partners must be willing to vote all their stock all the time
- It contains a master agreement with dozens of negotiated long term agreements
- Included are one-time agreements that govern day to day living
- Investments of social credits are exchanged between the partners
- The internal ledger keeps track of what is invested and what is returned
- Partners then send invoices to receive an appropriate return on investment
- The spousal exchange process must remain equitable for mutual happiness
- Both spouses must monitor the exchange process for equity on a constant basis
- If the equity slides toward inequity, partners must be held accountable
- Both partners must be aware of the Big Club Theory and keep their clubs polished

COMMUNICATION PITFALLS TO AVOID

Throughout the past chapters, holding other people accountable, conflict management, and the like, all are predicated on the idea that people are able to communicate effectively with one another. While the list below is no substitute for an in-depth treatise on face-to-face interpersonal oral communication, it is a list of the most common pitfalls that derail two people trying their best to work out solutions to their problems.

- These mistakes are very likely to occur in the process of making and enforcing agreements because these intricate maneuvers are ordinarily undertaken in the heat of battle. That, of course, would be the first pitfall. Figure out a way to tackle these agreement-related interpersonal issues at a time when both parties are relaxed and receptive.

- The first rule is to find a time when both parties are relaxed and receptive to discussing a way to revise the relationship and make it work better for both parties. Let some time pass from the last argument or disagreement so that the present discussion is not contaminated by leftover anger or anxiety.

- Tackle the negotiation soberly. Clear-headedness is a prerequisite for making genuine progress in negotiating about important life issues.

- The timing must be right, beginning of course by avoiding times when one or both parties are upset about something else. If we know our partner is not a morning person, do it later in the day. If our partner has just received bad news, wait for a better time. Issues like these cannot be handled rapidly, so carve out a time where there will be *enough* time to complete the discussions.

- We are all better communicators when we are relaxed, and most of us are the most relaxed in our own territories. Find a place where your partner feels at home, and use that location for important negotiations.

- Sitting at a square table to work some things out works better if the parties sit diagonal across a corner rather than across the table from each other. The table represents a physical barrier, and it impedes efficient and effective communication. The same lesson applies to sitting at a large table; sit across one of the corners.

- Stand or sit at about a foot or two away from the partner. Too much distance connotes reluctance to talk about intensely personal issues, and too little distance in intimidating.

- Choose language that is not inflammatory. We all know how to push our partners' buttons with words that have a long history of emotional significance. Use neutral words. It helps to rehearse your statements before speaking. This slows down the dialog, but impulsive speech could stop the dialog, perhaps even permanently.

- Plan the strategy for the discussion before initiating it. Make notes about the main ideas and structure them in the sequence that is most likely to flow smoothly and create the least destructive emotions along the way.

- Introduce carefully the entire dialog to include assumptions, goals, and other information that will keep surprises out of the ensuing conversation. Each new section of the discussion should be similarly introduced.

- Tone of voice and body language should be rehearsed in front of a mirror as preparation for important negotiations. The tone should be as neutral as possible, and the most important component of body language is eye contact. A friendly smile helps as well.

THE TOUGH & TENDER CAREGIVER

The TTC understands and acts upon the following principles governing the maintenance of relationships.

- Business and personal relationships operate according to exactly the same set of rules.

- Personal relationships require more energy to manage effectively than professional or business relationships because of a higher level of exchange.

- As a general rule, people will live up to their agreements only if they believe the agreements will be enforced.

- Agreements between relatives are no different from other agreements; failure to enforce them destroys the integrity of the relationship. Conversely, enforcing agreements with relatives is an act of love.

- All relationships are contracts governed by a Master Agreement, which consists of standing agreements accompanied by one-time agreements.

- A conflict in a relationship is destructive only if it is ignored. Properly handled, conflict contains the beginnings of new agreements, which can improve the quality of a relationship.
- When an issue is not very important to one person, converting conflict into negotiations is not necessary. Simply conceding the issue is more effective, provided the other person is willing to reciprocate on other issues.
- Issues of importance to both parties must be confronted quickly.
- Confrontation must take place tactfully and lovingly, focusing on what the confronter wishes to gain from negotiation rather than action required by the other person.
- In any negotiation, it is the problem that must be attacked, not the other person.
- In successful negotiation, both parties end up getting some of what they want.
- Negotiation works better if many alternative solutions are laid on the table before being evaluated.
- All agreements must be monitored to ensure both parties are living up to their commitments.
- Our willingness to penalize broken agreements is enough to keep most people from violating their commitments to us.
- Clear violations of an agreement must be surfaced quickly, followed by action if necessary to get the other person's attention.
- Important issues that create conflict should come up only once; they should be converted immediately to an agreement through confrontation and negotiation.
- A long-term relationship governed by a sound Master Agreement has an important byproduct: mature adult love, which consists of mutual advocacy and mutual respect.
- It is important to embrace sound principles of face-to-face interpersonal oral communication when handling the nuts and bolts of negotiating and enforcing agreements.

Chapter 5
ILLNESS AND DISABILITY BRING INEVITABLE CHANGES

Sex Suggestions for the Couple

ॐ∾ॐ

Now that there is an understanding of basic relationship theory and how marriages actually work, it is time to look at sexual intimacy. One obvious difference between spousal caregiving and other kinds of caregiving is the issue of sexual intimacy. It is difficult for many healthy couples to talk about sex openly, but once the relationship enters a caregiving phase the topic of sex is even tougher to talk about. We know that the only way to meet the sexual intimacy needs of the couple is for them to talk about all aspects of their sexual health.

Sex is clearly on the minds of caregivers who care for their spouses. One of the more popular online support groups available for caregivers contains various topics or "threads" that serve as areas of interest to caregivers. The thread called "affairs", which was started in 2004, has been viewed over 24,000 times. It was so busy a new "affairs" thread was started in 2006 and it has been viewed nearly 7000 times. By contrast, the actual postings for open discussion under those threads do not number nearly as high; only in the hundreds. It appears that caregivers are seeking answers for their pain, but that only a few are willing to put this quest in writing. The sensitivities surrounding this topic are raw and taboo.

Caregivers want answers to questions such as:
- How can I handle the sexual intimacy changes within the relationship?
- Where can I find out how to maintain intimacy without my partner feeling physical discomfort?
- What do I do about this feeling of loneliness?
- Do other people think about having an affair?
- Will talking to my spouse really help or make matters worse?
- Am I supposed to live a celibate life from now on?
- How can I find sexual satisfaction and still remain married?

These questions are extremely important and likely go unanswered using readily available resources. The information to help the frustrated caregiver is available (primarily from foreign sources given the attitudes of American society), but it takes time, energy and privacy to conduct online searches or peruse library resources. It helps to be specific in one's search; for example, specific questions about physical limitations on sexual activity related to specific illnesses and disabilities.

The authors advocate frank discussions with your partner and his or her physician. It may be necessary to sign a HIPPA confidentiality form because of the privacy issues involved. At office visits, come prepared with a list of written questions that are very specific in nature. If you find that the doctor is not comfortable talking about sexual practices, comfortable positions, minimizing pain, maximizing stimulation and so on, then talk with someone else. It is not unusual for a well spouse to seek second opinions for their partner since they are normally their partner's health care advocate. Sexual health issues are no different from any other health issue. Your partner's medical team is exactly that—*their* medical team. A professional health care provider's obligation is to their patient, not to their caregiver. Resolutions will only be found with open communication. With an ill spouse who is involved in the process of seeking information, the medical professionals will be more cooperative.

Nobody asks caregivers if they are sexually satisfied or if they wish to talk about the hardships of a diminished sex life. Finding resolutions is a difficult journey. This is even more complicated if the ill spouse wants sex and the caregiver finds this repulsive. Both individuals have intimacy needs, but fulfilling them is in conflict. The well spouse may be thinking, How can I take care of you physically and then be expected to have sex? The well spouse might need to say something like the following to their partner: "Am I your nursing assistant or am I your lover? I do not think I can be both, so you have to help me decide what we are going to do."

Caregivers express a keen interest in the topic of fulfilling sexual needs while caring for a chronically ill spouse, but in the caregiving literature there are few references to sex. As a group, well spouses are struggling with the issue of remaining faithful to their disabled spouses. But there is precious little help available. This is a serious issue for those dealing with a long-term, chronic illness.

Spouses with a terminal illness strike a different chord. The phrase "terminal illness" connotes an idea of swiftness to the end of life. Then the idea of sexual activity can rather easily be put on the back burner for the caregiver. But because medicine is so advanced, "terminal" can easily become "chronic," and then the back burner is no longer an acceptable way of addressing intimacy or sexual needs.

ORIGINS OF NORMAL SEXUAL AROUSAL

This may be an exercise of preaching to the choir because everyone who reads this book will have been sexually active during their lives. However, a little review of how arousal occurs will help us explore the impact of illness and disability on our arousal system. Our society places a lot of emphasis on the sexual arousal value of physical attributes of both men and women. Women's cleavage and exposed breasts, men's hairy chests, both men's and women's derrieres, sexy hair styles, men's facial hair, and so forth are what the media focuses on. Fortunately, for 95 percent of us, that is not the whole story. If it were, the rest of us would be celibate, or at least mightily deprived.

The rest of the story is that sensuality and sexuality is buried in the hundreds of subtle behaviors that most people overlook, but not our lovers and spouses. They focus on those signals or cues, and react with the experience of sexual arousal. In men, these signals include:

- A slight swagger when he walks toward his woman
- His wry smile when she models her new dress
- His rugged look when he needs a shave
- The roughness of his hands on her skin
- His standing closely behind her, hands on her waist

On the other side, women exhibit their own set of sensuality signals:

- She curls up on his lap unexpectedly and twirls his hair
- Her soft voice when she says how she feels about him
- Her shiver when his hands caress her bare shoulder
- Her embrace from behind
- Her asking him to brush her hair

The authors can just hear the reader saying, so what? We all know about romance and sex. So what? The 'so what' is that these meaningful signals tend to evaporate because of chronic illness or disability. They go "poof" and so does some of the romance. Chronic illness or disability interferes with this pattern of sexual and sensual stimulation and acknowledgement. The spousal relationship is not as much fun anymore in this arena. These exciting exchanges are diminished or gone, never to return in their original form. This can envelop the well spouse in regret and longing, particularly when the quality of the pre-illness relationship was good.

When we marry, mutual sexual satisfaction is up near the top of a list of needs spouses satisfy for each other within the marriage relationship. When one partner becomes chronically ill, as we described earlier, the original contract becomes canceled. The well spouse inherits a majority of the voting stock in the marital corporation in many areas, and thereafter calls most of the shots in those areas. The relationship is forever altered by the caregiving scenario, including the sexual arousal system described above.

Remember, everything changes. The distribution of household chores, how the couple earns a living, the physical living space, and of course how sexual needs are met, if at all. The sexual needs of the caregiver are likely to be the same as they always were, tempered only by exhaustion. What is the caregiver to do about these needs? In some cases, even the sexual needs of the disabled spouse are unchanged and they remain interested in maintaining the sexual contact they had always known. The caregiver must decide how this is going to be handled.

There is a way to negotiate a new sexual agreement with the ill spouse. First, we have to understand how the lack of sexual intimacy affects our health. We need to understand conditional love, what our marriage vows meant, and how to maintain civility. Our old normal would not have permitted us to do this, but our "new normal" requires us to revisit all our old assumptions about sex, morality, love, health, and the very nature of marriage.

HOW DOES SOCIETY TREAT THIS ISSUE?

This is a very prudish society. We find discussions of sex to be titillating, forbidden, touchy, mysterious, hidden, and just a little bit dirty. Many, perhaps most, married couples do not even talk about sex with each other. As David learned as a marriage counselor, for many couples the psychologist's office was the first place aspects of their sexual relationship ever surfaced. This is not the place for an academic exploration of the origin of sexual prudishness in America, but it is the place to emphasize that it is not good for our society. The United States has some of the highest incidence of sexual crimes in the Western world. The statistics are appalling.

However illogical, we get social messages that any variety of sexual activity other than "standard" (missionary position) is out of bounds. That certainly complicates things for spousal caregivers in several ways. Talking about sexual issues is not easy and finding a willing, comfortable listener is not easy. Figuring out how to handle your spouse and their limitations is very tough if the conversations about sex were nonexistent when both partners were well. What if the ill spouse is physically incapable of "standard" sex? According to some moral codes, the caregiver is out of luck. No other options can be considered.

Part of the challenge faced by caregivers in need of sexual intimacy is that they will need to swim upstream to participate in "forbidden" activities. Based on the information in Dr. Michael Brickey's book, Defy Aging, the absence of continuous and frequent sexual activity will shorten our lives. In fact, the well-documented rapid deterioration of caregivers' health could easily have something to do with their diminished sexual activity.

Now that we understand our 'new normal' has not diminished our need for intimacy, we must accept the fact that the missionary position is not always going to work the best. If there has been a hip replacement for example, a physical therapist can and should be consulted to understand what positions will allow for intercourse. Again, if the therapist shyly hands over a written illustration and cannot talk openly, seek another person who can talk and discuss the illustrations.

Some chronic illnesses require adaptive devices to be used to maintain balance and positioning so that a mutually satisfying encounter can be accomplished. These positioning devices, pillows, and support cushions can be located through a medical supply store. Many legitimate companies have supplies available under the heading "sexual health". Sadly, in some areas in the US it is illegal to purchase "marital" aides except from a "medical" supply company. Going about getting the assistive devices can seem embarrassing and feel like walking into foreign territory. However, the needs are real, they are recognized and the equipment is available. However, we also know that disability and illness can wear out the best couple relationships. There are some basic issues to examine fully to understand what could be happening to the marriage.

UNDERSTANDING CONDITIONAL LOVE

The false and misleading belief: *"love means never having to say you're sorry"* is a major problem for everyone, particularly for spouses, be they well or disabled. Where do ideals like this come from? The root cause of the problem appears to be cultural. It can be seen in petulant teenagers saying the ugliest things to their parents, things they would not dream of saying to one of their teachers. Their assumption, when questioned, is some variation of "They love me. I don't have to be polite to them."

So if someone loves us, we can afford to take their love for granted? That suggests something we refer to as *unconditional love*. The only form of truly unconditional love we know of is between a parent and minor child, especially for an infant. Normally, parents love newborns without strings attached. Of course, there are exceptions, but there is literally nothing a newborn can do to weaken the bonds of love felt by a parent.

In the courtship and newlywed stage of marriage, love often seems unconditional. Their vows bespeak of love lasting "until death do us part." However, we have established earlier in this book that marriage is a contract, and like all contracts, there are provisions that can be identified in the agreement. What is unspoken is "I will love you provided you do not abuse me, do not have sex with other people, do not squander marital financial resources, etc." This is, of course, conditional love. When the marital partner becomes disabled and unable to live up to the contractual obligations, their love is revealed to be what it has been all along; conditional.

WHAT ABOUT FRIENDSHIP?

In good marriages, the marriage contract works well. Courtship begins normally with friendship, blossoms into courtship and ultimately marriage. However, in the best marriages the friendship continues into the marriage. Some marriages maintain the romantic love and wonderful friendship for a lifetime. In these marriages, when one spouse is permanently disabled, the caregiving spouse has a long history to build on, and the friendship is likely to be so powerful that getting both sexual and non-sexual intimacy needs met is automatic.

☙❧

This is the precise problem Rhonda had with her marriage. There was something going wrong with Andy's health from the very beginning of their marriage. She did not have the memories of the youthful good times from which to draw during the caregiving days. She also did not have a genuine friendship foundation to help keep the relationship viable.

❧❧

Many couples are not so fortunate as to have memories and friendship to fall back on. Rhonda and Andy were not unique. In the typical marriage, the illness or permanent disability changes everything. As the well spouse takes over the caregiving duties and the household responsibilities, the friendship can continue in a different form, but it can never be the same. The new version is more like a parent being friendly with a child. In other words, friendship by itself is unlikely to satisfy the intimacy needs of the caregiving spouse for any length of time. However, that never rules out *civility*.

CIVILITY; THE BASIC BUILDING BLOCK

One should never have to remind anyone to be polite to one's husband or wife. After all, we are supposed to love our spouse. Isn't that why we married them? Well, it appears that this is a poor assumption. An example might set the stage for further discussion.

❧❧

Joe is a very talented executive with an advertising firm. He is the soul of diplomacy. With customers, he makes them feel they are the only worthwhile people in his universe. He handles his subordinates with great finesse, and they all love him for it. He treats his secretary like a queen and she would take a bullet for him.

But when Joe walks into the front door of his home in the evening, he is anything but the civilized leader he portrays at work. He has both guns blazing. He snaps at the kids, but saves his juiciest venom for his wife, criticizing her housekeeping, sneering at the meals she prepares, and calling her names like 'stupid' and 'lazy.'

Therefore, when his marriage counselor (David) asks him why he is so rude and hostile toward his wife, he replies, "I have to play a role all day. There ought to be one place in this town where I can truly be myself."

To which his counselor replies, "There is. You can truly be yourself sitting on the toilet with the door closed. However, when you are in the presence of other people, the relationship requires management to be successful. In fact, the more important the relationship to your long term well-being, the more careful you have to be. Words are like bullets. Once you've fired them, you can't take them back, and they leave bullet holes. Your wife will never forget that you have called her ugly names."

David's quote above was well rehearsed. This little speech, verbatim, was repeated at least once a week for 30 years. This kind of rudeness between spouses is so prevalent we can almost consider it an epidemic. Some version of this issue was a problem for maybe 80 percent of the patients in David's private practice.

☙❧

Verbal abuse is a huge problem in caregiving scenarios. Since so many intimate barriers are broken when performing intimate personal care, the rituals that kept a couple verbally respectful to each other through much of their marriage seem to come toppling down with changing the bandages and draining catheter bags. The ill spouse has no more intimate space.

Caregivers vent anger and frustration much of the time at inanimate objects. However, verbal assaults on ill spouses are likely to be dismissed as temporary reactions to stress by the overwhelmed caregiver. In understanding more about why caregivers lose their temper, volatility from the caregiver can be avoided. Most of us do not want to inflict verbal pain on our spouse. The combination of lack of gratitude from the ill spouse, as well as their frustration and anger, makes the caregiver's day seem endless at times. The stress can be overwhelming. Revisiting the tips in this book and knowing how to recognize limits and setting boundaries can help.

WHAT ABOUT WEDDING VOWS?

One of the most destructive "Deadly Misconceptions" is that "for better or worse, in sickness and in health" means exactly what it says. This phrase, "in sickness and in health" trips off the tongue with very little thought as it is said during the marriage ceremony. But nobody asks this question before the vows are spoken: "How sick is sick?" The truth is that when we took our vows to care for and to love our spouse in sickness and in health, we could never have envisioned a situation where they were so sick and needy on a permanent basis that it would threaten to suck the life out of their caregiver.

The same thought process applies to "for better or for worse." In the throes of a love affair, who would be able to imagine how bad 'for worse' could actually become? Could anyone envision having to lift someone in and out of bed to use the potty chair, clean them up afterwards, wash their bodies as if they were an infant, and administer injections daily, *forever*?

Who would have thought when those vows were said that financial, social, and psychological pressures could build to the point where you would want to end your own life? The caregiver needs to understand that for better or for worse, in sickness and health, does *not* mean exactly what it says. It is not to be taken literally because we doubt that any spousal caregiver understood initially the macabre implications of "'til death do us part."

Well spouses owe it to themselves and their ill spouses to make every effort to make their life happy and fulfilled, which includes sexual intimacy. Until the publication of this book, there has been no owner's manual for caregiving marriages. None of the customary expectations apply to marriage when a chronic condition intrudes. It is like being stranded on an island and we have to figure out what will and will not work for our survival. It is completely uncharted territory. The wedding vows simply do not apply when long-term major changes intrude.

Rhonda was quite mired in her wedding vow dilemma when David asked the support group about what their vows really meant when they got married. Below is her response.

෨෧

When she got married at twenty-two, she did not think that facing a permanent disability with her husband, as a young man, would be something she would ever face. She envisioned old age, perhaps, but not now. She thought "sickness" would be curable. She thought, at worst, she could, and would, willingly nurse Andy through a terminal illness until his death or remission. She accepted that they would face routine sicknesses and possible surgeries, but she did not have the capacity to see chronic, disabling, life altering, diseases; does anyone?

She would never have gotten married if she had a clue that his sickness would bring poverty and brutality into her life. No, that vow was not the oath she had taken. She did not imagine that "for richer or poorer" meant always being one paycheck from homelessness. She could not have conceived of the endless medical bills and the medication costs that would rob her of the ability to pay other living expenses. She could not have foreseen the emotional damage to their children, or the damage to her own self-esteem.

The mental clarity that developed from answering these questions about her marriage vows brought relief. She had never meant to give up her life for her husband's care. It did not feel like a sacrifice that was worth making. Not right out of the starting gate. She felt *cheated*. Living up to her religious doctrines had not brought comfort. God had blessed her with three wonderful children and she was not going to let them suffer another moment of stark terror. Nor could she have imagined being celibate as a young woman. She did not want to have regrets as an older woman, sad that she had been sexually unfulfilled and had not experienced wonderful love from a well man.

She had sought marriage counseling before she knew how sick Andy was going to get. She sought advice from the church counselor, but he told her to live with it, that it was her wifely duty. He told her to "try harder to be a better wife." She had taken that advice to heart, but she really believed she could not try harder than she had been trying for all these years.

Andy had been living in an assisted living facility (ALF) for a year, but her commitment to the marriage was still lingering and it felt like a death sentence. She had been intending to hang on until their youngest was grown, then she was planning to die. She fantasized about suicide constantly. At a minimum, she wanted an illness to strike her that would allow for an extended hospital stay so she could get some rest.

She felt all of her adult life had been wasted. She was nearing her forties without hopes and dreams. She thought throughout her twenties and thirties that life would one day get better if she worked hard enough, but it never materialized. It only got worse. In re-evaluating her marriage vows, she realized that the disease was not her fault, and that the broken marriage was the pot of gold at the end of the rainbow. Upon this awakening, she became preoccupied with the idea of getting out of the marriage. So after nearly twenty years of marriage, she filed for divorce.

కాళ

RENEGOTIATION OF THE SEXUAL CONTRACT

As noted earlier, when a disability or illness invades a marriage, the standing agreements governing the relationship must be renegotiated. This includes sexual activity. Negotiate about sex? Isn't sex supposed to be spontaneous? For many the idea that sex can be subjected to negotiation is shocking and out of bounds.

Negotiation about sex is really an ancient topic. When it comes to sex, the world's oldest profession, prostitution, is all about negotiation. Healthy couples may not think they are negotiating; he just puts his hands on her and waits to see if she responds. This is certainly nonverbal, but it is negotiation nonetheless. Couples become great at reading nonverbal cues.

Several different situations present themselves, and the sexual solutions available will depend on a number of variables.

Situation #1: The Ill Spouse is Capable of Standard Sex

Variation A: In this variation, if the sexual part of their marriage was terrific before the disability. The caregiver could lobby for a continuation of their sexual relationship undiminished, but making allowances for the fact that the sexual arousal system has been impaired. The sexual aides described below might help make up for what is now missing because of the illness (e.g., vibrators, massage oils, oral sex, pornography, and so forth).

Variation B: Even if the pre-illness sexual relationship was wonderful, the caregiver may *not* lobby for a continuation of their sexual intimacy. First of all, if the caregiver is going to perform intimate caregiving duties which violate all normal intimate space boundaries, then sex with the ill spouse is not likely to be all that appealing. Nothing destroys the sexual arousal mood more effectively than bathing, toileting and providing all the other necessary activities of daily living for a needy person. It would be difficult for the caregiver to then be expected to have sexual activity as a grand finale. It is precisely because of this that a non- standard agreement should be considered.

Some illnesses or injuries are disfiguring, and that too might make it more difficult for the caregiver to crank up romantic feelings for the ill spouse. This would not simply be because of the illness or disability, but fear that sexual activity might create pain or discomfort for their partner. Some ill spouses are so concerned about the changes in their body that they are intimidated by the prospect sexual contact. Again, any of these reasons would support consideration for a non-standard agreement.

There are situations where the ill spouse wants sex and is capable, but the caregiver is not interested. The requests of the ill spouse to have intimate relations can be treated as a *want* rather than a *need* and the caregiver can simply refuse to participate, hopefully in a way that protects the ill spouse's feelings.

It may be that the ill spouse is offering sex to entice the caregiver to forego an outside relationship. If the ill spouse is lucid, this could be the basis for renegotiating the sex provision of the new contract. Frequently, we find that the offer of sexual intimacy from an ill or disabled spouse to engage in sexual activity as an enticement, noted above, has less to do with an "affair" than it does the fear of abandonment. This will be a good starting point for contractual negotiation.

The ill spouse may not mind sexual relations outside the marriage as long as there is a commitment from the well spouse to continue to provide their comfort, care and companionship. If the ill spouse is cognitively impaired, the caregiver-the majority stockholder in the sexual realm-is not obligated to explain anything, and is free to seek sexual gratification elsewhere.

Variation C: If the quality of the sexual relationship in the marriage prior to the illness or injury was bad, mediocre or non-existent, it would be a rare caregiver who would choose to initiate a sexual relationship over the ashes of the old practices. More likely, the caregiver would not even consider kindling a passionate relationship where none had existed before. Such caregivers could proceed directly to consideration of a non-standard sexual arrangement.

Variation D: In another, increasingly prevalent situation, the ill spouse may have Traumatic Brain Injury-Acquired Brain Injury (TBI/ABI). They tend to be younger, and sexual activity has been a prevalent part of their life. This type of disability can affect emotional volatility and alters personality in ways that would be unacceptable in polite society. These patients tend to need long-term caregiving and are exceptionally difficult to work with. Alzheimer's-type dementias can make a caregiver face some unique decisions. Sexual activity with a spouse who cannot consent or respond with appropriate warmth is less than satisfying and may even feel like a violation. In either case, the emotional turmoil and uproar created by the nature of these patients will tend to make the caregiver look elsewhere for sexual gratification.

Situation #2: The Ill Spouse is not Capable of Standard Sex but Cooperative

Let us suppose the relationship was wonderful before the illness or injury. There are plenty of positive memories of a pleasant life together. In this case, sex is certainly still possible, and potentially desirable, but in different variations.

The options include erotic massage, mutual masturbation, mutual oral sex and use of various sexual toys to enhance sexual satisfaction. There are marital aids, such as vibrators, various creams and lotions for enhancing sexual enjoyment. There are, of course, erectile dysfunction medications. The couple might enjoy watching movies with sexual themes or pornography as a way of turning up the erotic temperature. Many couples, anecdotally, report that this is often enough intimacy with their spouse; no need to entertain thoughts of an affair or a non-standard sexual arrangement.

The suggestions above may introduce a couple to activities that were not part of their intimate life before the chronic illness, but that is precisely what learning to live with a chronic condition does to the marriage. Learning new sexual practices together is no different from the well husband learning to cook or the well wife learning to change a tire. Illnesses and disability brings new roles.

As mentioned earlier, there are legitimate marital aids that are available under the heading "sexual health" in many medical supply catalogs. The notion that adult toys are for a seedy crowd is unfortunate because we are sexual beings and disabilities do not change that. As loving spouses and caregivers we should first and foremost try to meet these needs with our partners. Vibrators and personal massage tools have their primary origins in the field of medicine. These are as legitimate as any other "over-the-counter" medical supplies. The authors also stress the importance of speaking with your own doctor regarding sexual activity if there are potential health issues involved.

Our ill spouses may be embarrassed to reveal their fears about sexual contact. If they are recovering from a stroke, they may be worried about raising their blood pressure via sexual arousal; they need to know about their limitations. A cardiac patient may worry about their cardiovascular fragility during sex, and have been afraid to ask their doctor about it.

Arthritis sufferers can benefit from massage, a potential entrée back into erotic touching. A licensed massage therapist can demonstrate techniques that can make your ill partner comfortable with massage—especially if the idea is new. A massage from an ill spouse can also allow them to feel their contribution to the arrangement has substantive meaning.

Occupational and physical therapists are a great resource for information on body mechanics regarding your partner's sexual limitations. Professionals in orthopedics and sports medicine can also be of assistance. Sexual activity in the water can be considered. The water activity is less strenuous on partners who have stamina issues and is non-weight bearing. Books are available on positions and flotation devices for support. This can also be found online.

Situation #3: The Ill Spouse is Not Capable of Standard Sex and is Uncooperative

In this situation, the caregiver is on his or her own, and would be free to choose any approach that was potentially satisfying. The caregiver can, of course, choose to be celibate. There is a good possibility that if the spouse is oriented and uncooperative, the quality of pre-disability sex may have been unsatisfactory. On the other hand, uncooperative can mean that the spouse is suffering from a dementia. They may be combative and uncooperative. Regardless of the type of "uncooperative," the old marital contract is null and void, the new contract has no provision for sexual activity and the vows of the original marriage are not in effect. This provides a unique opportunity, free of marital promises, to pursue a brand new course of action.

David and Kate initiated talk of his need to find friendship outside the home. Originally, it was about just getting out of the house. Then it developed into an awakening of long suppressed urges, which was a surprise to David who had suppressed all of this for the preceding decade. At first, Kate supported his quest for female companionship. It was a mutual agreement between them. Kate was content and even commented several times that she liked who he was when he came home from being with his friend.

Once it became clear to Kate that this was a developing emotional attachment, Kate decided she could offer David some form of sexual gratification if he would accept it from her. David by this time had no interest in Kate in any fashion because she had insisted that nobody, but David, could provide all that intimate care for her. After so many years of it, he could not think of being intimate sexually with her. The care itself destroyed so many boundaries and violated her intimate space to the point that no intimate sexual contact was even possible. Therefore, he politely declined her offer. By that time, he had also lost respect for her because of her refusal to take any action on her own behalf for all those years.

ॐ∽

CAREGIVER CELIBACY

Celibacy is thrust upon many of us. It is not something we would have ever considered as part of our lifestyle. Resentments usually accompany unwanted celibacy, but it is technically an option available to the caregiver with a sexually incapable, uncooperative or mentally disabled spouse.

Any discussion of caregiver celibacy is like plunging into the great unknown. We know very little about this topic. Among the questions that come to mind are the following:

- What percentage of spousal caregivers are celibate before beginning their duties as a caregiver?
- What percentage of spousal caregivers had an active, vigorous, satisfying sexual relationship with the ill spouse right up to the point of illness or injury?
- What percentage of caregivers were already not satisfied with the quality of intimacy with their spouse, and the illness just made matters worse?
- What percentage of spousal caregivers continue their sexual relationship unaltered even after the ill spouse becomes disabled?

What we do know is that permanent disabilities or debilitating illnesses occur at random. There is no evidence that the need for caregiving strikes one group more than another, or even one age group over another. We can assume that older couples probably face the caregiving dilemma more frequently, but even here, that would not rule out sexual intimacy as an issue. We know that age interferes very little with sexual desire and activity. Retirement communities are currently facing issues with sexually transmitted diseases. We are living longer these days. Continuing sexual interest and capabilities are a normal part of aging. The erectile dysfunction medications are also improving the quality of sexual activity in the older community.

ᚗᚗ

Rhonda was aware that something was wrong with her husband at least 10 years before the dementia diagnosis. That was while they both were still in their twenties. Long before Andy was being treated for Alzheimer's disease, he was taking testosterone replacement therapy and their sex life was virtually nonexistent. Hence, caregiving and sexual fulfillment covers a wide gambit of dysfunction and remedies. Therefore, it is not a huge leap to assume celibacy is frustrating to the average spousal caregiver.

One tipping point for David came as part of his practicing psychologist licensing requirements. He had to participate in seminars with CEUs (Continuing Education Units) that were pre-approved by his licensing board. He chose to take a course entitled, "Defy Aging," with an accompanying text of the same name written by Dr. Michael Brickey, another psychologist. It was a course about longevity, how to live a lot longer than normally expected. In the chapter entitled Sex, Dr. Brickey eloquently points out that continuous, vigorous sexual activity is absolutely essential to live well over the age of 100. By the time David read that chapter, he had already been celibate for about eight years due to Kate's physical and emotional limitations and her addiction to pain killers. It was at that precise moment that David began to examine his alternatives.

ᚗᚗ

Given the implications of Dr. Brickey's chapter on sex, it is safe to assume that celibacy is not an attractive alternative for a spousal caregiver trapped in Caregiver Hell. Celibacy does not appear to be healthy for anyone.

Most of the suggestions in this book apply not only to spousal caregivers of permanently disabled partners, but also to caregivers of temporarily disabled partners. Thus, when a spousal caregiver is orchestrating an arrangement to get sexual needs met, the future of the marriage must be carefully considered. If there is a good possibility, the spouse will be back to normal, negotiations should be about temporary arrangements.

After years of caring for an ill spouse, celibacy is increasingly frustrating. It is in these situations that caregivers start wondering if they should seek a different partner; that is, have an affair. This is why the "affair" thread of the online support group chat room has had 30,000 hits at the time of publication of this book.

Another alternative to celibacy for the frustrated caregiver is to take matters into their own hands, so to speak. Society generally has an opinion about all sexual variations and masturbation is no exception. It is considered "self abuse" by some, and others say it will make you go blind. There are many old wives tales about this practice (*you would think old wives would tire of making up this stuff*) implying that it is unhealthy, naughty, unspeakable, sinful or will lead to horrible consequences. That is ironic, considering the fact that masturbation is a universal practice that provides legitimate sexual release.

The down side to this typically solo release is that sexual desire is embedded in a whole constellation of intimacy needs. These needs cry out for the participation of a sexual partner. If the ill spouse will not or cannot be an effective sexual partner, then the spousal caregiver of a chronically ill partner should at least consider non-standard sexual arrangements.

Another important aspect to consider in this section is that sexual satisfaction in marriages goes well beyond the physical act of intercourse. We are talking about real emotional intimacy; the connection to another human with whom sharing emotions has been on equal terms. Illness and disability can force a well spouse emotionally into the cold. Their lover is dealing with problems of their own and adding to the pile of woes seems somehow inhumane. Therefore, the well spouse often starts to seek fulfillment elsewhere.

NON-STANDARD AGREEMENTS

Any discussion of non-standard arrangements for meeting sexual needs is fraught with ethical, moral and religious potholes. Perhaps a little perspective would be helpful. A large percentage of marriages, some say as much as eighty percent, dissolves after one spouse becomes permanently ill or disabled. That vast majority of well spouses moved on ostensibly to find another relationship in which a variety of their needs could be met. It would not be too speculative to assume that part of the well spouses' decisions to leave was based on improving the odds that their needs would be met in the bedroom.

෨෪෬

In the local Well Spouse support group, the participants were willing to discuss some of their unique methods for meeting their needs. One woman said that since her husband's stroke, she befriended a male well spouse. They went to movies and out to dinner once a week. She said that her husband knew about the friendship, and he did not care. She said that the attention from the man she was seeing was flattering.

She called the outings a "date" and they made her feel better about herself. It allowed her to go home rejuvenated for her caregiving duties. She stressed it was platonic because she was insecure about herself as a sexual being, but she needed the male attention.

A male participant said that his wife was terminal, and he would be fine being celibate because he knew it was not going to last forever. That is how he was coping. He also said that his wife had tried to maintain a normal sex life until it was physically impossible for her. This gentleman stays in touch with some of the group members and shared that after his wife died he felt worn out and emotionally drained, but he found a fulfilling relationship with another woman rather quickly. Because of his dedication to his wife's needs up until the end, he had no qualms about moving on so quickly. The authors observed that this man outwardly appears to be much healthier now than he was during the last year of his wife's life.

The group had other members who were entertaining affairs because their spouses were not capable of participating in an intellectual discussion regarding the matter due to their disease. A few were so angry about the unfairness of life, they could not think of much else until they got control of their anger. One participant was so disgusted by her duties as a caregiver that she never wanted to be near another man, and the idea of celibacy seemed like an attractive goal because her spouse was annoyingly hypersexual.

∾

Ideally, the ill partner would encourage the caregiver to fulfill those needs outside the marriage. But this is pretty rare. In most cases, that solution would not be available. Ill spouses suffer too much emotional pain without a full understanding of the legitimacy of the caregiver's sexual needs. In the absence of a renegotiated contract, the ill spouse is not likely to suggest alternatives.

One arrangement that falls short of a full-blown whirlwind affair is the *sexual gratification contract*. This is an arrangement that a caregiver makes with a friend that provides for periodic sexual relations without any other commitment or emotional attachment. Today's young people call this arrangement *"friends with benefits."* Either gender can initiate this arrangement with a friend. This kind of arrangement is actually quite popular. Often both friends are married to others, and this provides them with periodic episodes of intimacy with no strings attached. The only requirement is that both participants must be able to divorce their sexual desires from the larger concepts of romantic love. That is easier the longer the crushing burden of celibacy has been present in the caregivers life. Desperate times call for desperate measures.

Rhonda was open in the Caregiver Forum online about her sexual frustrations. People called and emailed her from all over the country to discuss her ideas about how to resolve the sexual dilemma.

Rhonda was not advocating any particular activity, but she was vocal about the need for open communication. People are not comfortable discussing sexual activity, yet it is a huge missing part of the spousal caregiver's life. Most of the interactions were positive, but Rhonda was quite open about the very views expressed in this chapter.

Rhonda experienced attempts by others to censor her views online. Some people quoted moral objections to alternative sexual arrangements. Being behavioral scientists, the authors were quite intrigued to examine, although unscientifically, the correlation to "moral" objections and tenure as a well spouse. Objections were more prevalent among those who either had not been a spousal caregiver for very long, had no experience in being a spousal caregiver or were caring for a terminally ill spouse where death was imminent. As the saying goes, "Where you stand depends on where you sit."

Another interesting notation was the fact that more men were interested in talking about the sexual deprivation. Conversations were usually filled with sorrow and struggles with marriage vows, but the palpable frustrations over unmet needs were becoming debilitating for some. The women with whom she interacted were usually under fifty years of age and were seeking a relationship outside their marriage that was safe and would not lead to emotional attachments. Women also fear how they will be viewed if others find out they are having an affair.

THE AFFAIR

The next step up (or down if, one has moral objections) is the full-blown *extramarital love affair*. For some caregivers, this would be easier than being a friend with benefits because sex would not be separated from romance. An affair is an arrangement that, under many circumstances, is truly a threat to the caregiver's marriage. Falling in love with someone else is exciting and can turn the head of the most dedicated caregiver. While there are no readily available statistics, a substantial proportion of caregivers who leave their partners could very well have had affairs as a prelude to divorce.

Some may object on moral grounds to this rather clinical treatment of the institution of marriage. The authors are supportive of organized religion. They understand that religious belief is the backbone of a majority of American families. The church or synagogue is a source of comfort and inspiration for a large slice of America. Those who turn to religious leaders for caregiving advice may be disappointed, however, in that religious teachings seldom make allowances for these burdensome caregiving arrangements.

Religious leaders normally have little or no professional training as counselors, social workers, psychologists or gerontologists. They are often extrapolating from their religious beliefs or drawing from their own relationship experiences. They normally mean well but frequently give irrelevant or even bad advice. At bottom, the needy caregiver is going to have to decide if religious teachings are the same as morality. The authors believe that, by anyone's standards, whatever course of action is best for the partners of a marriage is automatically the most moral and ethical path.

THE TOUGH & TENDER CAREGIVER

The TTC knows that nobody, including the ill spouse, cares a great deal about whether their needs are met. As with the frog in the frog pond, caregivers must initiate action, or their sexual needs will never be met. The TTC understands that everything about sex is negotiable. If the ill spouse is not cognitively impaired, the key to satisfying intimacy needs is good communication, with the ill spouse and with professionals in the community.

If a satisfactory solution to intimacy needs cannot be negotiated with the ill spouse, it may be necessary to consider sexual satisfaction outside the marriage. The TTC knows that in many situations, wedding vows can become outdated, so it may not be appropriate to feel guilty for contemplating a 'friend with benefits' arrangement or even an affair. The advice of family and friends, if sought, is likely to be useless. They typically recommend that you hang in there, stay celibate, and be unhappy because that is your duty. Such advice elevates suffering to the level of saintly sacrifice. Family members' advice might be contaminated by the possibility that if the caregiver has an affair, the caregiving duties might fall on them some day. You can just hear them exclaim, "Oh, My God."

Therefore, this is a decision the TTC must make alone. If negotiations have not produced an acceptable standing agreement about sex, there is not much point in asking the spouse's permission prior to taking action. The caregiver normally owns the majority of voting stock in the revised marital corporation, especially in the sexual arena, and is entitled to do what he or she deems best with no looking back.

Chapter 6
PHONY BALONEY

Overcoming Destructive Social Programming

♦≫≪♦

As bad as social brainwashing is for people in general, it is deadly for caregivers. Unfortunately, in a search for the specialized answers, caregivers have had to settle for the same misinformation available to the general population. Many of us place barriers in the way of taking effective action to mold the world to suit us. Perhaps the largest barrier we place in our way is philosophical. A philosophical obstacle is often insurmountable because it affects the way we respond to every situation and every decision we make throughout our lives. The philosophies we carry with us block us everywhere we turn. They prevent us from making constructive changes in our behavior as we seek happiness.

To be clear, a philosophy is a set of beliefs that we use as a guidance system for making decisions. A philosophy of child rearing is a set of rules we believe in that guides our disciplinary actions with our children. *In order for a philosophy to be a useful decision tool, it must accurately reflect reality*. If a child rearing philosophy is not realistic, our actions based on those beliefs will not shape a child's behavior in a way that satisfies the parents. Philosophies that are not realistic simply do not serve us. We must not be a slave to our philosophy. Our philosophy must serve us by helping us meet our needs.

Any philosophy we embrace that allows us to impose our will on the environment will serve us. Such a philosophy allows us to take action that meets our needs. A useful, realistic philosophy of self-interest must include the following basic idea: *it is OK to go after what we need*. Most people would be more likely to adopt this kind of philosophy if it also included some mention of not stepping on other people's toes, or interfering with their ability to go after what they need as well. It will be shown below that these extra rules are not necessary. If we are efficient in pursuing what we need, we automatically take others into consideration.

The authors hope it is clear from their personal stories in the first chapter that the very essence of what went wrong in their own lives hinges directly on the fact that they did not impose their will on the environment. Hence, there was no way that they could ever find peace and happiness that each human seeks.

THE BRAINWASHING—WHAT WE ARE TAUGHT

We are taught growing up that it is *not okay* to go after what we want. From the time we understand what our parents are saying, a steady and consistent campaign is launched to persuade us that what we want does not matter. We are told "no" when we reach for a glass on the table. Our hands are spanked when we enter the kitchen when mommy is cooking. They yell at us for eating with our fingers instead of a spoon.

When we are a little older, we hear the philosophy in simple terms: "It is more blessed to give than receive." "It is wrong to be selfish." We are rewarded when we act as if we believe all this, and punished when we ignore it. Over time, we incorporate these rules of conduct in our memory as a set of beliefs about how we are supposed to act. This becomes our philosophy.

A few more of these simply stated rules of conduct that have become societal expectations are as follows:
- Turn the other cheek
- To forgive is divine
- Silence is Golden
- Don't Rock the Boat
- Marriage if Forever
- What does not kill you makes you stronger
- Time Heals all Wounds
- Forgive & Forget

- Sticks & Stones
- Half a loaf is better than none
- Don't look a gift horse in the mouth
- Actions speak louder than words
- Live by the Golden Rule
- Don't Be Selfish

As we are growing up, nobody bothers to help us learn the difference between what we want and what we need in respect to making ourselves happy. It would be helpful if we were taught to distinguish between needs, wants and happiness. What we want basically falls into two categories, those things we want which are also what we *need* (e.g., food, recognition, companionship), and things we want that block or interfere with our needs (e.g., cocaine, to injure someone, the thrill of driving 100 miles an hour). Put simply, there are "good wants" and "bad wants."

Ideally, anything we want would be systematically compared with our needs to determine if the impulse represented a "good want" or a "bad want." The TTC would then ignore the bad ones and pursue the good ones. They would be able to say, "I want to eat a bowl of ice cream, but I need to watch my diet in order to stay healthy, so I'll pass." Or they might argue, "I want to stay home for my husband, but I need to get out and socialize for my mental health. So, I will find a sitter and agree to meet my friend at the movies."

Unfortunately, "bad wants" create a greater sense of urgency than "good wants". Therefore, we often pay more attention to the bad wants than the good wants. For example, a woman might badly need to resolve a conflict with her husband. She may want to avoid the conflict and this avoidance represents a "bad want." The "avoid" internal signal overwhelms her "resolve" and she adopts a "peace at any price" strategy. Sadly, the price she pays is that her need is not met and then other issues begin to arise and will likely undermine the pursuit of happiness within the marriage.

Of course, there are things we want which are neither good nor bad, such as a stroll on the beach or a new CD. There is no good reason to deny ourselves harmless indulgences if nobody gets hurt.

Parents can be forgiven for not teaching this distinction. It is hard enough for adults to understand what they need, and nearly impossible for children. To know what we really need requires the ability to visualize our own future, to grasp the long-term implications of today's decisions and actions. This ability develops slowly in human beings, and children simply do not understand.

However justified, our ignorance of the distinction causes many of us to apply the "don't be selfish" message to all of our desires. We conclude that if we want it, it is probably bad. For some of us, it gradually dawns on us that it is okay to go after some of the things we want but not others. For many of us, the rule haunts our every move. Every time we do something we really want to do, we feel guilty. We feel guilty if we take a vacation, eat too much, buy a new dress, get our car washed, discipline our child, read a novel, or drink a beer. To make matters worse, we pass by one opportunity after another to make our lives better, believing we would feel guilty if we capitalized on it.

છે⊸φ

Rhonda has had a terrible issue with this in the past. Every time she did something or acted in a way that served her, she thought that she was acting selfishly. She even told herself after a moment of happiness or succumbing to an indulgence that God would get her. This erroneous thinking was always reinforced by using the next negative event in her life as proof that she was going to pay for the self-described selfishness of her past action. What developed was a pattern of viewing every tough situation as a punishment and the inability to view the world with clarity. Hence, she thought her life was harder than it was for other people. Why does this keep happening to me?

છે⊸φ

The truth is that when a person is dealing with an unusually stressful situation, like a health crisis, a change in residence, a job loss, etc., every tough moment piles onto the next tough moment or event and seems like the cosmic scales have shifted unfairly.

છે⊸φ

A well spouse, Daphne, was dealing with her husband's sudden health crisis just after she treated herself to a night out with friends. This is something that she does quite infrequently since he is chronically ill. During that time of the acute hospitalization, her clothes washer broke down, her garbage did not get taken out timely, the dog ran away, her boss went out of town and left her alone to run the office. She missed her daughter's recital because of the long workdays to cover for her boss's absence. To Daphne, as she confessed, "Everything is going wrong, why me? It only happens to me, why is my life so hard?"

She finally decided it was because she had accepted the invitation to have dinner out and left her family at home. Because of the indulgence of a night out, she believed she paid a penalty.

≈≪

If you take out the health crisis from the scenario above, it seems like no big deal to any one else. It sounds just normal life. We all have chores, kids, unruly dogs, appliances and bosses. What is wrong here for caregiver is that it we are reluctant to admit what we need and then go after it free of guilt. Using the "magical thinking" that cosmic forces are keeping us down. Some other force is controlling our ability to find fulfillment.

WHY THE BRAINWASHING?

Self-interest began getting a bad name at the dawn of civilization. Human beings have banded together from the beginning to make life easier. Primitive man lived in a hostile environment that required people to live together to survive. A division of labor was required to hunt wild animals that were faster and stronger than individuals were by themselves.

From the beginning, individuals were called upon to make personal sacrifices for the good of the whole group. It must have been crystal clear to any witch doctor worth his salt that too much individual self-interest was a threat to the tribe. Individuals were asked to be farsighted enough to understand how they would ultimately benefit by contributing to the group.

It was probably no easier for primitive man to control his impulses and desires than it is for us. Immediate desires are more pressing and powerful than long-term needs. We as a species viewed self-interest as such a powerful force that it could only be tempered by an equally powerful, but opposite message: *Do For Others First*. Thus, even before the advent of organized religion, it seems likely that there has been a movement afoot lobbying for putting others before the individual, putting the group first. This message must have been invented by those who had the foresight to understand how everyone can benefit by collective efforts. It is as if these farsighted people also believed the only way to counter the powerful self interest idea was to convince people that self interest is bad. It can be assumed these leaders were ultimately looking for some kind of balance between self-interest and collective interests.

This powerful but extreme message continues to cause confusion today for most people. The message is the more insidious because it is contained in Western child rearing philosophies. We view the socialization process for very young people as designed to stamp out self-centeredness by getting toddlers to *"be polite, be thoughtful, think about others, too."* The hidden message is that it is wrong to think of your self-first. It even becomes a moral and theological issue when the self-centeredness is labeled *"original sin."* Moral development then becomes a process of stamping out original sin (selfishness).

Another force contributing to the power of this anti-selfishness belief is the wish of many people that the world be different than it is. Who among us hasn't wished that people would be nicer? It is hard to acknowledge and accept how truly mean-spirited and nasty some people can be. Some of us grab onto idealism as an antidote. If we just teach our children a spirit of *"brotherly love"*, then the world will be a better place. However sincerely we teach our children the rules of bridge, the world continues to play poker. It does little good to pretend the world is another way. Reality always wins out. It is far better for our children to be prepared.

TRAVLAND'S LAW—SELF-INTEREST IS INEVITABLE

❧

Travland's Law: People can always be counted upon to do what they perceive to be in their own best interests at the moment.

The words "at the moment" are extremely important because people always act in accordance with their momentary view that the action they take will help them somehow. In reality, impulsive actions often lead to second thoughts when they discover that their long-term interests are not being met. What often happens is that people have a lot of trouble admitting mistakes and making a mid-course correction. This inability to admit a wrong move can lead to days, years or even a lifetime of unhappiness because we were so stuck in our justifications for making a decision, right or wrong.

Interest in our own well-being is an extension of the survival instinct. If an individual is crossing the street and a dump truck is careening wildly toward him, he does not stop to analyze the situation and decide what course of action meets his needs. A direct message is sent from his brain to his feet and he moves out of the way, immediately. This is the survival instinct in action, part of our biological heritage.

We do not have a choice. In any situation, our first instinctive reaction is to think of ourselves first. How will this affect me? Will I be hurt? What's in this for me? What will this do to my home, my family, my spouse, and my kids? Yet the brainwashing immediately makes most of us feel bad for reacting this way. *"Oh my goodness, I'm not supposed to think this way."* This is then often followed by guilt feelings, some sort of rationalization (*"I'm really thinking of them."*), or a cover-up (*"I'll make them think I'm only thinking of them."*).

Often these disguises are very effective. We admire people who do volunteer work, thinking of them as charitable, doing for others out of the goodness of their hearts. But the truth is they do it for themselves, sometimes because the volunteer work is stimulating and their regular job is boring. In other situations, they have a strong need for recognition or power, which they do not get elsewhere. Our most sophisticated community leaders who must rely on volunteerism are acutely aware of self-interest in such work. They rely heavily on awards, public recognition, and other concrete kinds of "Thanks" which volunteers expect in exchange for their time. The leader who fails to recognize volunteers will not succeed.

An understanding of self-interest can improve relationships. It keeps us from having unrealistic expectations of others. One of the most reliable ways of predicting the behavior of others is to assume they will act according to what they perceive as their own best interests. If we understand this well, it will save us a lot of anger and disappointment. Realistic expectations are not likely to be violated by reality.

The deadly misconception that "the needs of the dependent spouse are more important than the needs of the caregiver" must be debunked because everybody's needs are important. The needs of the person being cared for (the dependent spouse) are oftentimes more visible and obvious. The noises made by those needs are almost deafening at times, but that does not mean those needs are any more important than the needs of the caregiver.

A very important principle needs to be enunciated here: *if the needs of the caregiver are not met, the caregiver cannot continue to be a caregiver.* If the caregiver cannot continue to be a whole person, he or she is not going to be much good as a caregiver. Then not only is the caregiver suffering, but the person receiving the care is going to suffer. Hence, everybody loses if the needs of the caregiver are not made a priority.

The above information is also a partial reason why the next misconception is so off kilter, "the dependent person's needs and wants are as important as the needs and wants of the caregiver." If we look at the difference between needs and wants, we can immediately see that there is something dysfunctional about treating needs and wants in the same category. Needs are fundamental to our well-being whereas our wants tend to be whimsical. Wants are more superficial or short term. People will suffer if their needs are not met, but they will not suffer if their wants are not met.

Unfortunately, in many caregiving situations the person who is dependent blurs the distinction between needs and wants when they ask for something, such as permission to watch a movie or to use a computer. They often fall into the pattern of implying that this is something they need. "I need to watch that movie." "I need to get online right now." The TTC is going to have to make a distinction between what the person needs versus what they want in order to carve out time for him or herself as a caregiver. Caregivers need go know that it is safe to say "no" to wants, but it is *not* always safe to say "no" to needs.

Another deadly misconception is, "it is always inappropriate say No to the requests of an ill spouse". The truth is that saying "no" is a lifeline for a caregiver. Knowing when you are able to say no, having the willingness to say no and not being "guilted" into saying yes all the time is part of the survival tactic.

Next, understanding that any caregiver with a chronically ill spouse has to learn the next myth to break the cycle; "Caregivers should not ask amateur or professional sitters to fill in for the caregiver". This misconception is one that is perpetuated by the very people for whom we are caring.

Some people feel that they have more control over their spouse as a caregiver than they would have over anyone else. So, at times they selfishly insist that the care they are being given comes only from one source, namely from their spouse. The TTC of a chronically ill spouse needs to have a whole cadre of fill-in and substitute caregivers that can be engaged on short notice.

ॐॐ

David fell for this self-serving argument and literally spent over two years allowing his wife to refuse all care that was not provided by him. This might have been workable in a situation where fewer medical needs were involved, but in Kate's case, it was total care. The physical strength it took from David was debilitating. By the end of nearly 20,000 hours of care without a substantial break, David reached his tipping point. If he had been aware of these misconceptions earlier

144

in his tenure as a full time caregiver, it may have paid off for both of them. He could have renegotiated the terms of his caregiver contract with Kate so everyone's needs could have been met more efficiently

ॐॐ

The next deadly misconception, "there is something noble about sacrificing your life for spouse," could not be further from the truth. Self-interest is vital to a caregiver because if the caregiver's needs are not met, the caregiver cannot function. We are in this life to get our needs met, like it or not. Therefore, we must find some measure of personal fulfillment and happiness in this life. Hence, there is nothing noble about burning out as a caregiver. That level of sacrifice ultimately serves no one.

ENLIGHTENED SELF-INTEREST

In keeping with the need for any philosophy to be realistic, there are two realities about self-interest that must be understood, one about self-interest in general which we have discussed as Travland's Law. The other one is about enlightened self-interest.

As discussed briefly in an earlier chapter, self-interest tempered by an understanding of our *long-term* needs is considered enlightened self-interest. For example, when we agree to attend a silly movie with our spouse it is in the hope that they will return the favor later. Therefore, when we accompany our spouse, it is for ourselves. A large percentage of our needs can only be satisfied with the cooperation of other people. What good is intimacy without another person? Our cat may respect us, but somehow it is not the same as respect from our peers. People are the source of our goodies.

The enlightened approach is to recognize this and plan ahead. We help our neighbor in hopes he will help us when we need it. We cooperate with our spouse and expect cooperation in return. We hope our mechanic makes a profit in business so the company will be there when we need it. In short, in order for us to win, others also have to win. Our children are much more likely to understand "do for others or you won't get what you want" than the philosophy of "it is more blessed to give than receive", which will quickly be proven untrue as they mature. In fact, there really is nothing that could be classified as genuine altruism. Everyone has their own self-interest in mind at some level of consciousness. They cannot always say it out loud, often because it is not considered socially acceptable, but it is true nonetheless.

We call this "relationship management" alluded previously. Some people believe that when we are nice to others it ought to be with no strings attached ("it is more blessed to give than receive"). We observe that the "internal ledger" keeps track of this investment whether we want it to or not. We know it is more efficient to admit simply what is really going on. We actually give with the expectation of getting something back. Some people denigrate this natural social exchange process by calling it "manipulation." That negative term only applies if one party is attempting to exploit the other person, if there is bad intent. If the intent is for both parties to win, the process is natural and harmless and is *relationship management.*

The TTC does not feel guilty for needing or wanting something. Needs are part of our biological equipment. That would be like feeling bad because we have toes. The TTC considers needs healthy, and the pursuit of those needs as a legitimate and rewarding activity. Those around the TTC benefit; they are grateful the TTC is so cleverly selfish, because they win too.

☞☜

Rhonda struggled with the guilt that kept rearing up when she put her own feelings first. When Andy, her husband, would get bad news, she would be aware that her first thoughts were, *"How will this affect me?" "How long will this nightmare last?" "Can the children cope while we figure out how Andy's needs will be met?"*

When David began speaking to her about this concept of self-interest, the clarity was profound. Feeling guilty made no sense. She needed to worry about her children. Somebody had to because Andy was no help at all with the children. If she permitted herself to explore how Andy's problems affected her without feeling guilty, then she could plan for their welfare. Her guilt feelings were interfering with her ability to take care of the whole family. She needed to be able to accept the reality of Andy's disease process and admit the marriage was not a marriage any longer. This had to be done for the sake everyone. After all, she needed to be well for the children and for her own goal of becoming a TTC.

In turn, Rhonda asked David some difficult questions of the same nature. Why was he allowing Kate to refuse others to help in her daily care? Why was he working from dawn to midnight tending to her every whim without a break and no support system? If he looked at his situation with an open objective mind, would he not see that his marriage was no longer equitable?

For both of them, giving to others to the point of exhaustion was not reaping any interpersonal rewards. They were living like zombies. They had to ask, why are we continuing to live this way?

❧❧

The TTC has adopted a realistic philosophy of self-interest, and thus is seldom disappointed in other people. Others are expected to pursue their own interests, and their behavior is therefore predictable.

❧❧

In their respective marriages, David and Rhonda consistently set themselves up for disappointment. They kept assuming that if they kept up with their side of the marriage, kept paying attention to their spouses' needs, then eventually they would get what they wanted from their spouses in return. They essentially failed themselves by not being able to stay focused on what they needed and permitted the interests of their ill spouses to prevail. As a result, they were both miserable and resigned to a bleak future.

Chapter 7
HOPELESS & HELPLESS

Assuming Responsibility for Our Behavior

తడ

Bad caregiving situations are a direct result of our own choices. Did we stay in the relationship too long? Did we throw caution to the wind? Were we willing to look the other way when something needed to be addressed? Now we are paying the price. As illustrated in the frog pond example, our needs will not be met unless we are willing to impose our will on the environment. If our needs are not met, we will not be happy. However, before we take action, we have to believe that meeting our needs is *our* responsibility. If we assume our needs are the responsibility of the environment or someone else, we will not lift a finger to help ourselves. We must assume total and complete responsibility for our lives.

Unfortunately, *blaming others* for our own unhappiness is something most of us do occasionally. Some people do it frequently. They blame God's will, the luck of the draw, fate, chance, or some other cosmic force over which they have no control. We discussed this a little in previous chapters.

There is a whole body of social propaganda, which encourages us to slough off our responsibilities. It takes the form of slogans, proverbs, sayings, myths, and other forms of social rules. Some examples include:

- You have to take the bad with the good
- Half a loaf is better than none at all
- Don't make waves
- Turn the other cheek
- Look on the bright side

- Silence is golden

The core message of these proverbs is that "since there is nothing you can do to change things, you have to accept whatever happens, and it is not my fault." Therefore, it has to be someone else's fault.

ASSUMING RESPONSIBILITY FOR OUR LIVES

Blaming others takes a variety of forms. The most common form has to do with how we distort language to make unacceptable behavior seem acceptable. For example, people are often afraid to take action that might ruffle someone's feathers, so they use the language to pretend their course of action is somehow rational and defensible. She might say, "Oh, I couldn't possibly attend the wedding without George." This woman is not telling the truth. The truth is that she is making a choice. She is choosing not to go without George. But she is reluctant to take responsibility for her decision. Instead, she is foisting the decision off on some cosmic principle that does not exist, such as "one cannot attend weddings without one's husband."

In this situation there is probably a lot more behind her need to pretend she has no choice. It is likely that she is afraid to ask George if it would be all right for her to attend alone. She might fear his reaction. Or, she might not want to admit how dependent she is on his presence. Something else is going on. Again, the truth is that she is *choosing* not to go without George and does not want to admit it.

Another example would be the obese man who claims that "I am just not able to eat less." He is implying there are forces beyond his control that are responsible for his eating behavior. We all know he is *choosing* to eat excessively, that it is precisely his choice that leads to his food intake. In all likelihood, he would have a lot of trouble admitting that his weight problem is totally his own responsibility. That would mean he *wanted* to be self-indulgent during meals, and that would mean there is an element of self-loathing and self-destructiveness to his behavior. On the one hand, that would be hard to admit, but on the other hand, that admission would be the beginning of healing. As Dr. Phil says, you have to own the problem to fix it.

When David heard someone use language to deny responsibility, his approach as a therapist would be "When you say 'I couldn't go without George' aren't you really saying 'I won't go without George?'" This would open up the therapeutic dialog about who is really responsible for her decisions.

WHY DENY RESPONSIBILITY?

Why would anyone refuse to accept responsibility for what they do and what happens to them? What barriers stand in the way of someone accepting the most elementary sort of responsibility for their own destiny?

First of all, many systems of religious belief promote the idea that our lives are in the hands of a higher power. Parents with these beliefs teach their children that we only have limited responsibility for our lives, which can undermine a child's determination to achieve mastery of his environment.

Caregivers trapped in Caregiver Hell often attribute their misery to some celestial luck of the draw. It is not their fault their spouse became disabled. What else can they do but go with the flow, take care of their ill spouse as long as necessary. To be sure, the caregiver is probably not the least bit responsible for the illness or disability. But the caregiver is indeed personally responsible for deciding how to handle the caregiving situation. Making sacrifices is a *choice*, not a *mandate*. Letting the ill spouse abuse them verbally is a choice made by the caregiver. Assuming complete responsibility for intimate care of the ill spouse is a decision made by the caregiver. Who is to blame for being trapped in Caregiver Hell? The person responsible is the caregiver.

This is illustrated in the case of dysfunctional caregiving, which often takes the form of caregivers giving up all responsibility for their own lives. With caregivers, it can take one of two forms. The caregiver may give up and allow the ill partner's wants and needs to consume them. Or, the ill spouse gives all power to the caregiver and the burden is so great that the caregiver succumbs to the pressure and loses their autonomy. Essentially, both parties in either form tend to blame the other for their own life decisions and simply exist mindlessly. This vicious cycle is so profoundly ingrained that it is difficult to unravel.

ॐ ॐ

One Well Spouse support group member, Mark, stayed in the nightmare with Ann because after years of hearing everything was his fault, he began to believe it. He had been away a great deal because of work. He felt he had let Ann down because of his absences decades earlier. There was also his coronary problem, which they both assumed led to his erectile dysfunction (ED).

Mark told the support group that he was no longer capable of physical intimacy. While it was likely a medical condition, Ann had told him over a decade earlier that he was to never attempt to have sex with her again because of the ED. It made Ann mad, as if he was doing this on purpose. He never consulted a physician about this since she was so adamant and hurtful. Mark told Ann then that she would one day regret the insulting way she shunned him as her husband.

What he did not tell her, he confessed, is that he was devastated by her rejection. He would tell himself that it was just as well that he never tried again. Ann never assumed any responsibility for the dysfunction, even though it is quite likely that her anger or her own physical disabilities could have contributed to the ED. They were supposed to be working on issues together as a couple, he thought. She could not afford to share any responsibility for the physical limitations of her caregiver lest he walk away. In discussions with the well spouse, support group members Mark concluded that Ann was using his guilty feelings about *his* impairment to control him.

Once Mark found the courage to become a TTC, he sought help from a physician and learned he did not have irreversible ED and received medical intervention. The Caregiver Hell yielded ED as part of the incredible stress Mark had been under for years. Once Mark learned how to handle the real problems in the relationship, that he was an enabler helping Ann maintain control of him through guilt, his physical abilities re-appeared.

ॐ ॐ

CONSEQUENCES OF AVOIDING RESPONSIBILITY

What happens to people who will not accept responsibility for their own lives? In the caregiving relationship both parties often abdicate responsibility for themselves. The caregiver says, "I cannot change anything because my spouse is sick." The disabled spouse says, "I cannot change anything because I am sick." So what happens? Nothing. The caregiver is paralyzed in the belief that since the ill spouse is not going to get better, nothing *can* change. The ill spouse accepts the status quo and quits trying to change anything; he or she succumbs to the disability and does nothing to help the situation.

In these situations, each party in their own way fails to accept personal responsibility for what is going on. This might be forgivable at times in the case of the disabled spouse; the limitations are real. The ill spouse, whose passivity often takes the form of passive-dependency, refuses to take responsibility for even the most routine of activities in the household. They play the "I'm too sick to care for myself" role and rely on the caregiver for everything. They tend to have spouses that are strong, take-charge people so they can depend on them in a pinch. The caregiver, by accepting this responsibility, becomes an enabler. The authors believe that well spouse caregivers have this role precisely because of their character. People without the attributes most long-term spousal caregivers posses give up on the marriage and its caregiving responsibilities, and leave the relationship long before burnout or any other difficult issues arise.

Another form it takes with the ill spouse is passive-aggressiveness. The ill spouses sometimes use their disability to dominate and control their caregivers. They know when the caregiver needs time for themselves, and deliberately intrude into the caregiver's schedule as a form of aggressiveness. The ill spouses who are most prone to this strategy for controlling their caregivers typically feel "owed." They feel their lives have been burdened unfairly with their disability, and somebody, somewhere, somehow, should pay them back for all this inconvenience. So they take it out on their caregiver.

These people intuitively understand which tactics, passive dependent or passive aggressive, are most likely to give them control over their caregiver, and then use the tactics they deem to be most likely to succeed. Well spouses who are strong and responsible can best be controlled with passive dependency whereas spouses who have a strong sense of honor or duty will respond to passive aggressive tactics. So what happens to caregivers who have come to believe they do not have the ability to fix their own situation? They may become depressed, withdrawn, attempt suicide, or perhaps drop out of life all together. They may figure, "What's the use? Nothing I can do will make a difference. "

One of the traps that caregivers fall into is a byproduct of being too responsible for everything. The responsible caregiver is so concerned about making sure everything in the household is handled that it crowds out the caregiver's concerns about his or her own needs. "I don't have time to think about what I need. Everybody is depending on me" is the refrain. This rationalization mutes the signals that would alert the caregiver to pay attention to their own needs. Subsequently, their needs are not met and the sense of urgency of unmet needs takes one of the following forms, or perhaps, a combination:

- Chronic anger
- Unhappiness
- Tearfulness
- Depression
- Sense of Futility
- Hopelessness

Caregivers often throw themselves on the kindness of strangers. They ask anyone and everyone for help, experimenting with new ways to spin their plight to elicit the most sympathy. Then they become angry when people do not volunteer to meet their needs. Sometimes they become bitter, eccentric, violent, or criminal. They often strike out at what they perceive as an uncooperative world. Caregivers are often unaware of this pattern, it sneaks up on them.

The caregiver has genuine options for making fundamental changes in the situation. The caregiver is not limited to indirect reactions like the disabled spouse. The only limitations on the caregiver are self-imposed and take the form of *erroneous beliefs*.

Throughout the book are listed Deadly Misconceptions about caregiving that influence how caregivers behave. For example, one of these is "we have a special responsibility to help those less fortunate." This is a misconception because our willingness to help others is situational. We seldom feel a special responsibility to help malnourished children in Haiti. Why not? They are a long way away from us, and we could not do much to make a difference in reality. In the caregiving situation, this is a misconception when certain limits are reached. For example, is the caregiver obligated to sacrifice his or her own health to maintain the health of the spouse? That would be ridiculous, of course, because if the caregiver's health fails, caregiving is impossible. We know spousal caregivers commonly work themselves into a position of failing health. It is well documented that spousal caregivers often succumb to illnesses before their ill spouse.

The other misconceptions in earlier chapters are equally erroneous, and set the stage for the caregiver to have any number of excuses for failing to take responsibility for themselves. The bottom line here is that believing this baloney will prevent the caregiver from doing the one thing that will fix the situation; *taking action.*

Without taking action, the life of the caregiver continues on a downward spiral of dissatisfaction with their life. At this point, the caregiver must accept responsibility in order to make a difference in their pursuit of happiness. If they do not accept responsibility, the consequences can make life worse. Until this paradigm of "it is not my fault I have to live like this" is broken, life will not get any better.

EVENTS BEYOND OUR CONTROL

Certainly, we must accept responsibility for what happens to us, but do we control everything? Obviously, there are events beyond our ability to influence or control, "acts of God," earthquakes, floods, tornados and the like. These represent certain limits to our responsibility. It is important to understand what these limits are so we can focus our energy where we have the most leverage.

It will be assumed that events are distributed at random. No system of cosmic evil or benevolence focuses ill will or special kindnesses on people because of what they deserve. Good things happen to bad people and bad things happen to good people. There is no system. Clearly, we are not responsible for these randomly distributed streaks of good or bad luck.

The frog is not responsible for the spraying of DDT that drastically reduced the population of bugs in the pond. It was not his fault. Does this mean the frog is helpless in the face of this onslaught? Should the frog hop around, wringing his feet saying, "Mercy me, now I'm a goner." Absolutely not. The frog is responsible for making adjustments in his approach to getting his needs met. In this case, he needs to spend a greater proportion of his time chasing bugs and less time sitting in the sun.

In other words, we may not be responsible for events in our environment, but we are certainly responsible for what we do in response to those events. The athlete who lost his legs in a terrorist car bomb explosion cannot be held responsible for being in the wrong place at the wrong time. However, he is certainly responsible for how he responds to this horrible misfortune. If he vegetates, gets depressed and becomes a ward of the state, it is because he *chose* that strategy. He has the option of retraining himself to become a useful and productive citizen in some occupation that requires brains and hands but not mobility.

BOUNDARY ERRORS

We are not responsible for random events, but we are responsible for how we respond to these events. This distinction is often hard to make when we try to sort out what is our responsibility and what is someone else's responsibility.

Growing up, most of us were taught some potentially confusing philosophy about our degree of responsibility for other people.

- *Love thy neighbor.*
- *Lend a helping hand.*
- *It is more blessed to give than receive*

These messages were not accompanied by detailed instructions laying out the limits on giving. We were not taught how much giving is too much. Nobody told us to limit the amount of sacrifice we make for others. We certainly were not taught that doing for others is often destructive. One way to clear up this confusion is to visualize everyone with a boundary around them that clearly separates one person from another. What is on my side of my boundary is my responsibility, and what is outside is not. Furthermore, what is inside the boundary of another person is their responsibility and not mine.

Type I Boundary Errors

There are several varieties of confusion about these boundaries. The Type I Boundary Error occurs when I blame somebody else for something that is my responsibility. It is quite common for teenage students who receive a bad grade to blame the teacher. The teacher was too strict, too lenient, gave us too much work, did not warn us before tests, gave essay exams everyone failed and so on. The little girl explains why she hit her brother with a baseball bat: "He made me do it. He made a face at me." The man beats his wife because "she deliberately provokes me." A man fired for insubordination blames his boss: "If he were able to make better decisions I wouldn't have had to go over his head." Flip Wilson said it all: "The devil made me do it."

People commit Type I Boundary Errors because they do not wish to be held accountable for the results of their own actions. They do not want to accept the blame for their mistakes. These same people are quick to accept credit for good things that happen, even when someone else deserves the credit.

છ્જ

When David was first married to Kate, she began gaining substantial amounts of weight in their first year of marriage. David asked her what was going on and what could he do to help her trim back. Kate was incensed by these questions. At first she implied that her mother had been monitoring her food intake her entire childhood, and she was not about to put up the same kind of harassment from her husband. Then she pointed out that the more he brought up the topic, the less motivated she was to do anything constructive about the weight. In other words, further weight gain would be David's fault.

Kate's early explanation for her weight gain gradually morphed into genetic explanations *(my genes make me do it)* and hormone explanations *(my autoimmune system makes me do it)*. If it was not David's fault then it was something else that absolved her of personal responsibility; namely the way her body works.

࿐

Rhonda faced a similarly troublesome *Type I Boundary Error* when her husband periodically erupted with hostility. He, his mother and sisters adamantly insisted that Andy did not have a problem with impulse control, that there was nothing wrong with him. When he got angry, it was only because Rhonda and the kids misbehaved or were uncooperative. None of Andy's ugly behavior was his fault. Neither Andy nor his family could own up to Andy's culpability in all of this violent behavior.

࿐

Type II Boundary Errors

These occur when I accept responsibility for the behavior of another person. Abused women frequently blame themselves for the violence: "It was my fault. I knew it would make him mad if I bought a new pair of shoes without consulting him." A man tries to help his wife control her excessive drinking by hiding the booze, thereby accepting at least partial responsibility for her self-discipline problem. A well-meaning, but misguided mother drives her son to school every day so he will not have to mingle with all those rowdy boys on the school bus.

Philosophical confusion can contribute to Type II Boundary Errors *(e.g., love thy neighbor)*, but ordinarily there are complex psychological motives at work. We sometimes leap into another person's boundary because we are trying to buy acceptance from that person.

If I help them out of their jam, they will think of me as a nice person. The abused wife cannot afford to acknowledge her husband's culpability because it would then be necessary for her to demand that he change his behavior, or else. The *or else* is too frightening for her to contemplate. Some parents accept responsibility for the behavior of a child because they see the child as an extension of themselves.

A person who commits Type II boundary errors frequently does considerable damage to the other person. The man who hides his wife's booze is not forcing her to accept responsibility for her own behavior. The misguided mother who drives her son to school deprives her son of the opportunity to learn self-protection skills. We may think we are helping someone by rescuing them, but we nearly always do more harm than good.

The following is a classic example of a Type II boundary error. It came to the authors via a family friend who needed advice on how to help his family out of what on the surface appeared to be a complicated situation and resolution would be difficult to achieve. Parenthetical analysis is following each email.

„›…

Dear Dave, I hope you are well. My sister, Jan, sent me these e-mails describing my brother, Bob's, plight and involves a social worker named Nancy. This plight, I think, is his fault. Bob was never much of an earner and spent all of his inheritance from our father. He has been barely employed and is occasionally a homeless young man. I think he's a lazy, self important, extreme narcissist who lives on what our sister sends him. I do not want to get involved. No, he can't move in with me (I have been asked all ready). Please let me know what you think from the e-mails. I want to know if I am wrong for feeling like this. Also, I need help in knowing how to respond to my sister. She is giving him too much & I am afraid for her well-being by getting this involved. She apparently is not getting the help from the local community and has decided to pull me in as well. Please. Thank you. Your Friend, Tom

„›…

What follows are excerpts of a series of emails between Jan and the Nancy, the social worker who is working with brother Bob. She is trying to placate Jan by explaining that continuing to rescue Bob will do nothing but harm him. Her emails demonstrate a rising level of exasperation with Jan's desire to rescue her brother.

৵৽৵

Jan, here is the information I reviewed in an attempt to help your brother find a suitable home. The phone number & address are in the application package. Your brother Bob needs to call the woman at the property to set an appointment & complete the application process. It is not on a bus line so he will have to arrange a ride. The only problem I foresee is that the first month's rent must be paid in advance—the rent, utilities and land rental plus trailer rental ranges from $345 to $485 a month and someone needs to guarantee that up front. The property manager stated that there are no advances in staying rent free cannot take on this liability without the prepayment. If he is working then there is typically no problem with someone who has special needs, but rent must be paid reliably as the park owners are not at all flexible nor are they understanding of personal circumstances.

Hopefully, Bob would be able to pay that from his job in January. However, unless he starts now to get help from the mental health agencies that new job might be very short term and having to leave would be painful. We can help with $400 for the first month only. I don't know how much more he will need. I have emailed question to the trailer park. Sincerely, Nancy, Community Social Services Coordinator

(Nancy offers advice and what help is available. She makes it clear that there are limits and Bob must be informed and willing to take action to help himself.)

Hi, Nancy, How can my brother, Bob, find a sponsor so that his trailer fee per month would be the $25.00 that is mentioned in the application paperwork? That would be the ultimate gift for Bob. That way, he could really make it! Thanks, Jan

(Jan's request for a "sponsor" indicates that she does not believe Bob can pay the $25. She is looking for someone else to be helpful.

Somehow, she must be hoping that the more Bob is given in the way of handouts, the more he will rise to the level of self-reliance. For example, stating that the $25 would be the ultimate gift and he would be able to make it this time. Is she hoping this time Bob will turn the corner?)

Dear Jan, I read through the application. The rent for the trailer is indeed $25 a month, but the lot on which the trailer rests costs 280-360. Here is what I found in the application: You rent the RV from the park for $25 per month. You will sign a lease agreement with them that allows you to get out of the agreement at anytime. Electricity ranges from about $40 per month to as high as $100 per month. You are in control of how much electricity you use. Most parks provide water, sewer and cable TV in the price of the lot rent. It seems to me that he could afford that with his job. He will probably take home $1000 a month and the trailers come with linens, pots, pans and furniture so his only expenses would be the 345-485 a month. Once you have a job, it is difficult to get time off for appointments. Perhaps he should go to (mental health services here which are free). If he goes through the homeless outreach which is downtown, they might make it easier for him to get an appt. I don't know of any organization that will sponsor him financially long-term. With his salary, he should be able to afford it. As I said, we would agree to subsidize the first month for $400. After that, I assume he will be self supporting. Downtown Charities doesn't do a lot here, as far as I know. I know the church does but they help only sporadically. You might want to search online and see if there are other options. Meanwhile, I will maintain contact with other people and see what other options there might be. Sincerely, Nancy

(Nancy is clearly stating that Bob needs to learn responsibility and that he is capable of making it on his own. Nancy carefully spells out the real expenses and informs Jan that self reliance is the only way for Bob to make changes)

Nancy, Hi, my concern is his inability to keep a job for very long. He will end up right on the street again. Going to get a Mental Health diagnosis would be a good move, but I wonder if he will participate in the process. He thinks he is fine and everyone else has a problem. Let me write him and see what I can do for him. Perhaps, the fact the trailer park can get him in quickly, and you kindly offered to support him for the first month, will be a balm to him. Thank you soooo much! Jan

(Jan still is not "hearing" the message that Bob is responsible for his own needs; note the use of the word "balm." It implies that Bob is a wounded baby. Jan is running to Bob's aid by saying "Let me see what I can do." The next excerpt is Nancy's final attempt to convince Jan to back off and stop being an enabler. Her verbiage is quite instructive.)

Dear Jan, I don't know you, nor your brother, but I have worked in inner city hospitals and I probably know a lot of men and women like him. So, take what I am about to say with that in mind. It may not sit well, and you will resist it. But, think about it............You are being blackmailed by you brother.

Until you stop rescuing him, he will not help himself. You do not need to do this. Tell him you do not have the money. Give him my phone number.

If he is working, he is warm. He has to use the resources that are available to him and you cannot be it for the rest of his life. When will he begin to trust the rest of society? He has to when all other resources have dried up. It may not be his fault he is where he is, but it is not helpful to him to keep him there. Just as kids are afraid to go to school but the loving parent makes them, as they know it is for their own good, you need to be able to do this for him. It would have been better had it happened when there is no threat of a freeze, but that's how it is.

I will not be blackmailed so as much as my heart aches for you, I am holding to my offer. He can go to the homeless shelters and all the places I have listed for you. Sometimes you can't save people from themselves. And unless you are willing to take this on for the rest of his life, it would be kinder to him to start now while he is young rather than when he is less able to learn new strategies. I hope there is some trusted pastor, counselor there to help you with these hard decisions. Your hands are full, your checkbook isn't. There has to be an end to this. I hope you can see it. I will email him as you requested (he must be in a nice warm library reading his emails while you wring your hands at home), but I want to know what decision you will be making first regarding your continued efforts to rescue him? Sincerely, Nancy

(This is a talented social worker, indeed. Nancy is to the point & telling Jan to stop her bad behavior. She is clear and this email exemplifies the point made repeatedly in this book regarding putting yourself first no matter how sick someone appears to be. Jan is causing herself harm, financially and emotionally. Bob has not acted in his own behalf and Jan needs to stop the behavior that are causing her harm and subsequently hurting Bob due to his increasing dependence on her tendency to rescue him. We hear from Jan one more time.)

Dear Tom, I have been trying to help our baby brother, Bob, both financially and with assistance in the community through indigent programs. I have sent him hundreds and thousands of dollars from my credit cards over the past years but, he still has not applied for the trailer I found for him even though I keep sending money to get him over there. Please read the huge list of e-mails back and forth between his Social Worker, Nancy, here and myself. I hope you are well! Any suggestions on how I can help our brother from this point? Your Sister, Jan

The final letter to Tom is clearly an attempt from Jan to pull more family members into her misplaced sense of obligation to her little brother. She had no business assuming responsibility for Bob. She is committing a classic Type II Boundary error. She may have fallen prey to misconceptions like "Love Thy Neighbor," or" Blood is thicker than water," or "I am my brother's keeper." It is important to note that when Jan does not get the answers she wants from the social worker, communication with Nancy ceases.

Type III Boundary Errors
Another type of error is to some degree a combination of Types I & II. Some people approach relationships as if they were creating a new entity instead of entering into a partnership. They merge or blend together while obliterating both individuals. Often these people think being in love means not having an identity anymore. They believe they are entitled to all the secrets of the other person.

Everything must be shared, nothing withheld. In effect, the boundaries disappear.

Poor self-image is probably the most prevalent reason people make Type III errors. They look for the strength of the other person to make them feel strong. All they really accomplish is to put control of their destiny in the hands of someone else. Their skills deteriorate from lack of use, and the need to find strength from someone else slowly becomes stronger and somewhat justified.

కూండ

An ill spouse, Kate, was not a college graduate, but was married to a man who worked in a specialized field. She was at home daily and began to crave a professional identity of her own. Kate did have a professional certification, but it was not a college degree. She had been in some type of competition with him since the day he "out ranked" her in education. With her disability, she was unable to work full-time and began an interest in her husband's professional life to a greater degree than ever before. She could tell others how proud she was of her husband's professional work, but could never tell him directly. He had to travel and she was constantly jealous of his trips. If she had to stay home, he should change his routine, she thought. She used to be able to travel in her own right and then she would accompany him.

She had few friends of her own and begged to go with him on his professional missions. Once in attendance, she attempted to co-opt the professional colleagues as her friends. She would stay in touch with these people, arrange social outings and often share personal information about her family dynamics via emails. For example, when Kate argued with her son's new mother-in-law, she contacted a professional colleague of her husband's to rehash the events and seek a "professional" opinion. Her husband was mortified that she had chosen to tell a business acquaintance about her "bad behavior" as if it was a suitable topic of discussion.

All of this was apparently in an effort to enhance her own social status, whether it was realized or simply in her mind was irrelevant. This activity seemed to fill a continual void in her self-esteem after the disability encroached. It was as if she was entitled to be half of a duo which was her husband's career. Given the illnesses with which she frequently struggled coupled with the lack of a degree, it is likely that this type of boundary error is related to her poor self-image. In acting out toward her son's newest relative and seeking an outside opinion, Kate was looking for justification to her actions that she did not get from the rest of her family.

Type IV Boundary Errors

People who commit Type IV errors assume responsibility for the relationship between two other people. A woman feels she is responsible for the relationship between her husband and her mother. When her mother complains to her about her husband, the woman confronts her husband on her mother's behalf. To stop making this error, the woman should refuse to listen to her mother's complaints, and refer her directly to her husband. She should let the relationship between them seek its own level by staying out of it.

Kate complained constantly about how the medical community was less than responsive to her, especially when it came to pain killing drugs. She appealed for help from David to convince the doctors to listen to reason about how much pain she was in, and to increase the dosage so she could rest. David always rose to the occasion and acted as Kate's advocate during appointments with her doctor.

By taking responsibility for managing the relationship between Kate and her doctor, David was not only committing a Type IV Boundary Error, he was acting as an enabler for her dependence. Of note, the pattern of David injecting himself into the communication between Kate and her doctors is that Kate's doctors began talking directly to David, not with Kate, during her appointments.

Once he became the medical advocate for her when she could still make her needs known, the conversations were exclusively with him. Kate's initial complaint was that the medical community was not responsive to her was exaggerated by the very action that was taken to remedy the issue. This boundary error is what undermined any improvement in Kate's ability to communicate with her physicians.

❧❧

This is the essence of this type of boundary error. When we get "in the middle" of a relationship between two people especially in behalf of our ill spouse, we unintentionally create the very situations we do not like. As with the above example, we are often the origins of their dependency. We talk for them at a doctor's appointment believing we are helping the situation. We handle the phone calls and setting of appointments. We begin to run the household without input from anyone else. Having the majority of the voting stock empowers us to run with it sometimes. Then we build up resentments that we "have to do everything." In turn, we unintentionally undermine the very thing we want from our ill spouse, their independence.

WE CAN INFLUENCE OTHERS

Since we are literally not responsible for the decisions and behavior of others, does this mean we have nothing to do with other people's actions? Not really. There is an obvious connection between what we do and what others do. For example, if we attack someone physically, it is predictable that they will defend themselves. If someone does not trust us, it is connected to the fact that we frequently break our word. But, the person who defends himself is still in charge of his behavior. He could choose not to defend himself. Someone could choose to trust us even though we break our word.

While we are not responsible for others, we have the power to influence what others do. Therefore, we must be responsible for the kind of influence we use, when and how we use it, how often we use it, and on whom. The influence we use will shape and mold the behavior of others, but without making us responsible for their decisions. Just because I say what I want does not make you give it to me.

Because we can influence others, we have an obligation to ourselves to be able to make accurate predictions about how others are likely to react. This is another aspect of taking responsibility for our lives. The more we know about how others react, the more power we have to control our destiny. In a very direct way, knowledge is power in this area. The naive employee can be trampled by office politics. Lack of political sophistication does not absolve the employee of his responsibility to control his career.

To put this simply, to assume responsibility for our lives we must seek out and put to use as much knowledge of human affairs as possible. To fail to do so is to diminish our control. Similarly, we have considerable ability to control physical events around us. The physical world is malleable. We can dig a trench in our front yard anytime we want to, and while the neighbors might object, the yard will not complain. We can exert as much influence as our skills, resources, and energy permit.

THE TOUGH & TENDER CAREGIVER

The TTC understands clearly and acts upon the following principles:

- We are responsible for getting our needs met. Blaming others is pointless.
- We must not take responsibility for the decisions of others. We are likely to harm them if we do.
- We are responsible for how we respond to events beyond our control.
- We can influence but not control the behavior of others.
- We can shape the physical world within the limits of our skills, resources, and energy.

Chapter 8
FINDING A
DIRECTION

Defining Personal Mission and Goals

∂∾∾6

ROLLING THE DICE

We have established in previous chapters that the world is indifferent to our needs. Unless we take action to impose our will on the world, our needs will not be met. We have also discovered that, despite what we are taught by society, it is natural and normal to take action on your own behalf, especially if it takes the form of Enlightened Self Interest.

In Hopeless & Helpless, we point out how difficult it is take responsibility for our own lives, and that it is especially difficult in the caregiver relationship. We know caregivers often fail to take personal responsibility for getting their needs met, but they also fail to assign properly a whole range of responsibilities in their lives.

It is in this chapter that the rubber meets the road. It is all about rolling the dice, setting a direction for ourselves so we may take appropriate action. Taking action without defining our needs first would be like Alice in Wonderland encountering the Cheshire Cat. She asks which road she should take and he replied that would depend on which direction she was heading. When Alice says she does not know where she is heading, the Cheshire Cat said to her then any road will do.

IT'S ALL ABOUT DECISIONS

It has been emphasized repeatedly that in order to get our needs met, we must accept responsibility for our lives and then impose our will on the world. Actions that modify the world are triggered by *decisions* that are responsive to our needs. For example, a decision to set up an individual retirement account is based on a need for financial security. One would have to know this need exists in order for the decision to be made. If the individual were not aware that he had a need for financial security, certainly he could find more immediate uses for the money. Without an understanding of what we need, our decisions would be guided by other internal signals, such as our emotions, impulses, and beliefs. If our needs happened to be met, it would be accidental.

Segmenting Our Lives

A useful tool for clarifying our need pattern involves viewing our total "life space" as a pie, with each slice representing a major realm of our life. Typical "slices" include:

- Career
- Spiritual
- Recreation
- Relationship with spouse (or significant other)
- Relationship with children
- Relationship with friends
- Financial
- Community
- Personal growth
- Education

In each of these categories, we can now ask ourselves what we need. This is an easier question to answer than a global "What do I need?"

Creating a Policy Manual

One powerful technique for clarifying our needs has the advantage of amplifying our psychological needs to compete better with other internal signals in the personal decision process. A policy manual in a corporation is a *decision shortcut*. It provides guidance that allows decisions to be made rapidly.

For example, the accounts receivable clerk in a large company is asked by a customer if he can delay paying his bill for 30 days due to cash flow problems. Fortunately, situations like this have been thought through in advance, with the results published in a policy manual. The clerk can quickly come up with a decision that best serves his company by checking the policy.

Similarly, it is possible to create a policy manual for our lives which makes provision for many, if not most, of our psychological needs. By using this policy manual as a constant source of guidance, we can more or less guarantee that our decisions will consistently serve our needs. The technique consists of creating a vision of the future, a kind of snapshot of how we want our lives to be at some specific point in the future. An integrated set of goals like this is called a *mission*.

The ability to create a mission is unique to the human species. It is this ability, to visualize some hypothetical state of affairs in the future and then commit ourselves to the attainment of this mission, that sets us apart from the rest of the animal kingdom.

Defining a Mission

Step 1—Segmenting Our Life Space
To get started, it is helpful first to segment our total "life space" into slices of a pie, as described earlier. Only this time the size of each slice should be made to represent our priorities among the realms. The bigger the slice, the more emphasis we place on this area. The pie should be drawn to reflect our *current* life. It will be necessary to experiment a good deal, drawing pies with different configurations until we are satisfied.

Since this pie represents our current priorities, this first step is potentially shocking. For example, the ambitious, career-oriented man may discover his career takes up three fourths of the pie, his marriage an eighth, with kids, leisure, spiritual, community, friends,

170

etc. crammed into the remaining eighth. This "workaholic" pattern is very common but also represents a time bomb that could explode at any time.

For the defeated or stressed caregiver, this exercise alone is likely to be quite revealing. Once we are able to look at how much of our life is devoted to the needs of the ill spouse via the pie chart, we begin to get a proper perspective on how we are failing to meet our needs. Where is the largest slice? Is it in meeting someone else's needs? Or is it meeting a want? The caregiver can acknowledge how many of their needs are not being met due to a lack of emphasis on self, much less being able to pay attention to wants. Can the same be said for our ill spouse if a pie chart was made for them? Are all of their wants being satisfied at the expense of our needs?

Step 2- Projecting Into the Future

The next step is to project ourselves mentally into the future. Five years out is an ideal time frame, far enough ahead to allow us to have a major impact on what happens, yet not so far that we are dealing with too many imponderables. The basic question is, what do I want my life to look like five years from now? Remember to include the assumption that five years will have elapsed for everything and everybody. Our seven year old will be twelve. A different president might be in the White House. Also, be careful not to limit the choices by carrying present circumstances automatically into the future. For example, don't automatically assume you have five more years of tenure on the same job.

It is helpful to do the exercise one segment at a time rather than trying to visualize the whole pie five years out. How important do I wish recreation to be (i.e., size of slice) in five years? How much time do I wish to spend on recreation? What recreational activities do I want to be enjoying at that time?

This process should be repeated for each slice of the pie. The results of each process should be *written down*. Writing down what we want has a kind of "magical" quality that ratifies the legitimacy of what we want.

If it is difficult to get started, sometimes a warm-up exercise helps. On a piece of paper, write down a complete schedule for yourself for an entire day. Start with time of awakening, account for each separate activity with blocks of time, and end with the time of going to sleep. But for which day? Pick a Thursday exactly five years from now. This schedule will represent how you wish to spend that specific day. It is important to make the schedule attainable rather than outlining a day on the beach in Tahiti. Schedule the day to fit your present value system, beliefs, and integrity.

For caregivers, this is an especially difficult exercise because you are likely facing the truth for the first time. Many of us caring for a partner with a chronic illness will not want to admit what we want our life to look like in five years, primarily because the fantasy that this will all get better keeps us going. When a caregiver stops and realistically tries to envision the future by writing it down, we are forced to admit that how our life functions today is *not* what we want for our future.

This is the first real step in the journey to becoming a TTC. The results of making a plan and changing how life currently exists does not mean a choice to live no longer live with your ill spouse. Quite the contrary, it means planning ways to make life better with your ill spouse so that there can be joy. The authors encourage the reader to have fun for a moment and really attempt to write down what you want for yourself. Even if the vision seems unrealistic, it can assist in goal setting and recognition of what *is* doable.

For those of us caring for a partner with a terminal illness, planning for the future takes a different shape. However, the goal is the same. Is there anything about today that (short of having no illness for your spouse) would you like to change when you look at your pie chart? What portions of the pie do you have control of so that if the illness is prolonged, you could make further changes?

చ్~ఆ

In this step, David had little difficulty defining what he wanted his life to be like five years down the road. He wanted some free time and to enjoy retirement. He wanted to have a comfortable social network. He wanted to enjoy his family; especially his only grandchild. He did not want to be continually worried about his financial stability because of plaguing health concerns for either one of them. David also wanted something he had never had, he wanted strong intellectual companionship. He longed for a wife with a sense of humor, a wife who was passionate about him, and who had the same needs and desires as he did. Was there a chance Kate could actually make that recovery she had always promised?

He was feeling used up and old. The projection for him was a fantasy; something he had been thinking about for the past twenty years. It still felt like it was never going to happen because he was stuck and had all ready been married twice. He settled for the life he had, but the exercise in dreaming was fun. Perhaps, the rest of the projections could be managed.

昆 昖

For her part, Rhonda prayed for and dreamed of having a healthy husband who demonstratively cared for her, took adult responsibility for the family, went to work in the mornings, held her in his arms, and was capable of loving her and the children in a way they have never been loved. That was the exact reason that she had been chasing a diagnosis for Andy all these years. If they could get him well, then things would be finally O.K.

Rhonda was tired and she wanted to be released from her Caregiver Hell, but in this step of forecasting, five years ahead seemed like an eternity. It seemed at the time that she could dream of anything she wanted and it would still be an impossible dream because of her obligations to Andy now firm in the diagnosis of dementia, and having three minor children to raise. What else was in her life segments also seemed equally unattainable. Financial improvement—she would even settle for paying the bills on time. Healthy kids and in five years at least one in college. Steady career in a field she enjoyed and better management of her time to attend to herself. Looking at the segments revealed nothing in a twenty-four hour period for herself. No wonder burnout and depression were lurking.

෴

Step 3—The Mission Statement

Once a desired hypothetical future state of affairs has been described in writing for each slice of the pie, the next step is an overall analysis of the big picture. First, by reading each description it should be apparent how important this slice will be to your overall happiness. While this is not exactly accurate, the size of the slice will roughly represent the proportion of your waking hours you will be willing to devote to each realm. Therefore, the first step in the analysis is to draw a new pie that represents how you wish your life to be five years from now.

The next analytic step is to compare each slice with the others to detect any inconsistencies or incompatibilities. Are these slices simultaneously possible? That is, are there any logical contradictions? Is there enough time in a day, a week, a month, to do what I have carved out for myself? If I have what I want in one slice, will I still want what I have described in every other slice?

Using the results of this analysis, it may be necessary to edit or otherwise revise the written descriptions. Once this has been accomplished, the results represent an *integrated mission statement.*

The mission statement should be reviewed every few months during the first year of its existence to ensure that it genuinely represents what we need. Because changes occur rapidly in caregiving, a quarterly update will keep the mission current.

෴

David's mission statement: *"I want to find joy again in my life. I will commit to myself that I will do each of the following at least once a month: play golf, have dinner out with friends and attend one symphony concert."*

Rhonda's mission statement: *"I will stop giving so much of my time to work and to my family. I need to recognize that I am doing the best that I can and the rest will have to take care of itself. I will pat myself on the back for all that I have accomplished and stop being angry at the world. I will consider that I cannot live in the same house with Andy and I will seek help when I need it."*

ॐॐ

Using the Mission Statement as Policy

While not exactly a definition of long-term needs, the mission statement is derived from a combination of them and represents priorities. In effect, the mission is the result of clear and precise thinking about what we need. In addition, the mission is a mechanism for amplifying the signal strength of needs we might easily overlook in making routine personal decisions.

Thus, the mission can be used as a substitute for internal scanning of internal need signals. Referring to the mission becomes a highly efficient way to make sure personal decisions are responsive to a broad range of needs.

For example, a woman discovers she will receive only a token raise in salary this year, even though she has worked hard and been productive. Her frustration triggers a decision about her career. She has worked as an accountant with this firm for two years now, but does not believe she is getting a fair chance regarding compensation. For guidance, she immediately makes reference to her mission statement, which specifies that in five years she wants to be supervising other accountants and earning roughly double her present salary. She realizes she needs additional accounting experience and a reputation for job stability in order to qualify for a position of more responsibility. She concludes hanging in with this job for at least another year would ultimately be in her best interests. Nevertheless, she also decides to examine her career management tactics to see if she can obtain more recognition than she has obviously received to date.

In an earlier example, a man is tempted to have an affair with an attractive young colleague. Before he decides, he consults his mission statement, zeros in on the section on Relationship With Spouse, and quickly realizes that an affair would blow these goals out of the water. He also makes passing reference to the *Financial* section of the mission, which really nails down his decision to pass up the temptation.

❧ ❧

David came to understand that he was using his interest in motorcycling and classical music as an inadequate substitute for what he really needed. He was suffering from a long-term intimacy deficit; there was no intimacy in his relationship with Kate. In addition to her physical limitations, her disdain for his interests also made him indifferent to her. By taking the time to create a new, invigorating life mission for himself, he was able to exit the debilitating caregiving duties. He was able to make meaningful changes and move in the direction of becoming a TTC.

❧ ❧

THE TOUGH & TENDER CAREGIVER

The TTC is acutely aware of internal need signals and focuses attention on them consciously whenever there is uncertainty about a course of action. The TTC has taken the trouble to define an integrated life mission and updates it regularly. This mission statement streamlines and simplifies many of the TTC's personal decisions, even large decisions. Furthermore, most the TTC's personal decisions result in needs being met, which leads to happiness. Having a clearly defined roadmap of needs to be met makes it much easier for the TTC to carve out a more fulfilling life. In turn, the result is a better life for the ill partner.

Chapter 9
NO DECISION IS A DECISION

How to Make Better Decisions

ॐ

Decision-making is a topic crucial to the survival of the caregiver. Caregivers who are trapped in a dysfunctional web of caring for someone are prone to making bad decisions about their lives. There are barriers the caregiver must overcome in order to make first class decisions about the often-ugly realities of caring for a permanently disabled spouse.

These barriers take the form of specific forms of *ignorance*. This chapter systematically addresses ignorance about the decision process. It sets out to define an effective and efficient way to make decisions that will ultimately redefine the caregiver's relationship with the dependent spouse. Caregivers must understand the *mechanics* of the decision process so they can approach life-altering decisions as rationally and systematically as possible and attain the elite status of a Tough & Tender Caregiver.

POOR DECISION PROCESS

Aside from incomplete understanding of the mechanics, the actual process of making decisions can be defective for other reasons. Some people are afraid to look indecisive. They confuse speed with quality of decisions. Snap decisions often can be traced to powerful emotional reactions triggered by a situation. The pain of the emotion causes the individual to embrace any action that reduces the immediate pain. The impulsive behavior becomes a bandage. Its primary function is pain reduction. Therefore, this behavior is unlikely to serve the long-term needs of the individual.

❧ ❧

David and Rhonda both had fallen prey to the snap decision trap. David often found himself giving in to Kate's whimsical demands for a specific type of junk food. He found that giving in was less hassle for him than saying "no." He might have served his long terms needs better by saying "no" because the poor quality of the foods she wanted made her medical situation worse. The foods would not support her diabetic diet, they would not promote healing and she was already too heavy. David frequently made the impulsive decision to give in to her demands rather than reason with himself about how he would be better off if he could draw the line on this kind of request. The price for saying "no" did not seem worth the hassle.

Andy enjoyed amusement parks. This activity was expensive for a growing family. However, his insistence to be entertained was stronger than Rhonda's will to say, "No, we cannot afford the expense because the mortgage payment is due." She would give in to the demand for a day at the park rather than argue, and she stopped thinking about how she was going to pay the bills.

❧ ❧

Failure to consider all the data available is a common reason for ineffective decision processes. Internal signals that tell us what we need are often so weak they get lost among stronger impulse and emotion signals. A similar defect lies in failure to anticipate what today's action will mean tomorrow, next week, or next year. We all tend to be a little shortsighted at times, and of course, children elevate this tendency to the level of doctrine. Decisions that fail to consider long-term implications are using incomplete data. Such decisions often do not serve us.

❧ ❧

When David gave in to Kate's impulsive demands, he put his stamp of approval on her pattern and increased the likelihood she would continue the behaviors. When Rhonda spent money on entertainment, she participated in the immaturity that dictated their lives and suffered the consequences of unpaid bills and poor credit.

༺·༻

DECISION PARALYSIS

There are people who simply refuse to decide anything when faced with certain situations. We might call this *decision paralysis*. This is a way of not facing up to their responsibility to themselves. Unfortunately, as we have routinely stated, no decision is always a decision. In this case, refusal to decide is a decision to accept whatever the environment chooses to dish out. The advantage they seek is that now they have someone to blame if the decision does not work out. These people often seek out relationships with people who will make decisions for them, then settle in for the long haul, accepting the crumbs others choose to feed them. They may be unhappy, but at least they do not have to accept the blame for their mistakes. In their minds, they did not make any mistakes.

༺·༻

This is a common tactic used by the besieged caregiver and Rhonda was no exception. When Rhonda had the opportunity to go to a movie with a good friend or just get away from caregiving for an afternoon, it presented all manner of complications for her. It would mean finding someone to stay with her sick spouse. It would mean a big fight with her husband because he never wanted anyone else to be in the house with him. Of course, it would mean getting someone to pick up the kids after school and stay with them. Therefore, Rhonda would use what she jokingly referred to as the *"constructive use of administrative delay"* and piddle around long enough so the outing became impossible. Now she did not have to take personal responsibility for saying "no" to her friend, and she did not have to take responsibility for an uproar with Andy. She tacitly made the decision not to rock the boat.

❧ ❧

The decision process can be defective because of missing data. Earlier we mentioned that many people have gaping holes in their skills and knowledge of human affairs. Our schools teach us math, science, and English, but they do not teach interpersonal strategies, tactics, goal setting, situation management, conflict resolution, negotiation techniques, or ways to hold people accountable. Yet, it is ironic that success in life can depend far more on these "people skills" than knowledge of math, science or English.

Data can also be missing because we see what we want to see. Our emotions sometimes cause us to make a premature commitment to a course of action that reduces emotional pain. This commitment can cause us to screen out information that would contradict the wisdom of the early decision. For example, he was so angry about his girlfriend's failure to phone him that he decided to drive to her apartment and camp out all night if necessary. He committed to this decision quickly, blocking out of his memory the fact that the last time he did this, she would not speak to him for two weeks.

CHAINS OF POOR DECISIONS
(Bad Decisions Beget Bad Decisions)

Once a decision is made and action taken, a completely new set of options presents itself. This is a different set of options than if another decision had been made. It is like winding our way through a maze; once we turn left the choices are different than if we had turned right.

Bad decisions have a way of presenting us with a set of bad options. For example, a man was killed on the highway because he lost control of his car at eighty miles an hour. This was but the final link in a whole chain of bad decisions. It all started because he had a powerful need to be liked by everyone. He had a reputation as a "giver;" those around him knew he would not say "no" if he was asked a favor. On the day of his death, he had decided to commit his time to too many people. That decision caused him to decide to wait until beyond the last minute to begin his trip to another city for an important meeting. That decision led to a decision to drive recklessly. One bad choice led to a chain of bad choices.

In another example, a 38-year-old woman is extremely unhappy in her marriage. Her husband treats her with disrespect, even contempt at times. He is insensitive to her needs and ridicules her attempts to obtain emotional support from him. Why is she in this predicament? Tracing the decisions backwards, she had decided not to confront him with her complaints. Why? Because she lacked the personal confidence to pull it off. She was afraid to rock the boat. Why did she lack confidence? Because she chose to get married at age 17 rather than accumulate experience taking care of herself, building her skill, knowledge, and confidence. Here again, bad decisions led to more bad decisions.

⁓⁓

To illustrate the notion that bad decisions beget bad decisions:

Four months after Andy and Rhonda started dating, they were engaged. She then graduated from college, got married and five months after the wedding, they were expecting their first child. Almost immediately upon returning from their honeymoon, Rhonda realized something was wrong with Andy. He had bouts of temper that scared her. He was not the responsible man she thought she had married. She was forced into a position of acting like his mother. He was difficult to awaken in the morning. He was seemingly depressed and took no initiative in establishing his life as a grown man with a new bride and a baby on they way.

Being strong, Rhonda assumed the role of primary breadwinner, financial planner and all the other marital responsibilities. Andy never objected and the pattern continued. From that point in the marriage, Rhonda continued to make a series of decisions that set them up to fail both financially and as a couple. She never stopped to think about what was happening long enough to make sound decisions. She never examined what was really going on.

In summary, they moved nine times in 13 years. They had three children and were constantly changing career paths because of the moves. She kept looking for ways to force Andy to be the husband she had been seeking. All she knew was that she was unhappy and she wanted it fixed. All the decisions she made about their life created more turmoil. Rhonda had no idea Andy was ill. Unable to decipher his odd behavior and the impact on their marriage, Rhonda did not stop the carousel long enough to look at how her decisions were making things worse. In retrospect, they were made without any forethought and little planning. She was chasing a dream and repeated bad decisions.

Once she decided that Andy must be sick, Rhonda went after a diagnosis for him vigorously. His behavior escalated and after a great deal of searching for a "cure", many tests and five neurologists, she found an answer in his diagnosis. Rhonda's entire adult life had been filled with discontent and now she hit a brick wall because she did not know how to make appropriate decisions about her life. She did not understand what either of them needed. She had been seeking a brand of fulfillment suggested by of all the caregiver myths.

The Ideal Decision Making/Action Process (Long Version)

A rational decision/action process involves the following elements:

- a situation requiring a decision
- data (both internal and external)
- an analysis of all relevant data (what has been happening to arrive at this point)
- the invention of realistic alternatives
- an analysis of the pros and cons of each alternative

- the selection of one alternative that maximizes advantages and minimizes disadvantages
- planning how to take action
- the initiation of sustained action to implement the decision
- evaluation of the outcomes of the decision

External data includes signals that we receive from the environment and from other people about the situation. These include significant facts about the situation, time constraints, temptations, the wishes of others, and so on. Internal data consists of signals from inside ourselves telling us about our impulses, emotions, needs, beliefs, etc. Skills and knowledge are also internal data.

When we encounter any kind of situation, be it a problem, an opportunity, someone making a demand on us, or a change of any sort in our environment, some kind of decision is triggered. If the situation is new or novel, one we have not encountered before, the long form of the decision process is most appropriate.

Once a novel situation has been identified, the first step in the process is to gather all the relevant information. We should ask ourselves the following kinds of questions.

- What is this situation like? What's important about it?
- What do other people need from me in this situation?
- How much time do I have to make a decision?
- What barriers and constraints are present?
- What resources are available to me?
- What is my first impulse?
- What emotional reaction do I have to this situation?
- Which of my beliefs provide guidance for situations like this?
- Which of my skills is available to help me?
- What are my long-term needs in this situation?

Data Analysis

Once the relevant data have been gathered and understood, the next step is to evaluate the significance of the pattern of information. We should be asking questions such as these:

- Do I need to go after additional information?
- Is it safe to ignore whether my physical needs will be met?
- How important is my first impulse?
- How does my fear stack up against the importance of getting my long-term needs satisfied?
- Because what people want of me conflicts with what I believe in, which is most important to me in this situation?
- Could I eliminate one of the barriers in my environment if I had more skill?
- What happens if I give in to my first impulse?

Inventing Alternatives

Having gone through a detailed analysis by asking questions like those above, we should now have a good idea what realistic alternatives are available to us. Usually there are two or three from which to choose. For example, a broken TV set might yield the following alternatives: 1. get it fixed, 2. buy a new one, or 3. do without.

Analyzing Alternatives and Deciding

For each alternative, the advantages and disadvantages should be cautiously weighed, carefully looking for all the pros and cons. These should be carefully considered until one alternative clearly leaps out as superior. One beauty of this process is that, by this point in the decision process, there is usually no debate about which alternative makes the most sense. People afflicted with "analysis paralysis" have artificially biased the data in order to justify not making a decision. Ordinarily, decisions grab us once the analysis has come this far.

It helps to understand that there are seldom perfect decisions, choices where there is no price to be paid. Tradeoffs of some kind always seem necessary. Robert Heinlein recognized this in his famous **"TANSTAAFL"** principle; *There Ain't No Such Thing As A Free Lunch*. Decisions jump out at us because the least costly alternative is usually obvious.

⁊⚬⚭

David's alternatives seemed limited until he went through this systematic process. There was a Well Spouse Association outing arranged by members of the local group. This would provide him with a badly needed respite. How would he be able to get away from his caregiving responsibilities for that long? He could ask his daughter, Betsy, but he had tried that in the past. She always had something else to do when he needed her for respite. Or, he could hire someone without Kate's knowledge and spring it on her at the last minute. That would minimize the complaining and possible meltdown. Perhaps, he could invent a business trip that he knew Kate would understand. Betsy would stay with her mother for a business trip. In other words, lie about it. This last option seemed best, it worked, and David spent a respite weekend recharging his batteries.

In David's situation, the TANSTAAFL principle came down to this. The price he would have to pay for lying to his wife was that he would feel regret. The question became, is the pain of feeling regret large enough to supersede the pain of continuing the caregiving grind without a break? Which pain was going to be greater? Obviously, the discomfort of staying with Kate without a break was huge, and the pain of feeling regret about lying was tiny by comparison. Thus, David lied and never regretted it. For without the respite, Kate's care would have likely suffered.

⁊⚬⚭

Setting the Decision in Motion

Once the decision is made, the next step involves planning how to put the decision into action. How should I get started? Who should be informed? What resources will I need to use? What will I have to learn first? What time frame should I place on this? How will I know everything is going as planned? How will I know when I'm finished?

Now it is time to push the "go" button and set the plan in motion. By this time, moving from planning to action should be natural. However, in many situations, thinking about what to do is one thing, doing it is something else. We may have to bolster our courage. We may have to contain our enthusiasm so we do not blow it. Some degree of self-discipline is usually involved (see Chapter 10 regarding self-discipline).

さ※

David pushed his "Go" button by explaining the "business opportunity" to Kate, pleading his case with daughter Betsy, making motel reservations for the respite weekend, and contacting his client about the deception in case Kate called him to verify that this was a legitimate business trip. Fortunately, this client was also a friend and knew David's plight.

さ※

It is useful to develop the habit of analyzing each important decision. Did this turn out the way I thought it would? What problems did I fail to anticipate? Will this decision hold up over the long haul? Were the tradeoffs indeed acceptable? Answers to these and other similar questions will contribute to our becoming a better and better decision maker over time.

The Ideal Decision Making/Action Process (Short Version)

While the total process described above is ideal for new situations, the overwhelming majority of our personal decisions are made in response to familiar situations. The complete process is far too cumbersome to handle more routine decisions. Instead, there is a short version available.

Beginning in childhood, we all develop a set of *decision rules* that make many routine decisions nearly automatic. The brain seems to work this way. A situation comes to our attention, triggering the need for a decision. Our first reaction is to scan our memory banks (like a computer) for a decision rule that covers this situation. If one is found, the situation is referred to the applicable rule, which makes the decision for us. The decision is nearly instantaneous. If no decision rule is found, the long form of the process should be used.

As we mature, we accumulate thousands of decision rules, such as the following:

- It is okay to give people feedback about their personal appearance only if they request it.
- If someone lets you into traffic, you should acknowledge it.
- It is okay to stop work for a break only if work is if the break is short
- Displaying aggression toward another person is appropriate only as part of organized sports or in self-defense
- Once I have told someone my time of arrival, I must keep my word
- One should have no more than one sexually-active relationship at a time

How Decision Rules Are Learned

There are two primary ways decision rules are learned, either by way of instructions from parents and other adults as we grow up, or by way of our own experiences. Decision rules are learned from early childhood in the form of principles. Examples include:

- Look both ways before crossing the street.
- When someone does something nice for you, say "thank you."
- Finish your work before you play.
- Run cold water on burns.
- Finish everything on your plate.

These principles are also learned by reading books, attending church or by observing the behavior of others (e.g., a child learns decision rules by watching a sibling get into trouble). We also learn decision rules by trying new things and observing what happens. You may have heard the old saying: Good judgment is based on experience, and experience is based on bad judgment. We learn by making mistakes, and we create decision rules to cover these situations if we are paying attention.

Now granted, there are people who make the same mistake repeatedly, somehow expecting a different outcome each time. This is not a mentally healthy way to conduct life. To a psychologist, this is considered neurotic behavior. It is important to learn from our experiences, especially our mistakes, because that is the stuff of wisdom.

The following are examples of decision rules based on experience.

- Touching a hot stove leads to pain.
- Staying out of work can get you fired.
- If I spend my whole allowance the day I get it, I will later wish I had not.
- Failing to cooperate with my father leads to pain.
- Driving too fast can result in a speeding ticket.
- Staying up too late means I will be sleepy the next day.
- Kicking a bigger boy on the playground leads to pain.
- Insulting your wife leads to sleeping on the couch.

THE TOUGH & TENDER CAREGIVER

The TTC knows that it is a huge mistake to allow life to wash over us, for us to accept passively whatever others dish out. To find a measure of joy and personal fulfillment in life, the caregiver must be proactive and not bury his or her head in the sand and allow others to make decisions that rightly belong to the caregiver. For example, in some situations, the disabled spouse's family has no interest in assisting with caregiving. The in-laws and other extended family members are thrilled that these responsibilities are not falling on them. They tend to be oblivious to the fact that the caregiver's needs are not being met. They can only care that they are not being inconvenienced. Unless the caregiver steps up to the plate and takes control of his or her own life, caregiving for the chronically ill spouse can be a death sentence.

TTCs understand that life is a succession of decisions, that there are small, medium, and large decisions to be made in life. The larger the decision, the more helpful it is to take it slow, gather information, and weigh the pros and cons of each alternative before deciding. Small decisions can be impulsive without much danger, but large decisions are usually full of traps to be avoided.

TTCs also understand that no decision is a decision. It represents a passive acceptance of whatever the world chooses to dish out. It is an abdication of responsibility. It puts control in the hands of others.

TTCs are critical of their own decisions. An attempt is made to evaluate how decisions are turning out, what the consequences are. It is healthy to examine periodically our own decision rules, whether we learned them from others or by experience. In theory, the quality of our personal decisions should improve the older we get. Continuous improvement is part of TTCs' commitment to themselves.

Chapter 10
DEVELOPING SELF-DISCIPLINE

Taking Organized Effective Action

ॐॐ

"You ask me why I do not write something.... I think one's feelings waste themselves in words; they ought all to be distilled into actions and into actions which bring results."—Florence Nightingale, Founder of the modern profession of nursing

ॐॐ

Caregivers caring for an ill spouse can rather easily fall into a pattern of putting everything else on the back burner. Society sends the strong message that responding to the needs of the disabled or sick partner is "Job One" for the caregiver, the very first priority. When the caregiving burden is overwhelming, the worst-case scenario can mean no groceries in the house, dirty laundry everywhere, stacks of unpaid bills, unreturned phone calls, foul odors wafting through the house, and children doing pretty much what they want without supervision. The neighbors and extended family shake their heads, going "tsk, tsk" and thanking their lucky stars that their lives are not as bad as this.

In this scenario, apathy sets in. This caregiver is under siege, unhappy, longing for relief with none in sight, giving in to circumstance with acceptable resignation, and ultimately not caring about those things he or she used to care about.

So what does it take for the well spouse use to start the process of recovery and move to the elite status of TTC? How do we develop an upward trajectory out of this morass? How can the caregiver "wake up" to the fact that systematic action is going to be required to find resolution?

In order to focus the caregiver on the all-important issue of self-discipline, we will assume that the lessons of Chapters 1 through 9 have been understood, and that the reader is ready to move forward. In other words, the caregiver who is about to read this chapter understands the following:

- The caregiver understands relationship management theory
- The caregiver knows how to negotiate and enforce Master Agreements
- Nobody cares if the caregiver's needs are met
- It is OK for the caregivers to focus on getting their own needs met; in fact, it is essential
- The only people who can resolve the caregivers' dilemma are the caregivers themselves
- Caregivers will not find relief by thinking different thoughts. Action is required
- The caregiver has defined his or her most pressing needs
- The caregiver has decided to take appropriate action.

The next step is that caregivers must learn how to call upon the correct amount of self-discipline to implement the decisions they have made, and to stay the course once action has been initiated.

FIGHTING OFF THE SOCIAL PROPAGANDA

Not only does our social propaganda discourage us from taking full responsibility for our actions, the proverbs strongly suggest to us that there is no point in trying to change things. Self-discipline isn't going to help. So, why bother putting forth all the work involved in planning and executing a plan when it won't make any difference anyhow?

- Whatever will be will be
- It's God's will
- Beating our head against a wall
- The glass is half full
- Sometimes you're the hydrant, sometimes you're the dog
- Swimming against the tide
- Banging your head against the wall
- The best laid plans of mice and men
- Man plans, God laughs

The message in these proverbs, clichés, and sayings is that *trying to impose your will on the world is futile. There is no point in trying.* These are messages of passivity. The proverbs contain an anti-action bias. The authors have an hypothesis that these proverbs and sayings were originally invented by the following kinds of people:

- Lazy. They were looking for an excuse to remain passive.
- Depressed. Their worldview was gloomy, precluded optimism.
- Discouraged. They had burned out in hopeless causes.
- Angry. They believed the world was deliberately uncooperative.

Well spouse caregivers cannot afford to be lazy, depressed, discouraged, or angry. This is a time for focused action. It is a time to mobilize all available energy to make radical changes in lifestyle. The TTC will be able to confound and dazzle family and friends who have come to see the caregiver as defeated, destined to remain in Caregiver Hell.

Any effort we make to impose our will on the environment must be carefully guided and controlled. Random efforts will lead to random results. The energy we direct at the world must be orderly and systematic to achieve TTC status. The need to gain control of our behavior begins with the decision making/action process itself.

When action begins, self-discipline is essential in allowing us to focus on the action program called for by the decision. Without self-discipline, we would yield to temptations, distractions, competing activities, the reactions of others and so forth. We must be able to make ourselves do what we need to do, especially when we do not want to do it. We need a kind of *constructive tunnel vision* to make it happen.

Other requirements of successful living also involve self-discipline. Preventing the formation of bad habits requires such control, as does breaking the habits that already exist. We often must force ourselves to go through certain interpersonal processes, such as conflict management, agreement making, and negotiation in order to get important needs met.

In short, self-discipline is an all-purpose tool for shaping the world to meet our needs. The absence of this tool can truly cripple anyone's effectiveness and therefore make happiness unattainable. In the case of caregivers, absence of self-discipline makes attaining TTC status less likely. Without self-discipline, the caregiver is merely pretending to fix Caregiver Hell. All efforts will fail.

DEGREE OF CONTROL

In order to develop and exercise self-discipline, it must first be assumed that we are willing to accept total and complete responsibility for our behavior. Unless we are unconscious or functioning abnormally, any complex behavior we display is deliberate and under our control. (Reflex behavior, such as blinking or flinching, is automatic and is not considered complex behavior.)

When caregivers argue that they cannot say "no" to their ill spouse's wants, they really mean they *choose* not to say "no" because there is a price tag attached. The ill spouse will protest when told "no" so it is just easier to capitulate. The truth is that the caregiver must often pay a price for their disciplined resolve. The price to be paid could be being yelled at. The price to be paid might be that the ill spouse will call the caregiver names and remind them of their vows. The price may include a dose of biblical quotes implying the caregiver is shirking a cosmic command to continue with the self-sacrifice.

The price of failing to take charge is a much larger than enduring someone's displeasure. It involves failure to get ones own needs met, failure to display personal integrity, failure to take charge of one's own life, and perhaps the largest price of all, the failure to ever be happy.

When a man "loses his temper" in an argument and punches someone, has he really lost control? No, he has merely chosen one kind of behavior (punching) over another (yelling). He may claim later that he lost control, and he may even believe it himself, but this is a cover-up. He wants others to believe he lost control and that the punch was not his fault (the devil made me do it). The simple truth is that he chose not to discipline his own behavior.

ॐ॰ॐ

While not all abusive spouses are ill, Rhonda's spouse was the same type of man described above. His disease process was damaging the part of the brain that controlled impulses. Therefore, Andy was unable to control his behaviors or at least very long when challenged. One doctor described Andy's disease as a thermometer without a thermostat. He could go from cold to boiling in a matter of seconds. No warning. No clues. When this happened, the family knew to take cover. Andy even agreed to try anger management classes to stave off the loss of control for as long as possible.

ॐ॰ॐ

Caregivers with spouses who have been diagnosed with Traumatic Brain Injuries (TBI), Acquired Brain Injuries (ABI), and fronto-temporal dementias (FTD) are dealing with loved ones who probably have a diminished ability to control their impulses. Caregivers in this situation are correct to assume their spouses have some control over their behavior, but their emotions are now more volatile than ever before. Because impulse control is diminished, and aggressive behavior is so dangerous, there is no guarantee negotiation will be successful, or that agreements will hold up. But there is likely no harm in working toward some agreements, and at least the caregiver can announce what tactics will be used in case the ill spouse becomes violent (e.g., call the police). The only practical advice for caregivers of spouses with these forms of brain damage is; protect yourself and children.

Other suggested interventions have come by way of a network involving TBI spouses. Leslie trained her small children that when their father could not find something they *"needed to hit the floor and start looking for it."* It never mattered if they knew what their father could not find, they just needed to jump into visible action to keep daddy happy. Another example is from Marcy. She said her husband was indifferent to the world and would become irritated at being interrupted while staring into space. She quickly learned to ignore his presence and live her life as if he were a "piece of furniture." He could make his own meals and he went to bed when he felt like it so she left him alone. It minimized outbursts and she was able to have some semblance of peace even if she felt like she was not married anymore.

We will not even attempt to develop self-discipline unless we first believe we can control what we do and how we do it. Therefore, we must start with this fundamental assumption: we cannot control our spouse behavior, but *our* behavior is firmly under our own control.

A DEFINITION OF SELF-DISCIPLINE

Growing up we were exposed to a meaning of the word 'discipline' which is very close to how the word will be used here. Discipline meant forcing us to conform to the rules of conduct specified by our parents. They handed us a structure within which to live, and demanded we live within it, (or else). Disciplinary procedures in organizations are used to require that employees adhere to the rules (structure) of the organization. Penalties or punishments are held over employees' heads to "encourage" them to abide by the rules, just as threats of parental punishment help children to "remember" to do as they are told.

From these examples it can been seen that a system of discipline consists of three elements: 1) a structure, such as a set of rules, that serves to guide conduct, 2) a resolve by the individual to keep his behavior within the structure, and 3) penalties for failure to remain within the structure.

Self-discipline requires behavior to conform to some kind of structure. That structure takes the form of the personal decision making/action process described in Chapter 8. That process might be thought of as a machine with a large hopper into which problems, opportunities and other situations are poured. A crank is then turned, and out the bottom come solutions, resolutions, and other kinds of action that meet our needs.

❧❦

While David was caring for the overwhelming physical and medical needs of Kate in their home, he noticed that she would call for him to bring her something unimportant at exactly 9PM each day. He believed that this was a game she concocted that was designed to wreak the maximum amount of havoc. Essentially, she was bored and his commanding him became a game. He resolved, privately, to force her to wait for whatever she asked for until he found it convenient. At first, he caved in within 5 minutes of her request, despite his private resolve. But, as he grew bolder, he found the courage and resolve to honor his own structure, and simply refused to enter her bedroom unless it was an emergency. This willingness and ability to apply discipline to his own behavior allowed David to stamp out Kate's intrusive habit. He was taking responsibility for his behavior in the attempt to regain his dignity and feel less like a servant.

❧❦

The structure which must guide our behavior, also includes our collection of decision rules. If a rule exists to cover a familiar situation, we must force ourselves to follow the rule. The second element of self-discipline is voluntary compliance to the structure. We must make a commitment to crank everything through the decision/action machine. The same act of will that kept us from breaking our parents' rules must be used to keep us from breaking these decision/action rules. The resolve that makes us comply with rules of the organization can make us comply with our personal decision making process.

Failure to force our behavior to conform to an orderly decision/action system gets us in trouble of two different ways. First, decisions made outside this structure are unlikely to meet our needs. This causes unhappiness. Second, such "impulsive" decisions often endanger our well-being; they bring us into conflict with others or with society. The penalty is unhappiness. The ability to anticipate the penalty provides incentive to stay with the orderly decision process.

In summary, self-discipline is voluntary compliance to an orderly personal decision making and action sequence to avoid future unhappiness.

ॐ ॐ

Self Discipline = Structure + Resolve + Penalties

ॐ ॐ

WHY DO PEOPLE LACK SELF-DISCIPLINE?

We say that someone lacks self-discipline if they display impulsive behavior in more than one or two realms of their lives; that, of course, is for the ordinary person. While the caregiver is not lazy and not likely displaying impulsive behavior, they are often discouraged, depressed and angry. They may also be tired and apathetic. Self-discipline requires considerable resolve. People who are depressed and apathetic can barely crank up enough resolve to use the bathroom, let alone shop for groceries, clean the bathroom, fold laundry or vacuum the rug. Overcoming the apathy requires energy or a desire to influence events, but without these, disciplined action is unlikely. Caregivers can be so exhausted that it seems unimportant to design a structured action plan and set it in motion, despite the fact that this is the only way things will ever get better.

Most of us have at least one area in which self-discipline is weak or absent. Examples include the highly disciplined attorney whose one weakness is for cherry pie, or the airline pilot who cannot put a novel down once started.

ॐ ॐ

David needed sustained time away from Kate. Instead, he looked for any excuse to go to the grocery store, and ended up doing this daily for ten minutes spurts. If David had put his needs first, such as a need to be away from home, he would have imposed a time structure on his situation that would have allowed him to be away for hours at a time. It would have required a plan, and planning requires resolve and discipline. Lacking these, David lived a reactive life style and left the house for the most minor excuse, for short periods. None of these short breaks were the respite he actually needed. Therefore, David was never rejuvenated. His friends called it "spinning" because he was in constant motion, with no real benefit. This only made Caregiver Hell even more painful for David.

Rhonda lacked the self-discipline to do grocery shopping, attend to the laundry, wax the kitchen floor, or cook meals. She did go out with her sister to tea, she did go to movies, watched TV, and surfed the internet. She had trouble sleeping and infrequently got enough sleep to do simple tasks well. It may not be fair to use the concept of self-discipline in a dysfunctional household. Rhonda was depressed and in survival mode. Self-discipline is a luxury in this type of environment, but is does not mean that self-discipline should not be a goal.

అం అం

ANALYSIS OF SELF-DISCIPLINE PROBLEMS

A teenager on his way home from a beer party tries to take a corner too fast and wrecks his car. The situation did not trigger a successful search for an applicable *decision rule* (slow down for corners), either because none existed because of his inexperience, or because earlier in the evening a related decision rule (don't drink and drive) did not kick in. In the absence of a decision rule, his resolve could have helped, but the immediate thrill of speed or his beer-pickled brain prevented a rational decision process (*structure*). The *penalty* consists of some or all the following: physical injuries, increased insurance rates, no car to drive for a while, angry parents, legal bills, and embarrassment.

A college student studying for tomorrow's final exam in English receives a phone call inviting her to a party that is just beginning. The situation immediately triggers a decision rule (finish your work before you play), but the situation also triggers a powerful internal signal (feeling lonely and unloved). Reluctantly she resolves to subject the situation to the decision structure and does some thinking about it. The decision rule is on one side of her internal argument, and the emotion is on the other side.

To tip the decision toward studying, she would have to anticipate correctly the consequences of a poor English exam grade. Unfortunately, her good grades came without having to study in high school, so she erroneously concludes she can muddle through. This allows the emotion to overwhelm the decision rule and she goes to the party. The penalty consists of a poor grade on the exam and the possibility she will have to repeat the course, forcing her to decide between attending summer school or graduating late. Angry parents and embarrassment are additional penalties.

❧❦

Rhonda, in the example above, also fell back on decision rules she had learned from harsh experience. Unless Andy eats at a certain time, he becomes aggressive.. Therefore, the decision rule was, "Take the family out to eat exactly at 6 PM." This meant Rhonda had no time to cook after a long day at the office and picking up the kids. Other decision rules came out of Rhonda's Caregiving Hell:

- Take Andy to play poker when he wants to go; having Andy out of the house in the evening is the only way Rhonda had time to help the children with homework, or take a shower.
- Don't ask Andy to drive anywhere. He always becomes distracted.
- Don't leave the children with Andy. He can play with them, but he cannot supervise them.

Rhonda's penalties for ignoring these decision rules were predictable; a black eye, terrified children, no food in the house, car repairs, injured children, or one of Andy's tantrums.

∂⤜∾⟡

USING SELF-DISCIPLINE TO BECOME A TTC

Self-discipline can be improved by using a variety of different strategies. This discussion applies to routine decision situations that most of us encounter on a daily basis. It does *not* apply to bad habits where long-standing faulty decision rules have been over-learned. This is addressed in Chapter 11.

1. Take full responsibility for your decisions. You are in charge, not your ill spouse. If you understand that you and you alone will be accountable for your decision, a level of caution should result. Ask yourself, what outcomes of this situation will I be willing to live with?

2. Develop a mission statement for yourself. The existence of a mission amplifies long-term needs, reducing the influence of impulses, temptations, emotions or demands of the ill spouse, all of which can detract from the real issue; need satisfaction.

3. Make a commitment to improved self-discipline. Decide that keeping your behavior under better control can contribute to your happiness. Remember, self-discipline is a form of self-love. You have to love yourself a lot to deny yourself the short-term gratification of giving in to the demands of other people.

4. Use experience to create new decision rules. The more decision rules we accumulate, the fewer novel experiences we encounter, thus reducing opportunities for impulsive behavior. Deliberately look for themes and patterns in your experience that can be used as decision rules in the future.

5. Develop the habit of slowing down the decision process. You do not get points for quick decisions except in emergencies. Become more thoughtful; take time to ponder your options when faced with unfamiliar situations.

6. Talk over decisions with someone. Find someone willing to listen to your approach to handling situations and solving problems, and invite their candid observations. Do not be defensive or they will tell you what you want to hear instead of what you need to hear. It is important not to choose non-caregiver friends or neighbors, or family members, to confide in. Their input will reflect their agendas and common social misconceptions about caregiving.

7. Analyze bad decisions. Trace the origin of decisions that have resulted in outcomes that do not meet your needs. Try to understand the patterns of circumstances that lead to impulsive decisions so they can alert you to slow down and use the decision making/action process.

THE TOUGH & TENDER CAREGIVER

In general, the TTC is highly disciplined. Even spontaneous behavior has been subjected to some form of analysis to insure that some of the caregiver's needs will still be met despite sacrifices inherent in caring for an ill spouse. The TTC admits that events are indeed under his or her control; nobody else is to blame for outcomes. New situations are treated with caution and patience, whereas familiar situations make use of proactive (not defensive) decision rules.

TTCs make good use of the resources available to them, including trusted advisors (who are unlikely to be family or non-caregiver friends) to evaluate the quality of their decisions. They also routinely evaluate what went wrong in the decision process when their self-discipline occasionally fails. TTCs have a positive self-image, and consider tight self-discipline to be a form of self-love.

Chapter 11
CONTROLLING BAD HABITS

How to Identify and Fix Destructive Behavior

చం ఈం

In the popular culture, discussions of bad habits include alcohol and drug abuse, nail biting, hair twisting, driving too fast, procrastination, and the like. However, in the world of spousal caregivers, there is a set of bad habits that sneak up on us. They are subtle but destructive in the impact on the well-being of caregivers.

Caregivers who find themselves in tough caregiver situations are vulnerable to the development of bad personal habits. The frustration level of spousal caregivers can become so painful that they will try anything to gain relief. This is fertile ground for the development of a whole class of bad habits that are particularly common among caregivers.

THE MECHANICS OF BAD HABIT DEVELOPMENT

Virtually all bad habits originate as reactions to powerful emotions. There are few things in life more filled with powerful emotions than the spousal caregiver's life. The sequence begins with a situation that triggers a strong emotion, such as anger or fear. The emotion has become attached to the situation for any number of reasons. For instance, Rhonda would experience "fear" in response to Andy's violent outbursts. David would experience "anger" in response to Kate's demands.

Whatever the current or historical connection between a bad habit and an emotion, traumatic caregiving situations often lead to an immediate and overwhelming emotional reaction that the individual experiences as extreme discomfort. The emotional reaction is so powerful that it overwhelms external signals as it amplifies internal signals. It is like comparing a bright, flashing neon sign with an ordinary billboard. The internal emotional signal dominates the individual's attention.

Because the emotional reaction is so uncomfortable, the individual begins an immediate, sometimes random search for some kind of activity that will reduce the pain. The person is looking for an *emotional bandage*. The first action that reduces the pain, even a little bit, is seized upon as an all-purpose remedy. The pain-reduction rewards and strengthens the "solution," and a habit has been set in motion. The next time this particular emotional reaction occurs, the individual immediately remembers what relieved the pain last time, and the behavior is again displayed.

Food Habits

People who are experiencing a strong sensation of anxiety often find their stomach "in a knot." Food can calm the stomach down, which makes over-eating a natural reaction to powerful anxiety. One of the most common bad habits among frustrated caregivers is the abuse of food. We hear about "comfort foods." Not only is food comforting, but also consuming "comfort foods" is a rare form of indulgence, a treat, in a caregiver's life. Comfort foods have this name for several reasons. They typically are the foods that remind us of a better time, a happier place and our own childhood when we were cared for by another person. Because they are indulgent foods, they were rewards during our lifetime. We had ice cream cones when we were at the park, a slice of pie after a Thanksgiving meal, a birthday cake on a special day. For some people comfort foods are grandma's cookies or mom's mashed potatoes.

These foods also legitimately make us feel better, too. That is why some of us claim to be emotional eaters. Without going into a realm of science outside our area of expertise, a brief commentary may be of help. Comfort foods are typically those foods that are high in carbohydrates. Carbohydrates are essential in the production of serotonin. Serotonin is a neurotransmitter that is important in many systems in the human body, particularly mood, appetite and human sexuality. There is much more information about serotonin and its importance available via the internet, but this chapter is about bad habits.

But eating is more than just a rush of serotonin. Eating can symbolically fill the void of emptiness accompanying loneliness for the caregiver grieving for lost companionship. Foods can represent a way of rewarding ourselves if we feel others have not properly rewarded us for our efforts in the daily chores of delivering care. Caregivers tend to feel "owed" all day, every day, and food feels like a kind of payback. Often when we feel anxiety, our stomach aches or feels like it is in a knot. Food counteracts uncomfortable stomach sensations and brings temporary relief.

Abusing food often results in one of many forms of a *vicious circle* that perpetuates rather than solves the underlying problems in the caregiver's life style. Eating comfort foods (because we need to reward ourselves) gives us a brief feeling of happiness. It does not last very long and we consume more foods high in carbohydrates chasing the "high" of feeling better. In turn, we overeat. Overeating causes weight gain, which frustrates the caregiver and results in anger directed at oneself for putting on weight. This self-loathing creates more anxiety, which requires more eating to calm down, resulting in more weight gain and the vicious circle continues.

When the food is served in a restaurant, the eating process can become a rare bit of entertainment in what was otherwise another crushingly dull day. The foods we typically order from a restaurant will likely be filled with carbohydrates and fat. They give us all of the same sensations with the added bonus that the portions are too large; so we overeat.

৯৯

Rhonda could always get her husband to go to a restaurant even on a bad day and extended family would gladly meet them at a local place for a quick bite. Comfort foods and restaurants became her refuge.

৯৯

The real problem with the food "bad habit" or addiction is that, while we can live without alcohol or drugs, we cannot go "cold turkey" and live without food. Every day we have to ingest the very substance we are trying to avoid. We have heard it said about food addiction "every day you fall off the wagon no matter how committed you are to stopping."

Personal Hygiene

Caregivers often become apathetic about their own personal hygiene. Assuming that the spousal caregiver is not working outside the home, the daily grind of caring for one's spouse becomes mind numbing. This bad habit begins because caregiving requires such a concentrated focus on the other person that the price many caregivers pay is to stop paying attention to their self-care. It is like there is only so much room in their brain for caring, and all of it is used up caring for the ill spouse. There is no room left for self-care. Personal hygiene takes on an "indulgent" feeling and we use any down time for other necessities, like sleeping.

It is common for caregivers trapped in Caregiver Hell to go for days without a shower, to stop brushing their teeth, to "forget" to change clothes. After all, they cannot go anywhere anyhow, so why bother? The days all feel the same, so "I'll bathe later." This precipitates another variation of the *vicious circle*. My neglect of personal hygiene and personal appearance causes me to feel bad about myself, intensifying my pain, which makes me feel I do not deserve to be cared for, which prolongs and intensifies my self-neglect, and the downward spiral continues.

For those well spouses who work outside the home, it may be surprising to learn that human resource management personnel and corporate executives are quite aware of the adverse impact working caregivers have on their company's productivity. Simply put, our bosses can tell when we are neglecting ourselves either by our outward appearance or our lost time. We are not keeping our vicious circle a secret.

の◦ふ

David fell into a pattern of neglecting himself. He stopped taking regular showers, wore the same jeans, shirt, socks, etc. for days on end. He stopped caring properly for his teeth. As a result, when his caregiving duties ceased he had expensive dental bills.

In retrospect, it had been a dysfunctional response to his wife's demands while they were living together. Kate had been insisting that she needed some expensive dental work because her teeth were starting to fall out. Rather than have a full set of dentures to compensate for the losses, she was seeking full implants. This would have been a huge expense and Kate did not seem to understand that the oral surgery was risky. Tired of arguing, David, thought the requests was a waste of money considering her overall health status, so he joined her in a battle of poor oral health.

অ⊸⊖

Chores

Bad habits creep up on us, a little like the *boiled frog syndrome* described earlier. It is common not only for caregivers to begin to neglect their personal hygiene, but their environment as well. It is not uncommon to find household chores neglected. The garbage piles up in the kitchen, dirty clothes are everywhere, every surface is dusty, there is dried food on the carpets, the hard floors dirty, and there is no clean window in the house.

This bad habit has its origin in apathy. Homeowners normally keep their place neat and clean because they take pride in their homes. However, caregiving without appropriate support or respite can lead to burnout, and burnout makes us stop caring about our homes and ourselves.

For some spousal caregivers working outside the home, work is the only respite we experience. We are aware that the *real* workday begins upon arrival home. The bad habit to not complete chores seems to start with putting off a chore because we are tired, then we are resentful that we have to do everything and it culminates with a vicious cycle of not doing any of them.

Passivity

Healthy people keep almost everyone at a healthy distance, both physically and emotionally. This self-protection mechanism keeps others from intruding into their private space and private thoughts. Those trapped in Caregiver Hell often fall prey to relaxing those boundaries and letting people do what would normally be unthinkable; namely, inject themselves into the caregivers's world without an invitation.

The bad habit for caregivers is that we are usually so desperate for social networks that we allow this to take place without complaint. Normally, we screen people out of our inner circle whose presence we know is toxic. We let them stay because we are so desperate to find acceptance, and they throw us bones occasionally, so rather than removing the toxic individual, we give in to their presence, and the passive acceptance is the bad habit.

ৡৣ

Rhonda allowed Andy's family to set the agenda for Rhonda and her children nearly every weekend. They would create some kind of family event or outing, and Rhonda went along with it. She was exhausted most of the time and did not have the energy to challenge Andy's sister because it would just result in a huge uproar, and she needed the peace. However, she also needed her family engaged when they were all home from school because Andy needed to be entertained. She often considered letting Andy and the children go without her so she could rest, but when she tried it a few times, one of them would always come home injured somehow. The respite was not worth the pain and not participating in the activity was not worth the argument with Andy. Either way, Rhonda's bad habit elicited some kind of cost, but she was unaware of the habits or the way out of them.

While visiting with his wife and child, Bob, David's grown son, would dictate how the entire household ran during their visit. Bob insisted that David could not put away the clean dishes and that the dog's tinkling tags must be removed because those activities would awaken Bob's child. Bob refused to eat certain foods in the house and insisted that foods be prepared a certain way. He demanded that David purchase items for leisure activities prior to their four day visit.

Bob leveraged to compliance by implicitly threatening that if things were not done his way, the visits would cease as would contact with David's only grandchild. Before he became so immersed in caregiving, David would never have allowed himself to be blackmailed. The caregiving had damaged David's self-esteem and had deprived him of appropriate social contact. Bob apparently recognized this change in his father and took full advantage.

ॐॐ

Anger

The frustrations of Caregiver Hell make one chronically angry. Chronic anger is essentially a bad habit. If we tell ourselves that life is futile and nothing changes then we are justifying the anger. The authors have seen caregivers develop such a short fuse that anything can set them off. These people become extremely angry at the smallest provocation, and in some cases the anger flashes unexpectedly in public.

ॐॐ

Rhonda carried around that kind of burnout-inspired anger for years. It manifested itself at home in bursts of temper directed at Andy and at the children. An interesting by-product of her unchecked anger, and that of Andy's, was that the children began to display the same unchecked anger at one another. *"Letting it fly"* became the norm in the home for everyone. Even more dramatically, the anger was directed at retail clerks, waiters, or bystanders who did something that annoyed Rhonda. She became an avenging angel of sorts, administering blistering tongue-lashings to whoever was in her sights. Anger was a habitual way of life.

David did the same thing with his niece Tiffany when she wanted to come for a visit. His withering criticism of her "rudeness" was all out of proportion to her sin.

಄ೲ

Role Addiction

Caregivers become addicted to the role. In self-defense, burned out caregivers can fall into a pattern of building a "new normal" around the presence of the ill spouse and caregiving duties. The duties of caregiving become an all-purpose excuse for whatever the caregiver wants to do, *or wants to avoid.*

Earlier in this book was talk briefly about a new normal, but that is in the context of building a better life with the ill spouse. When the new normal is a crutch to avoid living, it has no positive qualities. The authors suggest an examination of what the new normal really became after the onset of disability or illness. Has the identity of "well spouse" become our new claim to fame? Do we get "goodies" because we are the poor suffering well spouse?

The problem with this consuming identity is that we stop viewing looking at ourselves with high regard. We become one thing, a caregiver, and we stop moving forward in life. It is all "on hold" until our caregiving days cease. Some of us then do not know what to do with ourselves in the "normal" world. If our self-concept is that of spousal caregiver and we find we are no longer a caregiver, we hit a metaphorical brick wall and lose our identity.

಄ೲ

Andrew has been caring for his ill spouse most of his marriage. He has built an entire lifestyle around her care. He uses her illness to send out appeals online for financial help because the expenses are astronomical. Andrew has confessed that he thinks people should help them because nobody chose this illness and he cannot work full-time because of his wife's care needs. The health care system is failing them and Andrew thinks an appeal for public aid is fair and due to him. His whole world is "devotion" to his wife and health care reform.

Andrew cannot emotionally afford to contemplate a life that does not circle around her. Therefore, he has kept his wife alive, barely, for years. When she is in the hospital, which is frequent, her near-death experiences have become a circus. She signed numerous living wills when she was able to express her wishes and there is usually a DNR (Do Not Resuscitate) order on the chart. Andrew's wife knew this was coming and prepared to minimize the problems for Andrew. However, every time the need to invoke the DNR arises, Andrew refuses to allow the DNR to be honored. He continually makes the doctor rescind the order at the last minute because he cannot bear the thought of letting her go.

As unbearably sad as all of this is, Andrew's *whole identity* is that of spousal caregiver and thoughts of losing his wife is akin to losing his own identity. He also believes that without her alive, somehow, he loses credibility both as a well spouse and with his advocacy work. If she dies, he will just be another widower, nothing special and will have no purpose in life as he grows old without her.

ৰু৽ড়

Entertainment

A caregiver bad habit can take the form of an aversion to the environment in which the care is given, normally the family home. That form involves looking for any excuse *not to* stay home, regardless of the consequences financially or socially. Sometimes the entertainment bad habit overlaps with another bad habit, neglect of chores. The entertainment habit can manifest itself in the home as well, and can in the form of computer games, online chat rooms and other mental "escapes" like reading incessantly or watching television. Nothing else is done except delivering basic care to the ill spouse.

ৰু৽ড়

Known for needing to entertain Andy, Rhonda began looking for any entertainment activity to occupy her family. Formal entertainment activities would be calmness she sought in her daily life. Entertainment and "busy" days became addictive. When she began to make decisions to heal her wounds, it was as if she experienced withdrawal symptoms learning how to enjoy quiet time, read a book or refuse to spend money entertaining the children. They were all used to living on the "run."

∻

Alcohol

For many people, alcohol is a depressant, and can temporarily numb awareness and calm symptoms of anxiety. This characteristic, and its ready availability, makes it the drug of choice for many caregivers.

∻

David's unhappiness and isolation translated into an issue with alcohol. He began to use it at night to relax and over the decades of living with Kate's disability, he would drink. He was attempting to blot out the calls for help during the hours he wanted to be "off the clock". He rationalized the drinking as a way to have at least eight hours of uninterrupted sleep, or recovery time. The truth is it was forcing him into longer periods of sleep where Kate had to wait for him and he did not care when, or if, he woke up.

∻

Defensiveness

The atmosphere of caregiving households can become very tense. The ill spouse can be constantly concerned about health issues and whether his or her needs will be met with the same care today as they were yesterday. Caregivers often have given up so much in the service of their caregiving duties that they are constantly frazzled, feel owed, and are extremely angry. In this environment, defensiveness is the order of the day. Everyone is on guard. The caregiver is waiting for the ill spouse to ask just "one more thing" that will be the tipping point. The ill spouse is waiting to be denied "one more thing" to justify an explosion.

❧❦

Years after Rhonda and Andy were divorced, Rhonda's two daughters continued to elevate defensiveness to a high art form. While living in Rhonda's dysfunctional household growing up, whenever they were challenged, it nearly always was followed by angry criticism or blanket disapproval. Their father used yelling as a primary mode of communication and their mother was constantly making excuses for his behavior. She "forgave" their chores. Therefore, nothing was expected of them. They had no responsibilities and Rhonda truly thought this was the way to apologize for the "tough life they had been given."

The children's conditioning in this environment has caused them to make excuses for whatever behavior they chose to exhibit. They did not do their chores because they forgot, or they had homework, or the expectations were not made clear. It was never their fault and they knew how to make Rhonda assume the burden. For these children, defensiveness had become a way of life. It can be considered a bad habit with its origins in a worn out caregiving environment.

❧❦

Miscellaneous

The category of miscellaneous bad habits includes a wide variety of behaviors which, if displayed occasionally, would be considered innocuous. Examples include nail biting, hair twisting, nose picking, chain-smoking, excessive eye blinking, incessant gum chewing, and that always-annoying verbal habit of punctuating nearly every statement with "you know?" or "like." These behaviors flourish in tense environments, and the burned out caregiver household certainly qualifies.

ADVANCED FORMS OF BAD HABITS

Any of the previously listed bad habits, plus others can go on indefinitely. Caregivers often get into long-term bad habits that lost their function, which would have been to alleviate anxiety. These habits are considered "functionally autonomous." The behavior has lost its bandage *function*, has become *autonomous* (independent) of its original purpose. A habit in this form is often especially puzzling because it appears to serve no function for the person and it continues without conscious awareness.

The mechanism by which this attachment occurs is known as classical conditioning. In his well-known experiment, Pavlov succeeded in conditioning dogs to salivate at the sound of a bell by repeatedly pairing the bell with food. What began as bell/food/saliva eventually became bell/saliva.

Another advanced form of bad habit might be thought of as the "vicious circle," described earlier in this chapter. Here the penalty experienced by the individual for displaying the bad habit is emotional pain, similar to the pain which originally triggered the habit. This penalty then triggers an immediate recurrence of the habit, and the cycle goes on and on.

Motivation for Eliminating Bad Habits

Before embarking on any strategy for eliminating self-defeating patterns of behavior, it is necessary to admit the habit exists. We are responsible for our lives. Making excuses or blaming others may help relieve us of the pain of owning up to our own conduct, but the facts do not change. We are responsible for the behavior, and only we can change it.

Caregivers wrapped up in their own versions of "Caregiver Hell" with their ill spouse are often defensive about their bad habits. Their reaction is usually a variation of the following theme: "What do you expect from someone in my circumstance?" Eric Berne in his classic book <u>Games People Play</u> describes a "game" entitled *"What Do You Expect From A Man With A Wooden Leg?"*

Caregivers in these horrible circumstances have been known to use their circumstances to justify any avoidance behavior. This makes it especially difficult to help caregivers conquer bad habits unless they are willing to make a total commitment to altering their caregiving arrangement. Then it is easier for them to assume responsibility for their behavior, and thus change it.

Having made this giant step, it is important for caregivers, and others, to be willing to try new things, to experiment with what we do, what we believe, what we think, what we assume. The key to change is to try something new. What follows is a list of strategies for accomplishing change in bad habits. They can be used by themselves or in combination.

STRATEGIES FOR ELIMINATING BAD HABITS

The caregiver without professional help can implement some of these strategies for eliminating bad habits. These include Strategies 1 through 4. Strategy #5, Intensive Feedback, requires the assistance of another person, but not necessarily a professional counselor. Strategies 6 and 7 definitely require the assistance of a professional counselor. They are listed here to educate the caregiver about what options exist, and what to expect if that choice is made. Strategy # 8, Magnify Penalties, and Strategy #9, Prevent Behavior, can be accomplished without professional help.

Strategy #1: Targeted self-discipline

Sheer determination to stop a bad habit should not be discounted. Almost any bad habit can be stopped by force of willpower if someone is sufficiently motivated. Sometimes a new piece of behavior that also reduces some of the pain will be easier to substitute for the bad habit. Chewing gum relieves tension a little, and can sometimes help someone quit smoking. Old-fashioned self-discipline is probably the most common method used for breaking bad habits. This is by far the most common technique used to quit smoking and lose weight. However, it is extremely difficult for caregivers because our support systems and desire for change waivers based on our ill spouse's health status.

Strategy #2: Insight

Most people understand amazingly little about their own bad habits. The ignorance is partly due to the automatic way many habits originate. It happens quickly and without conscious or deliberate effort on our part. Another reason for the ignorance is that knowledge of the mechanics of how habits begin is rare. It is simply a mystery to most people.

The puzzlement increases with functionally autonomous habits where the original emotional "middle man" has disappeared. There is no function, no apparent purpose served by the behavior. Insight can put a bad habit in better perspective. Discussion and analysis can make sense of the bad habit and provide a conceptual cubbyhole into which to tuck the behavior.

Through discussion it is frequently possible to identify what actual function a bad habit serves, or served originally; that is, what discomfort the behavior relieves. For example, talking can establish the connection between binge eating and loneliness, between alcohol consumption and the pain of rejection, between stimulant abuse and boredom.

Talking can also clear up misinformation and result in our bad assumptions being challenged. Tackling problems on our own is a little like stirring the same old mud. However, talking with someone can add fresh water to the mix that gradually clarifies things.

While it is possible to achieve insight through thoughtful self-analysis or by reading a self-help book (such as this one), the fastest, most efficient method is by talking with someone who is reasonably objective. Mental health professionals do not have a franchise on the ability to help someone with a personal problem. A sympathetic friend or family member can frequently provide all the insight required to conquer a bad habit.

Talking can help in another way. Knowing we have a bad habit and hiding it from others can create constant internal tension. Tension interferes with self-discipline. Letting someone else hear about our little secret without being condemned can relieve tension and make for a more relaxed, objective approach to fixing the problem. A good friend will also reassure us that we are not alone, that others have experienced similar difficulties. This kind of information also helps reduce tension. For example, after years of living with poor dietary habits of comfort foods and restaurant eating, Rhonda can only stay focused on a healthy diet regime if someone else knows she is trying to adhere to a healthy diet and is aware of her current weight. As long as her weight is a "secret", she is not as disciplined and she gains weight back. Eating poorly is a hard habit to break.

Strategy #3: Substitute Behaviors

Sometimes it is possible to break the connection between emotion and behavior or between situation and behavior (when the emotional component has disappeared). This is not a "pure" strategy in that some self-discipline is required to experiment with a new response to the emotion, or the situation. But, there is a trick to it. The new behavior chosen to replace the bad habit should serve a discomfort-reducing function as much as the bad habit does. For example, tranquillizer abuse counteracts uncomfortable tension, but so does jogging, which can sometimes be effectively substituted.

Insight can also help find substitutes. A little creative thinking about the function a habit serves can often generate several alternatives. It also helps to be persistent. If one substitute does not work, something else should be tried.

Strategy #4: New Skills

While bad habits get started as a bandage for painful emotions, they are sometimes reinforced partly by the absence of acceptable alternatives. For example, the shy person who avoids social situations may lack social skills and literally not know how to handle these situations. Sometimes they stammer when talking to a stranger. The verbal habit "you know" can be eliminated by substituting another kind of verbal filler, such as a combination of silence and head scratching, to let the listener know the person is pondering something.

One clue to which new skill should be learned lies in the answer to this question: "What would I rather do when I feel this way?" The trick is to identify a skill which allows us to handle situations in ways that truly suit us. Bad habits seldom yield outcomes that suit us afterwards.

The so-called "therapeutic community" approach to treating drug addiction is founded on the teaching of new skills. This approach is based on the observation that most addicts have poor interpersonal skills and an unwillingness to accept responsibility for their behavior. The therapy consists of confinement in a tightly controlled community in which every move of the addict is watched. Staff members provide constant tutoring, and manipulate rewards and punishments to strengthen new skills. Once the new skills are learned and well practiced, addicts can leave with the ability to handle situations in ways that truly suit them.

Strategy #5: Intensive Feedback

At times people are not conscious of exhibiting a bad habit. The habit has become so ingrained and automatic that it feels normal when it happens. Such people cannot make a deliberate attempt to control the bad habit if they are not aware the behavior is occurring.

A simple technique for improving awareness of a bad habit is extremely effective. It is called a *feedback contract*. The victim of the bad habit identifies someone close by who has a lot of contact with the victim, someone willing to help. (Caregivers of ill spouses should avoid asking non-caregiver friends and extended family for help—see "Who Not To Confide In" below) The victim then a) admits the problem exists, b) asks for assistance in the form of constant feedback each and every time the habit is exhibited, and then c) promises not to become defensive when the feedback is forthcoming. It may be necessary to provide the person giving the feedback with specific words to use in initiating feedback to prevent automatic defensiveness by the caregiver.

Mechanically, the process looks like this. At first, there is no awareness of the behavior. When the feedback process begins, awareness occurs *after* the behavior is exhibited, say five seconds. As the feedback process continues, awareness occurs earlier and earlier in the sequence, moving from five seconds to three seconds to one second. But at some point awareness occurs at the time the behavior occurs but not early enough to catch it. Finally, awareness occurs *before* the behavior is exhibited and, with a little practice, can be completely stopped.

༅༅

Well spouse, Cecile asked her friend Jim to help her eliminate her outbursts of anger in public. She admitted that these flashes of hostility were inappropriate, and she always felt bad about them later. She and Jim worked out a set of signals that Jim could use in public without calling attention to them (in this case, Jim pulled on his right earlobe), and Cecile agreed to stop herself each time. After several weeks of this kind of feedback, Cecile was able to catch her own mounting frustration and exit situations before she let her anger fly.

༅༅

The feedback is extremely helpful in eliminating automatic types of bad habits such as facial grimaces, tics, blinking, "uh huh" or "like" and similar verbal habits, grunts, throat clearing, and nail biting. Alcohol abuse and smoking also contain elements of automatic behavior and can often be helped with this technique.

Strategy #6: Desensitization

This strategy can break the bond between situations and the bad habit we are trying to eliminate. An example would be anger management. Placing a caregiver into increasingly provocative situations while applying relaxation techniques can gradually desensitize the individual to these forms of provocations, and reduce the automatic display of hostility. It can also work to desensitize an individual to situations normally stimulating overeating. Repeated exposure to situations normally stimulating the eating of comfort food can be paired with other forms of anxiety reduction, such as relaxation responses, talking, or listening with a different mindset.

In terms of the mechanics of the process, desensitization often works best by breaking down the situation into sequential segments and desensitizing each step separately. Fear of riding elevators can be approached by first standing in front of an elevator for a long time, long enough to quell the fear of being close to an elevator. The next step might be to arrange for the elevator to be turned off with the doors open, and standing inside long enough for that fear to diminish. Next, the doors are allowed to close, and again time elapses, along with the fear. The next step is to ride the elevator down only one floor, then two floors, and so on. This gradual approach addresses each stage of the fear and reduces it before moving on to the next stage, thus "disconnecting" the emotional reaction from the situation.

Strategy #7: Structured Behavior Modification

Another approach that uses segmentation relies on the creation of a behavior change plan that lays out a step by step modification process. It usually begins with research into the exact nature of the bad habit—how often does it occur, what situations trigger it, how long does it last, etc. The next step is to make a chart specifying what progress is to be made at what time intervals.

For example, a caregiver discovers during the research phase that she smokes the most during and after lengthy, daily confrontations with her ill spouse. At these times, she smokes five cigarettes in an hour. Her chart specifies that she will cut this to four cigarettes the first week, three the next, and so on until she quits. Other situations which trigger excessive smoking will be similarly charted, so that by the end of the time period, all situations that lead to smoking will have been neutralized.

There are especially poignant examples from the caregiver literature. Caregivers who abuse alcohol drink more when the demands are greatest from the ill spouse, normally during the evenings. Demands of a disabled or chronically ill spouse have patterns unique to each situation. It is enlightening to chart the frequency and loudness of the ill spouse's demands, and compare that with the pattern of whatever the caregiver is abusing. The results can be startling.

Achieving the small objectives in a systematic program of behavior modification provides enough of a reward to sustain the new behavior for most people. Sometimes it helps to build in additional rewards—a new hat, a concert, out to dinner—for successfully completing a particular stage of the plan.

Strategy #8: Magnify Penalties

Bad habits lead to penalties. If the penalties are less painful than the emotion that triggered the habit, the individual experiences a net gain in comfort by displaying the behavior. Anything that would make the penalty more painful would serve to make the behavior less desirable, and therefore less likely to occur.

We often manipulate in our minds how painful the penalties appear to be. This is done by ignoring or refusing to focus on the real implications of the bad habit. The pain of the penalty can sometimes be magnified by discussing with someone what bad things keep happening because of the bad habit.

For example, compulsive eating leads to obesity. Through candid discussion, the victim might be forced to a conscious realization that the penalty is enormous and deadly. We can manipulate penalties another way. Often smokers intensify the penalties for continued smoking by announcing to the world a stop smoking campaign. The prospect of embarrassment at failure to quit adds incentive to keep self-discipline intact.

Strategy #9: Prevent Behavior

This is a radical strategy involves voluntarily creating physical barriers to exhibiting certain behavior. Examples include individuals who padlock their refrigerator to prevent binge eating, or someone who wears gloves for a time to prevent nail biting.

DO NOT CONFIDE IN CERTAIN PEOPLE
THEY DO NOT CARE AS MUCH AS YOU THINK

Several of the strategies listed above for controlling or eliminating bad habits involve discussing matters with someone. You need to be very careful with whom you talk. While this may be difficult at first to understand, your extended family and non-caregiver friends may not be trustworthy with your private information and concerns. The non-caregiver friend or family member usually means well when they offer an ear to listen. Unfortunately, they often miss the mark when trying to offer advice after they "hear" your concerns. They likely try to show empathy, but the authors have formulated some opinions based on interviews and their own experiences.

扶扶

David felt he had a solid relationship with his grown children. Bob was married and had a family and Betsy had a long-term relationship. David was eager to have important people in his life understand that he had reached the end of his rope. He needed them to support his decision to live no longer with Kate. They had already expressed their unwillingness to care for Kate to allow David an extended respite when needed. Confiding in them about his decision due to his exhaustion turned out to be a disastrous mistake.

When David took Bob and Betsy into his confidence, they were horrified. What do you mean, put mom in a nursing home? They were angry. David thought the anger was out of proportion to his supposed bad deed. At first, David took the rap, thinking he had not shared with them enough details of the daily hell of caring for their mother, nor did they know how bad their marriage had been all along.

As it turned out, that was not it. They saw a threat to their inheritance if David went on with his life. This situation became all about money. Bob even said, incredibly, that he had made no provision for own son's college, and had been hoping David would take care of that. Betsy said that she would help with her mother for a $120,000 deposit into her checking account for home renovations. And, no, there was not going to be ownership in her home for either of her parents. This was to be considered an "opportunity cost" if David did not want to live with Kate. David was devastated to see they really did not care about his health.

Despite the absence of support from his children, David placed Kate in a nursing facility with the understanding that she was going to rehabilitate before coming home because David could not do it any longer.

As threatened, Bob retaliated by cutting off David's contact with his grandchild. The good relationship David assumed he had with his own children turned out to have been a gross miscalculation. The lesson here; be careful in whom you confide. Those who are not caregivers will never understand.

⁐⁐

"THE MEASURING STICK THEORY OF FRIENDSHIP"

Non-caregiver friends and family members often use the caregiver's life as a "measuring stick." They listen and they show grief, but the truth is that in their sympathy, they actually walk away feeling better about their own lives. They mean no harm, but they cannot help thinking (or worse gossiping) about how they are glad this is not happening to them. It takes the form of the following comments:

- "Boy, I thought my life was bad until I heard about yours."
- "I was feeling sorry for myself, but knowing what you are going through, I feel better."

Some of us are offered unwelcome interference that makes our days actually harder, but instead of saying "Thanks, but no thanks," we take the tidbits that are offered out of desperation. As a general rule, non-caregiver friends and family members offer what they find most convenient to give rather than bothering to find out what the caregiver really needs.

⁐⁐

Nancy, whom Rhonda thought of as a dear friend, had a special attachment to Rhonda's children because of all they had been through in the past years. During some of her worst days of caring for Andy, Nancy babysat with the children. Rhonda was cautious not to abuse the friendship; Nancy was paid for her time. They had frank discussions about how the help was necessary; Rhonda did not want Nancy dipping into her own family finances to help them. Rhonda told her she was grateful for the assistance and for a long time, it was an amicable working relationship; and the friendship appeared to be intact.

The babysitting evolved into Nancy unexpectedly making dinner for the family. Rhonda felt awkward about the extra expenses she must have been incurring for those meals and began reimbursing her for the food. Nancy began taking liberties with the relationship. She started by telling Rhonda she did not approve of some Rhonda's decisions about her own household. She did not like the new friendship she was developing with other caregivers. Nancy consistently defended Andy's actions when told how aggressive he had been the night before. This was strange because Nancy knew he had this serious disability. Gradually the relationship with Nancy evolved into something intolerable. She used the "favors" she was doing as an opportunity to lecture Rhonda. She seemed to have an agenda, and it may have been that Nancy's marriage was nearly as troubled as Rhonda's. If Rhonda was not doing things her way, it was a threat to the way Nancy was managing her own private hell.

Rhonda began to realize that the "friendship" was a true testament to Travland's Law. Nancy was doing what she perceived to be in her own best interest at the time, not what was in Rhonda's best interests. As Rhonda became better informed and mentally healthy, the more annoyed and opinionated Nancy became. The two of them are no longer friends. Rhonda strongly believes that once she got well and was no longer living in Caregiver Hell, the "measuring stick" that had made Nancy feel better when she was around Rhonda disappeared. *"Thank God, I am not Rhonda. My life could be worse."* no longer applied and she had no further use for Rhonda.

One of the hardest lessons for Rhonda was to find that when she shared her real thoughts and feelings about caregiving the very people she trusted judged her. If she said she missed having sex, missed being cared for by a man or wanting a healthy husband, she would hear words akin to *"how dare you?"* Once she confided in someone close to her that her intimacy with Andy was nonexistent. This friend responded with *'What do you mean, you just had a baby?"* Well, a nine month old is not "just had," and that was following nine months of pregnancy. That adds up to nearly two years. Was that how other 36-year-old women lived, she inquired. There were just no real answers.

Rhonda would share her thoughts with friends about the apparent uselessness of Andy's expensive medications. If no help was to be forthcoming, was this life worthwhile? Should she even keep buying those medications or was it just to cover the doctor's liability in offering treatment? To her friends, those questions seemed like disloyalty and complete disregard for her husband. They would gasp, "*We all have problems.*" They also said "*God never gives you more than you can handle.*" "*It is your duty because of your vows.*" "*You just cannot stop giving a medication.*" No person seemed to understand except for the other caregivers.

Finally, there are indeed days it feels like you have been given more than you can handle. Caregivers often feel alone and that the world has turned its back and the burdens are too much. Caregivers usually do not want to be reminded that they are weak for feeling overwhelmed. It takes the emotional strength of Hercules to get through a day as a full time caregiver.

☙❧

THE TOUGH & TENDER CAREGIVER

To enjoy TTC status, caregivers must recognize the bad habits they have developed along the caregiver journey and take corrective action. The TTC is quick to admit the habit exists and looks for a technique to eliminate the bad habit before it creates significant interference with need satisfaction. The TTC knows to ask for help when things are difficult, but knows to find a neutral party or, in some cases, a professional counselor. The ideal confident is someone without their own agenda, someone who is not using the TTC as a stick to measure the quality of their own life. The safest source for good conversation is another caregiver.

Chapter 12
THE LEARNING CONTRACT

Gaining the Most from Our Experiences

೨ೂ

The poor caregiver caught in Caregiver Hell cannot win for losing. Not only does society indoctrinate us into believing we should not look out for our own needs, that marriage is forever and other myths about relationships, we are also told that it is pointless to educate ourselves. This anti-intellectual bias comes to us courtesy of maxims and proverbs like the following:

- There is nothing new under the sun
- I learned everything I needed to know in the 6th grade
- No news is good news
- What goes around comes around
- History doesn't repeat itself
- Ignorance is bliss

The quality of our personal decisions and actions should continue to improve as we grow older and gain experience. We should continue to become more effective and efficient in meeting our needs. If all goes well, the percentage of our needs that are met, and the degree to which those needs are met, should continue to increase. In short, the older we get, the happier we should become.

For the spousal caregiver, the process of getting better at getting our needs met should not be affected by our caregiver duties. If anything, the quest to become a TTC makes it even more critical to profit from our mistakes. In order to keep growing, it helps greatly to make a pact with ourselves. Thus, the *Learning Contract* is a commitment we make to ourselves to extract every ounce of learning from everything that happens to us. This vow keeps us open to new learning in every aspect of our lives. As the old saying goes, "good decisions come from experience, which comes from bad decisions."

We learn in a variety of ways; from our successes, from other people, from watching television, from reading books, from classroom teachers, and from simple observation of how things go. But, the most important lessons we learn are from our own mistakes. The most profound lessons of life are learned in this school of hard knocks. Profiting from our own mistakes is the primary emphasis of the learning contract and this chapter.

One wag said that neurosis is best exemplified by the person who makes the same mistake time after time, each time expecting a different outcome. Caregivers with ill spouses do this constantly.

☙❧

David kept feeding Kate junk food at her request, all the time buying into her argument that these little snacks between meals were so small that they had no bearing on her bulk. He kept expecting her to lose weight.

Rhonda kept on entertaining Andy and ignoring how dysfunctional their lives had become all in an attempt to pacify Andy. She hoped this would eventually pay off in that he would start being nice to his family and they could stop living in fear.

☙❧

BELIEFS THAT DO NOT SERVE US

Beliefs are principles we learned along the way that guide our decisions. We use our beliefs as a policy manual, making quick reference to them as shortcuts in the decision process. Christianity's Ten

Commandments (e.g., thou shalt not kill) are examples of useful principles for decision guidance.

Beliefs should serve us. We should not serve our beliefs. But all of us learn some principles that, in the end, do not serve us. In order to improve our decision 'hit rate' we must be able to identify the root cause of poor decisions. More often than not, the bad decision was based on a bad belief. To improve the quality of future decisions, the bad belief must be identified, articulated, and smashed to smithereens. The following beliefs or Deadly Misconception are very common in our society, but seldom help us:

- Justice will prevail
- It is wrong to be selfish
- Children should be seen and not heard
- Love conquers all
- People will treat us the way we treat them
- Hard work always pays off
- Good always triumphs over evil
- Always lend people a helping hand

MODIFYING OUR BELIEFS

Since beliefs are used as guideposts for decisions, over time a connection develops between certain beliefs and corresponding specific behavior. As a positive example, our belief that it is wrong to steal is triggered when we covet something we would like to own. This gets connected to the behavior of refraining from stealing the coveted object. When our beliefs consistently lead us to self-defeating behavior, it is important to replace those beliefs with others. For example, a woman had constant conflict with her mom. Whenever they talked by phone, or in person, Mom criticized her constantly. Mom did not like her daughter's lifestyle, choice of companions, taste in furniture, child-rearing approach, etc. Nothing seemed to please her.

When she received this criticism, the daughter almost always felt anger and guilt for not being the "perfect" daughter. Each conversation made her feel unworthy. She frequently tried to be diplomatic and suggested that Mom should tone down the criticism, but without effect. The daughter failed to use effective techniques for stopping this barrage because of a belief she embraced. She believed: *Out of respect for one's parents, one must tolerate all their criticism.* Let us call this Belief A.

Belief A is so entrenched that it is the driving force for the daughter's behavior, "putting up with the criticism," which we will call Behavior A. In order to eliminate Behavior A and the associated anger she feels, it will be necessary to get rid of Belief A and substitute another, more realistic belief in its place. We will call the new one Belief B, which might be stated as follows: *The relationship between and parent and a grown child should be governed by the same rules that apply to any other relationship between adults.*

In order to adopt this new, more realistic belief, one must understand that this new belief leads to a radically different kind of behavior, which we will call Behavior B: the daughter threatens to discontinue the relationship with her Mom unless the criticism stops, and mean it.

Even though this next step is extremely difficult for someone committed to Belief A, the way to begin to accept Belief B instead is to deliberately display Behavior B; that is, confront and threaten the Mom. Choosing an appropriate time and place, Mom should be told, face to face if possible, something like the following: "Mom, I have asked you repeatedly to stop being so critical of me, and you have ignored my requests. Now I have no choice but to insist that you make a change, immediately. Otherwise I will not visit you or talk with you on the phone."

A word about *personal courage*. Mom is not going to be happy with this change in the dynamic of her relationship with her daughter. This will hurt her feelings because she thought she was helping her daughter. So she will be angry, over-react with prolonged silence, or even counter-attack. The same is true of the spousal caregiver seeking TTC status. Change is hard for most people, and initiating change is one of our greatest challenges in life. Putting a stop to self-destructive behavior on the way to enhanced personal fulfillment is often painful. Problem solving is almost never without some kind of cost. In these situations, the payoff is frequently a hundred times more significant than the price.

In the example above, once Mom has been confronted, Belief B is immediately strengthened. Beliefs follow behavior. Our minds will not tolerate a contradiction as blatant as between Belief A and Behavior B. They are mutually incompatible. By deliberately displaying Behavior B, we force the mind to help justify the behavior. The mind does this by strengthening Belief B. As Behavior B occurs again and again in different situations, Belief B gets stronger and stronger, while Belief A fades away.

&ro&

After they were divorced, long after Andy had been diagnosed with dementia, Rhonda wanted badly to believe that he wanted to maintain a relationship with his children. For months, Andy would call periodically and ask to see the children, and Rhonda would pile the children in the car, spend hours visiting. Along the way, she would respond to Andy's other requests, such as giving him spending money, to be taken to lunch or some other favor. Andy's interest in the children seemed secondary to his other desires. She jumped through hoops to honor his requests because she wanted Andy to care about his children.

Through observing these interchanges, David suspected that Andy was incapable of genuinely caring for the children. This type of indifference, he noted, is typical of the kind of brain pathology with which Andy was afflicted. David explained to Rhonda when Andy wanted something from her he was using the children as a tool to get her to comply with his other requests.

The belief that Andy cared about his children was hurting Rhonda, and hurting the children. Rhonda was inconveniencing herself, spending money she did not have and then having to explain to the children why the visits (or phone calls) were not going any better. The kids always felt hurt, as if they were the ones having to force "Dad" to interact and care about them.

With closer observation, Rhonda began to agree that perhaps Andy actually could not care about the children because of legitimate mental limitations. It was one thing to understand his medical condition intellectually, but another to feel it. This made her increasingly disturbed by her interactions with Andy. She felt even more used and abused. The children had been suffering because they were afraid of Andy's temper and had trouble sleeping for days after such encounters.

David suggested to Rhonda that because her belief was not accurate, and that Andy was incapable of normal fatherly interest for the children, forcing the visits was hurting all of them. By forcing Andy to behave in a way that was unnatural, she was also indirectly, harming Andy. David suggested a course of action designed to smash through the brick tower Rhonda had built around that specific belief—that Andy had normal parental feelings for his children.

David suggested that she begin postponing activities and delaying his requests that did not fit her schedule or benefit the children. She should tell him "no" when she did not have extra money or time to spend entertaining him. David explained to Rhonda that Andy's behaviors would be extinguished once she stopped responding to all of his requests.

Rhonda followed this advice, which was extraordinarily difficult. She would put Andy off, make excuses, take his request "under advisement," or promise to ask the children if they wanted to see their father.

Early on in the process, he would call back days or weeks later and repeat his request, but when he realized that money was not free flowing and the children were not eager to see him, the calls stopped. She also told the older children that they needed to be responsible for interactions with Andy under supervision. Andy needed to know what they thought and how they felt.

At first, this was all very difficult for Rhonda. It was painful to contradict powerful impulses to put the children together with their biological father. She also felt enough responsibility about the divorce itself to feel pain at not responding to his requests for favors. But, over a period of a few months, Andy's calling stopped entirely, and Rhonda's new belief took over; namely, that Andy was indeed not capable of caring about his children as would a normal father.

The result was that Rhonda and the children were able to re-define the terms of visitation that suited their needs. When Andy calls, the children speak to him more freely because the boundary errors have been corrected and the children understand they have power to pursue the relationship on their own terms. Andy has found a new sense of independence because Rhonda backed away.

↝↜

The principle in this section is this: *To replace one belief with another, behave as if the new belief were true and accepted. Over time, the old belief will fade and be replaced by the new.*

STRONGLY HELD BELIEFS

When we have used beliefs for a very long time as a guide for decisions, each decision made in response to that belief is like another brick in a tower encircling the belief. The tower grows ever taller and gradually encases that belief, protecting it from modifications. When someone challenges a belief that is so protected, the challenge bounces off harmlessly with no noticeable effect on the belief. This is not a problem when the protected belief serves us well and, in the case of caregivers, enhances our TTC status.

However, in the case of beliefs that are better off replaced, a way must be found to demolish the protective tower. When caregivers find themselves sucked into a self-destructive pattern with a chronically ill or disabled spouse, it is likely that the behavior is tied to some kind of belief. In this case, the caregiver might mistakenly believe that caregivers are obligated to be at the disposal of the ill spouse. In order to move to TTC status, the caregiver will have to use insight to recognize this bad belief for what it is, and use self-discipline to plan a course of action to destroy the brick tower and modify the belief. In these cases, the tower-destroying behavior would be to experiment with simply ignoring the desires of the ill spouse and arranging for someone to fill in. Caregiver would then simply announce the following to the ill spouse: "I will be out for the rest of the afternoon. Phyllis will be staying here with you. I know you don't want me to leave, but I have to go. I'll see you around 6 this evening. Good bye."

GROWTH RULES

There are a number of rules that, if followed, allow us to continue to improve the quality of our personal decisions and actions.

Rule 1—Be Open To Learn Something New

There is an old story about the relatively unskilled employee who had been in his position for ten years. His supervisor summed it up beautifully: "He doesn't have ten years of experience. He has one year of experience ten times."

It is important to be open to new information, understanding, and experience. We must be curious about many issues. We should stay up to date on innovation, read about a wide variety of topics, and keep up with current events. The rule means adopting a mindset, an attitude about the unfamiliar, the novel. It means suspending disbelief long enough to understand new experiences. Knowledge is power, and more knowledge is more power to control our destiny.

Rule 2—Evaluate Important Decisions

As discussed briefly in the chapter about decisions we know that decisions do not always turn out the way we thought they would. When outcomes were not exactly anticipated, something was undoubtedly wrong with the decision process. There is a wealth of information in such decisions that can be used to improve similar decisions in the future.

Do not overlook discrepancies as "not our fault," or rationalize them away as being "almost right." Close only counts in horseshoes and hand grenades. Dig in and assess what went wrong. Even when everything turned out right, it may have been for the wrong reasons. There is something to learn by evaluating every important decision. Was there anything you would have done differently in the process of getting to the finale?

Rule 3—Look in the Mirror First

Before allocating blame to others, bad luck, fate, or acts of God, it helps to first assess our own contribution to the problem. The primary advantage of this tactic is that there is precious little we can do about fate, luck, the actions of others or God. But there is a great deal we can do about ourselves. For example, a salesperson loses a sale due to pricing confusion after the contract was signed. She was tempted to blame initial misinformation from the factory she represents, but by looking in the mirror first, she was able to identify her contribution. It turns out she had a bad habit of failing to crosscheck factory information against a published formula that would have allowed her to smell a rat early in the game and rescue the sale. As Pogo said, "We have met the enemy, and he is us."

Rule 4—Forgive Yourself for Making Mistakes

Mistakes are the stuff of growth. It is a waste of energy to beat ourselves up because we erred. We could be using that same energy to figure out what went wrong. Some of us are prone to experience guilt feelings at the drop of a hat, perhaps, because guilt-inducing tactics were used frequently by our parents, mentors or teachers to control our conduct.

A commitment to the learning contract is a perfect antidote for this tendency. Mistakes come to be viewed as opportunities to increase our sophistication rather than cause for self-flagellation.

Rule 5—Beware of the Status Quo

In order to meet our needs on a continuing basis, we must accept change as a way of life. Employees who resist change in companies because "we've always done it this way" tend to block progress. Growth is unlikely when historical precedent is elevated to the level of doctrine. This rule must of course be tempered by another principle: if it ain't broke, don't fix it. This means that change should take place only if it leads to greater effectiveness in meeting our needs.

Rule 6—Be a Good Listener

It is quite natural to quit listening to someone who disagrees with us, or to hear only what we want to hear. Considerable psychological research supports the common sense observation that we listen more attentively to messages of which we agree. However, we learn a great deal more by absorbing alternative points of view.

It is especially useful not only to listen to those who take issue with our views, but also to actually probe and question the reasoning behind such opinions. This takes self-discipline and a commitment to learning. But who knows, we might learn something.

Rule 7—Be Grateful for Feedback, Even If It's BS

It is helpful to establish a reputation for receiving feedback gracefully. As hard as it is to muster up the courage to give others our opinion of something they have said or have done, it is nearly impossible if we believe they will become defensive. We can thank others for the consideration they have shown in reacting to our behavior, even if we do not intend to take the feedback to heart. If nothing else, at least it is polite. The adage, "even your best friends won't tell you" reminds us that, in general, we do not receive information well. Being able to overcome that obstacle can enhance a caregiver's life.

Rule 8—Practice Being Open

When we share how we feel or what we really think with someone (within the bounds of tact and diplomacy, of course), we invite scrutiny of our feelings and ideas. Many of us perpetuate downright screwy ideas because we do not share them with anyone. A cut on the finger covered by a tight band-aid cannot form a scab and heal. Similarly, ideas that never see the light of day cannot be improved.

A variation on this theme occurs when we are afraid to tell people who we really are for fear they will not like us. We hide behind a mask of someone we think others will like better. Unfortunately, this common practice perpetuates itself. Since our real persona is never seen, our real qualities cannot be improved. This means we never grow, which increases our motivation to remain hidden behind a mask. People with low self-esteem perpetuate their own misery by this vicious circle.

A word of caution is in order. Candid conversations with non-caregiver friends, relatives and in-laws are fraught with danger. As pointed out earlier, these people are likely to have their own agendas that are at cross-purposes with your own. Caregivers seeking the rarified atmosphere of TTC status should not let the camel's nose under their tents.

THE TOUGH & TENDER CAREGIVER

When we are growing, continuously becoming more knowledgeable, and making better and better decisions, our feelings about ourselves become more positive by the day. The experience of growth is exhilarating, a "natural high." The TTC tends to look at events optimistically and displays enthusiasm about everything from a beautiful tree to sex. Activities are more fun and relationships more satisfying.

Thus, we can get "hooked" on growth. The sensation of movement can develop a momentum all its own. Growth furnishes its own reward for the TTC. It opens up a whole cornucopia of new goodies. Life is a new adventure every day. The TTC caregiver wakes up excited about what each new day will bring. What a trip! This exhilaration can be a springboard to help the caregiver climb the ladder to Caregiver Heaven.

Chapter 13
PRACTICAL SOLUTIONS FOR THE TTC

Strategies for Solving Major Problems

ॐ∼ॐ

The completely frustrated spousal caregiver, at wit's end, needs to know what options are available. What can be done? What is legitimate? What is the correct sequence of events in which to start the action? Here are some answers, in roughly the sequence to consider them. Each option on the list will be examined in detail.

- Admit that total burnout will lead to disaster
- Admit indifference is dangerous
- Seek professional counseling
- Find a support group that is geared to the needs of the caregiver, not the ill spouse
- Find a confidant for ongoing emotional support
- Impose a schedule on the ill spouse
- Make excuses to get out of the house, lie if necessary
- Research available respite care in the home
- Research available home health care agencies
- Research available day programs for chronically ill adults
- Consider an assisted living facility for the ill spouse
- Consider nursing home placement for the ill spouse

- Divorce as a last option
- When the caregiving ends; what next?

BE HONEST ABOUT TOTAL BURNOUT

As caregiving drudgery drags on, the typical spousal caregiver experiences a variety of physical and mental symptoms. These range from chronic headaches, rapid heart beat and high blood pressure on the physical side, to depression, panic attacks and violence directed toward the ill spouse on the psychological side. Burnout is no laughing matter. As a byproduct of caring for chronically ill spouses, caregivers themselves become ill, and the medical costs are astronomical. The human cost is even more tragic. Forty percent of caregivers of chronically ill or disabled spouses precede their ill spouses in death.

TTCs understand the dangers of burnout, monitor their own status on a regular basis, and are poised to swing into action at the first indicator. The first things to look for include a rising sense of frustration, eroding civility in conversations with the ill spouse, increased complaints from the ill spouse, or an increase in sexual yearnings for which there is no readily available solution. Using cues like these, the TTC knows that Caregiver Hell may be around the corner, and that some kind of action must be taken.

ADMIT THAT INDIFFERENCE IS DANGEROUS

Indifference is indeed dangerous. As we addressed, the opposite of love is indifference. Indifference to our own well-being can bring about depression. Indifference to our partner can bring about neglectful care. Dedicated caregivers are unlikely to recognize that they have begun feeling indifferent to their spouse. It creeps up on us as we go about our daily lives.

What does indifference feel like? We look at our spouse, and instead of feeling love or compassion or a clearly defined obligation, we feel nothing. Indifference feels like not having feelings for someone.

Indifference causes us to do the minimum required but no more; there is often nothing left to give. Perhaps it takes the form of waiting a little longer to change a diaper. What is the use in hurrying if the mess is still going to be there later? Why force a combative spouse into the shower if he is not going anywhere? Or maybe you didn't see the need to fill the prescription right away because the medications never seem to help. You no longer respond to friends and family when they call; you cannot leave the house and you are tired of explaining. Does she yell and you ignore her? There is no joy in any of the interactions with the ill spouse.

When we feel nothing for our partner, we must make a change. We are lacking the loving compassion that initially held us there. Most would think that if we do not feel love then we must feel hate. But that is not the case in caregiving. If we hated our spouse, we would not have taken on the caregiving role. Indifference cannot continue with damage to one or both partners. Possible actions include figuring out a way to reduce burnout (such as renegotiating the Master Agreement), change methods for delivering care, or choosing to exit the relationship so that care can be provided by the right people for the job. Some combination of these actions might be appropriate.

SEEK PROFESSIONAL COUNSELING

This is not an idea that the caregiver under siege will warm to instantly, usually because of pride and society's inappropriate attitudes about the mental health professions. There are some genuine potholes on the pathway to truly effective counseling. Well-trained, competent counselors are hard to find

Most counselors do not know enough about caregiver burnout. Seeking counseling requires one to bare one's soul, difficult for anyone. Counseling can be expensive and seeking counseling requires one to admit one needs help.

Society has an anti-counseling bias. Perhaps, the best way to find a well-trained professional counselor who understands caregiving is to get a referral. Sometimes medical doctors have a handle on who is good and who is not. Also home health care nurses, other caregivers, and geriatric care managers might have information, as well as assisted living facility and nursing home administrators.

It is advisable to arrange an interview first with the counselor to evaluate the counselor's background, training, and experience with caregiver situations. It is also useful to discuss fees, payment method, confidentiality, length of visits, and frequency of visits the counselor recommends. It is also possible to check on counselor credentials on the internet and with licensing boards.

As far as training is concerned, the best-trained counselors are psychologists, social workers and other licensed mental health professionals. The laws governing who can hang out a shingle and claim to be a counselor are usually full of loopholes and poorly enforced. Those who call themselves counselors with no additional information about training or credentials are unlikely to be of much help, but some "coaches" are trained in the areas of which might be useful to focusing on how to improve living situations and relationships. There are no doubt some effective "pastoral counselors" but they are unlikely to have the right kind of professional training. Also, pastoral counselors are likely to put a religious slant on any advice, which can perpetuate certain caregiver misconceptions.

Use caution when considering spending money for "help" on such things as holistic therapists, new age counselors, or fortune-tellers. They want your money, but may have little to offer in the way of real help.

Assuming a referral, professional credentials and licensing, the next thing to evaluate during the first or second counseling session is rapport. The counselor should make caregivers feel comfortable by being good listeners and being non-judgmental.

To get the very most out of professional counseling it is essential to be completely candid. Leave nothing out or it will cripple the counselor's effectiveness with you. Good counselors have heard it all, so embarrassment should not be an issue.

OBTAIN GRIEF COUNSELING OR COACHING

As we covered in the beginning, death is not the only reason for grief. Caregivers of chronically ill or disabled spouses grieve for the future that has been ripped away from them. They grieve for lost companionship, lost tenderness, lost romance, lost walks on the beach, lost intimacy, lost carefree moments. As Rhonda put it, she grieved for the future she would never have. However, she learned that she was responsible for letting it happen. We have to learn that the grief related to losing control over our own destiny is because we allowed it to happen. We let the ill partners' limitations dictate how we lived our life.

It is helpful to find the right person to help us retrace our actions, glimpse where we let go of our control, and how reclaim it. Fellow caregivers and members of support groups are often good listeners, but a professionally trained grief coach can zero quickly into the most important issues, and will provide practical tips to make the pain more bearable. As with other categories of professional counselors, a well-trained and competent grief counselor is hard to find, so it helps to do research.

FIND A CAREGIVING COACH OR MENTOR

As caregiver coaches themselves, the authors understand that caregiver coaching is an emerging practice specialty. These professionals support the unique needs of family caregivers by blending the knowledge of family systems and skills of a coach. It is possible to research the availability of coaches using the internet, your local physician, various agencies that provide social services, such as public health departments, departments of social services, health insurance providers, hospitals and of course the local Hospice.

It is vital that you screen coaches regarding their professional credentials, and the orientation they use for their coaching. As a relatively new field, coaching does not require an actual license, nor are there universal professional standards in place. Anyone can call themselves a "coach" and for that matter, one can purchase "coaching certification" from a variety of web sites. Always check out the background of those who market themselves as coaches. They should at least have a bachelor's degree if they purport to be any kind of professional.

Also, beware the caregiving coach who wants to make you a better caregiver by suggesting ways to try harder or only to write in a journal. This emphasis normally includes no practical help for the frustrated, grieving, depressed caregiver. Be a little cautious about faith-based programs in that their message could be more theological than practical. You are in need of genuine solutions that produce real change.

FIND A SUPPORT GROUP

Finding the right support group can be difficult. Support groups tend to focus on one kind of disease process, such as Alzheimer's disease, or multiple sclerosis. Depending on the exact nature of the ill spouse's disability or disease, it may be possible to find one of these focused groups. The down side is that these groups often focus on how to *be* a better caregiver by delivering education about the disease process, not what most spousal caregivers need. Rhonda attended a support group for caregivers who were taking care of loved ones with Alzheimer's disease. She was not comfortable and she left feeling defeated. The age group was not that of her cohorts and the recollections of "good times past" was something to which she could not relate. It is essential to find a support system that can be beneficial.

These some support groups can be unintentionally harmful by implying that it is not appropriate for caregivers to complain. Also, caregivers in some of these groups engage in subtle competition to determine who is the most dedicated and justify their own hard work as a caregiver. The authors think such competitors may be displaying how close they are to being burned by the heat of Caregiver Hell. Because these competitive caregivers are misguided, they will dominate sessions by sharing their success stories and spewing how happy they are to be caring for an ill spouse, their mother or other family member.

The happy tales of these competitive souls may leave the rest of us, the support group attendees, wondering what we are doing wrong—we are not that happy. We begin to think we are bad people because we do not feel this same joy in the tasks of being a homebound nurse. Instead, we leave the support group meetings thinking about to the last time we yelled at our spouse or groaned when they needed the bathroom for the hundredth time.

Look for support groups that *nurture* the caregiver. It is entirely appropriate to quiz a group leader about the overall tone and philosophy of the group. Find out who is sponsoring the group, and the mission of the sponsor. Then find out all you can about any specific support group, regardless of what they call themselves or who sponsors it. Judge for yourself the tone and philosophy of the group by interviewing a participant or the leader. The internet is so vast that it is likely you can find an online forum that is exactly targeted to your situation. Do not forget about the Well Spouse Association, the organization that was of such great help to the authors. Spousal caregivers fit in no matter what the disabling situation.

If there is nothing, even online, that seems like it would be helpful, an activity group that is not a support group, such as a bowling league or bridge club, at least puts caregivers into contact with people. Caregiving is such a solitary activity that social groups can at least bestow some normality on the caregiver. Complete isolation is the breeding ground of depression and irrational behavior of one sort or another.

FIND A CONFIDANT OR ONGOING EMOTIONAL SUPPORT

Caring for an ill spouse can be an especially lonely and thankless job. Particularly if the pre-illness marriage was good, the illness or disability can rob the caregiver of their best friend. Aside from the all-important function of staving off loneliness, a confidant can help the caregiver in quest of TTC status to stay focused on the goal. Caregivers get lost in misery. We are bogged down in the dirty details of caregiving. We often need help to see the big picture, to look at the situation from 30,000 feet rather than 6 inches. A confidant can remind us of what is possible, and help us monitor our progress toward ultimate relief.

A word of caution is in order here. Do not expect the confidant to volunteer time as a substitute caregiver, or run errands for you. As soon as the confidant suspects you want respite care or messenger services, in addition to a person to talk to, the confidant may disappear. Confidants are pure gold playing only that role, and they are hard to find. Do not fall into the trap of exploiting a friendship. Be polite, grateful, and generous with the confidant. You need the confidant more than they need you.

ॐॐ

David once needed a night away. He thought he would ask Kate's best friend, Bonnie, to assist for the evening. Bonnie came to their home quite often and would spend the night when she did not want to drive back home. Bonnie and David had been each other's confidants for years, too. Bonnie's husband had been ill often and she seemed to understand David's need for respite. The couples had decades of friendship behind them.

Because of the longevity of the friendship, he made his plans in advance assuming Kate's friend would gladly stay the night with her. Upon hearing his request for staying the night, Bonnie, declined in a huff of anger stating that she could not care for Kate and to never put her in that position again. David was flabbergasted and realized that offers of help were actually perfunctory acts of social niceties.

෨෬

As mentioned earlier in this book, non-caregiver friends and acquaintances, relatives and in-laws are not good choices for a confidant. Much as we want to believe those close to us will be sympathetic, chances are excellent that their self-interest (see Travland's Law) will overwhelm their compassion. Find someone who has no stake in the outcome of your struggles to attain TTC status.

The ideal confidant might be a non-spousal caregiver. Those who care for elderly parents, for example, have experienced the sacrifices involved and the daily details of intimate care, but might have few preconceptions about caring for an ill spouse. There might be non-spousal caregivers in social groups, such as a bowling league. Staff members of home health care agencies might know of someone who would make a good confidant. Physicians and nurses who care for the ill spouse would probably be able to steer you to someone. A member of a support group is one place to look for someone. The only down side is that caregivers who attend support groups sometimes are victims of the Deadly Misconceptions themselves and attend such groups to commiserate with fellow martyrs. Such a person might make matters worse; just keep looking until it "clicks."

IMPOSE A SCHEDULE ON THE ILL SPOUSE

Depending on the quality of the pre-illness relationship, ill spouses have been known to take unfair advantage of their caregivers' good nature. Caregivers are naturally compassionate, and are especially prone to self-sacrifice in situations where someone is sick or injured. For many, this might have begun in childhood in the form of nurturing injured birds or sick puppies.

Allowing what is inherently an unbalanced relationship to shift toward even greater inequity is dangerous. The TTC stays alert to demand-creep, the subtle and gradual escalation of demands. Unchecked, this pattern can run the caregiver ragged, and hasten burnout.

In an ideal world, the caregiver could approach the ill spouse, point out the problem, and ask for some cooperation. In situations preceded by a wonderful pre-illness marriage, that might work well. The ill spouse may even suggest a new schedule. In some instances, the ill spouse will resist giving up perks, even in the service of a better relationship with their caregiver. Since they own the majority of voting stock, caregivers technically do not need to ask for permission to create a schedule and make it stick. Caregivers would improve their journey to TTC status by devising a schedule that is responsive to the needs of the ill spouse but, most importantly, to the needs and wants of the caregiver. The schedule can then be announced, described and implemented.

For example, the caregiver might build a schedule around mealtime, and bedtime. From 7 to 10 AM, the caregiver is available to prepare breakfast, attend to toileting needs, change sheets, and prepare a bag lunch to be left with the ill spouse. From 10 AM until 4 PM, the caregiver has no responsibilities to the ill spouse. From 4 PM until 7 PM, the caregiver attends to dinner, bath, and tucking the ill spouse in for the night. That leaves from 7 PM until bedtime as free time for the caregiver; to watch TV, read a book, do crafts, or visit with a friend. The caregiver can impose a new structure on the caregiving arrangement that will provide respite for the caregiver on a daily basis.

Schedules do not have to look like a conventional day. Perhaps your ill spouse does not sleep well during the night and you are up all night every night. Unconventional schedules are certainly possible, as with workers on the night shift. They eat dinner at 8AM, for example. Nothing prevents the caregiver from creatively scheduling around the natural rhythms of the ill spouse.

MAKE EXCUSES TO GET OUT OF THE HOUSE—LIE IF NECESSARY

If for some reason the schedule option described above is unrealistic, the next best thing is to create "reasons" for getting away. It could be shopping, going to the bank, looking for a gift for a friend's birthday, or looking up some medical information at the library. Little white lies like this should not be necessary if the relationship between spouses is mutually satisfactory, but if civility is periodically lacking, the excuses can head off needless yelling and anguish.

RESEARCH AVAILABLE RESPITE CARE

Caregivers are often familiar with the concept of respite care. However, actually pursuing it may seem more complicated than it is. Respite care should actually be at the top of the list as an option to avoid burnout. Going this route need not involve the use of family or friends.

With the internet, available programs and eligibility information are literally at your fingertips. Our experiences indicate that working through an agency or an adult sitting service is safer than hiring a stranger. Agencies pre-screen sitters and are bonded. The wrong person can be a problem inside your home because of potential theft, disregard for duties and crossing professional boundaries.

For example, Peter interviewed several agencies and individuals to provide respite for his wife. Tammy, a certified nursing assistant, was hired as an independent contractor. This was going to be her second job when she was not on duty in the nursing home. Initially, it was working the way they planned. After a few weeks, the aide became unreliable using car trouble as the excuse. Then she wanted to borrow money, and she began spending a lot of time complaining about her personal life, both to Peter's wife and to others using the family telephone.

Tammy's personal problems began to affect how Peter's ill spouse interacted with Tammy. Peter's wife was afraid to request assistance from the aide. She felt she was a burden and did not want to upset Tammy. This paradigm is common and because some of our dependant spouses are trying to please us, this intimidation can go unreported. Our ill spouse may wait until the situation is intolerable to tell us there is a problem with the aide's performance.

The lesson here is to be vigilant about remaining the employer, not the friend. For many caregivers, it is the first time they are in the position to be the "boss" and it can be uncomfortable. Caregivers have enough problems without the addition of respite care providers' issues. They are being paid to perform a service and the caregiver is in charge. If it is not working out you have to let them know or let them go.

In another situation, Kelly, an independent contractor for sitting services, was hired to care for Maggie's husband. Kelly came with references and interviewed well. The ladies became friendly. Kelly was hired to stay for weekends. Six months into the relationship, Maggie noticed that jewelry was missing from the house and so were some checks she kept in the desk. Maggie had a hard time believing Kelly would do this. After reporting the theft to the police department, Maggie learned that befriending caregivers is a tactic used by professional thieves.

In an unbelievably silly example, Jenny hired a sitter to stay with her mother. While Jenny was away, Shirley, the sitter, thought she had found "breath freshener" on Jenny's key chain. When Jenny returned home, she found Shirley writhing in pain on the floor by the front door. What Shirley had assumed was breath freshener was actually mace and she had sprayed it in her mouth. Needless to say, care had not been provided that day.

The point of these stories is not to make a caregiver afraid of trying to hire an independent aid or sitter, but rather to suggest caution. It may be worth the extra expense to hire a company that conducts background checks. The prices are nominal considering an independent contractor is likely to be less expensive than using an agency.

The companion companies or home health agencies are a little more expensive, but they provide stability and can rotate employees to ensure convenient coverage. If you are dissatisfied with service, there is a supervisor to call. Insurance policies and charitable programs can sometimes help offset the expense of an agency.

Another option is a respite program at a long-term care facility (nursing home) or assisted living facility (ALF). Many of these facilities offer short-term (temporary) admissions. Many well spouses have promised that they would never admit their husband or wife to a nursing home, and the very topic can elicit a resounding "No way." Caregivers often feel guilty for considering this option, but there are some real advantages to a temporary placement.

The lucid ill spouse can be involved in a frank discussion as to why the temporary move is necessary for the caregiver. As we have pointed out repeatedly in this book, it is damaging to both partners if the caregiver's needs are not met. The upside to this option is that caregivers can seek respite inside their own home, catch up on chores they have been putting off or catch up on long overdue sleep in the comfort of their own bed.

The real bonus to this option is that after the first facility placement for respite is successful, the ill spouse is more likely to be agreeable the next time the caregiver needs a break. After all, for the ill spouse it is also a break from the caregiver. This gives them the chance to have a change of scenery and invoke some independence they may have lost.

Many of these facilities are good at treating the ill spouse as a special guest. The programs are part of their marketing strategy. The intention is to be the facility of choice if or when long-term placement becomes necessary. Caregivers should look for these opportunities. Provided the level of supervised care is appropriate, a retirement community ALF can allow the caregiver to schedule extra services, such as salon services or shopping trips.

RESEARCH AVAILABLE HOME HEALTH CARE AGENCIES

Home health care agencies serve an important function for ill patients who are being cared for at home. These agencies hire professional nurses, usually Licensed Practical Nurses (LPNs) and Certified Nursing Assistants (CNAs) to provide the hands-on care, supervised by a Registered Nurse (RN). They maintain a relationship with a select number of physicians in the community. The physicians often recommend follow-up care by a home health agency, and will recommend the one with which they are affiliated. They will write an order to use home health care, which directs the efforts of the agency and sets the stage for health insurance to pay for the services.

Normally the doctor's order specifies how long the care should be provided, and that will influence how long the insurance will pay for agency visits to the home. The patient can request the in-home care continue after the insurance runs out, but that would be "private pay," or at the expense of the caregiver or patient.

It is essential for the caregiver engaging the services of a home health care agency to arrive at a mutually satisfactory definition of who will actually provide the care. Many such agencies operate on what might be called a "turnkey" approach. They envision themselves as trainers or teachers, showing the caregiver how to provide the care and then supervising the caregiver. If the caregiver is willing and able, an arrangement like this is workable, especially if the health insurance provides for a very short agency presence and if the care required is not too technical.

However, if the care required in the home is potentially dangerous, such as when it involves communicable diseases, requires sterile bandaging, or involves wound care, the health care professionals themselves should provide the actual care. Caregivers may have to insist on this approach, because agency personnel can assume that the caregiver wants to do the work, or insist that the caregiver take an active part in the process as part of "training." For the caregiver it is best to perform only the services you select, feel comfortable doing and can routinely deliver. Nobody wins if care delivery is not handled properly.

❧

David engaged a home health care agency to care for Kate's open wounds. The professionals tended to apply one bandage to her multiple wounds, and then insist that David tend to the rest. David was too uninformed to say "no" to all this and too naïve to recognize the legal problems. He did not have the wound management education to assess the implications of why the wounds kept getting worse and worse. Finally, Kate required wound care in a hospital, partly the fault of the agency.

৵৹

RESEARCH AVAILABLE DAY PROGRAMS FOR CHRONICALLY ILL ADULTS

As with all the options, an internet search can help create a list of programs and contacts to begin planning. Some day programs specialize in specific illnesses or disabilities.

The ill spouse may reject the idea of 'daycare,' but the good programs are stimulating and fun. They provide appropriate physical activity and socialization that our ill spouses are not likely to get at home. There are programs throughout local communities that cater to early onset dementia and other more youthful disabilities. Our needs are changing in U.S. health care and so are the community-based programs.

If all the leads for day programs for your ill spouse seem to be getting nowhere, a little creativity may be in order. What activities would my ill spouse enjoy without me, such as card games? Bridge and poker can provide for the opportunity to host a game at your house. Set-up would be an added responsibility, but with preparation, it can provide enough time with others in the house to let the caregiver leave for a couple of hours. The authors have found ill spouses enjoy entertaining without the well spouse around. It lets them be "normal" for a while.

Along these same lines, the caregiver can host a meal and invite the ill spouse's old friends. The friends may feel guilty about not coming by more often to visit. In a larger group setting, they will feel more at ease. Use the guilt to your advantage by leaving the house while they visit. If a meal seems too expensive, try potluck (everyone brings a dish). Or, invite them over for wine and cheese and make it a BYOB (you provide the cheese). The party could be fun.

The point is to brainstorm about what would engage your spouse, provide a few hours of separation and fulfill both sets of needs.

In another variation, a monthly card game can be held at the homes of other people. You transport your partner to the game and depart. The same suggestion is made for meals out with friends.

If the ill spouse had been involved in leagues or clubs, it may be a good time to look at rekindling the involvement. For example, cancer survivors and MS sufferers, who are not at fully healthy, may have dropped out of their club involvement during treatment or periods of declining health. Now they are feeling a little better, they feel out of place and are intimidated to return to their social life. Many clubs members will express genuine interest in assisting you in getting the ill spouse involved again.

One option proposed to some caregivers for early/mild dementia patients is to find a safe place for the ill spouse to volunteer. This takes planning and research, but can be helpful in the proper setting. Some volunteer coordinators for organizations will be accommodating if they know in advance that reminders and cuing will be needed for your loved one.

Some of our ill spouses suffer from multiple disorders. If the program specializing in one of the disorders is not working out, try going after service under the flag of another disorder. For example, Andy had dementia of the Alzheimer's type. He is younger than most of the typical victims of the disease. The Alzheimer's support group he first attended was not meeting his needs. He could not relate to their issues because the other participants were up to thirty years his senior.

His wife looked for other options by making a list of what else was wrong with him. What she found was a program that catered to people suffering with anger management problems. For a month, he attended an anger management group five days a week. He loved the outing. Did it help him? No, not really, but it was a help to *her*.

When that program concluded, she had already found a support group for depression and he attended until it ran its course. She followed that group with one that dealt with people suffering from bipolar disorder. Friendships developed eventually and Andy was able to join a regular card game. The lesson here is to be creative when looking for *your own* escape.

CONSIDER AN ASSISTED LIVING FACILITY OR NURSING HOME FOR THE ILL SPOUSE

As mentioned earlier, this decision is difficult for all partners and it may mean a caregiver is breaking what once was a sincere promise. Nevertheless, sometimes breaking this promise is the most humane thing we can do as a caregiver. There are some real benefits to consider of a long-term placement. Placing an ill spouse in a facility does not mean you have relinquished your identity, compassion or role as a caregiver.

On the contrary, your role as caregiver will be at least as important as before. Your spouse will need you in a role of advocate, adviser and friend. Those roles may be more in keeping with your original marital relationship. You may find your relationship is more rewarding than when you had the entire responsibility at home.

Professionals will provide the care your ill spouse needs, and you as a caregiver will begin to recover from possible burnout. For some disabled spouses, the placement in an ALF allows for a resurgence of independence they thought they had lost. Assisted living facilities have certain self-care and independence criteria that a resident must meet to stay there. If those criteria are not met, a nursing home must be considered.

Caregivers frequently commit the kinds of boundary errors discussed earlier in the book. By helping them so much, we inadvertently hurt them by doing too much for them. We wait on them; they get used to it, and become too dependent on us. The ALF setting allows them to regain some of their independence, which will enhance their dignity and quality of life. Our ill spouse may not consider this a compassionate choice, at least initially, but our job as caregivers is to stay objective and be strong when necessary. Nevertheless, if we know that the move was best for their well-being and ours, then the choice was a good one. There is no reason to feel guilty.

In general, nursing homes have a poor reputation. The stereotype is unfortunate and based on the publicized practices of a few problem facilities. While there is some variation in quality, there are a great many very good facilities with dedicated employees. The employees are specialists. They are well trained at all levels to provide the best care for our loved ones. When the ill husband cannot swallow properly, the dietary department must meet his dietary needs. When the ill wife cannot toilet herself, the nursing staff must help her. When our life partner suffers a stroke (even if it was years ago), the appropriate therapeutic disciplines will make every effort to help the patient regain whatever independence is possible.

Professional staff members in these facilities have chosen to work in a long-term care setting; most do it with pride. Most of the professionals did not become full time employees at a nursing home by default, as some caregivers may have assumed. They deliberately chose "long-term care" as a specialty rather than pediatrics, surgery or psychiatry. Each department provides unique services to ill spouses, exceeding in quality what is normally available in the home.

Here are some of the ways caregivers can continue to stay involved with their ill spouse. Be involved in the life of your spouse at the facility. This can range from frequent visits to staying all day, depending on your schedule. You can help your loved one eat or you can eat with your spouse. Order a meal from dietary or bring in your own; talk to the staff, tell them "thank you." Let them know with civility when they are doing something you do not like. Talk to the care providers first before going to their supervisor or to the facility administrator. The respect you demonstrate to them will be rewarded with more attention to your spouse. Do not be remiss in complimenting the staff. Often the compliment and "thanks" will be deeply appreciated. As with many things in life, we hear the negative, but not the positive. Then let the supervisor and administrator know about the compliment. When the entire staff knows we are involved and interested in the care our spouse is receiving they are all on alert.

If you have your spouse's permission (via HIPPA forms) to attend, you will be invited to participate as a part of the care plan team. This is a regularly scheduled progress review by all departments to make sure your spouse is thriving in this environment. Participate in "family" events planned by the activities department. The visible and sociable spouse (not a chronic complainer) at the nursing home will be a regular reminder that the spouse's care is being scrutinized. The comfort of family members is also a concern of the "customer service" program of the facility. Your spouse is covered by a Residents' Bill of Rights. Know them and hold the facility accountable for honoring them. Encourage your spouse, if possible, to participate in the Resident's Council.

જે•ન્ડ

Sally was very much in love with her much older husband, Paul. He developed dementia and declined rapidly after diagnosis. Sally could not handle all of Paul's needs in their home, but she did not want to spend her days without him. She came into the facility every morning for breakfast, stayed with Paul until after dinner, and helped him get ready for bed. Sally became part of the facility's volunteer program. She helped with activities and offered suggestions to the staff to make life better for all residents. On those days when she played tennis, she came for breakfast, left to play tennis, and returned in the afternoon.

The placement of Paul in a facility did nothing to affect adversely their lives. She adhered to the life style they had enjoyed as a couple. She continued her hobbies and Paul was able to be with his wife every day. They were both happier than if Paul had remained in the home.

જે•ન્ડ

There are times when nursing home placement is necessary and unexpected; there is little time to plan for the admission. The suggestions above are still valid; *stay involved* with your spouse during his nursing home stay, even if it is viewed as a short-term stay for rehabilitation. If the spouse is resisting placement, it is important to try to 'sell' them on the idea rather than showing exasperation at the caregiving burden. The diplomacy will make for a better stay for the spouse and lessen the likelihood they will feel abandoned.

ॐ॰ॐ

Rhonda warned Andy that another outburst of violence was going to lead to permanent separation. Even if he could not help it (that it was the disease and not his fault) she could not live like that anymore. So, the next time he behaved in a threatening manner, he was escorted from the home. He resided in a string of ALFs until he found one that suited him and the surrounding financial constraints. He began over the course of a few years to develop some of the long gone independent skills that he had abandoned in allowing Rhonda to take over his life.

Kate and David had been discussing the options as his Caregiver Hell escalated. Her wounds were not healing and her skin was a serious concern for him. A doctor told David that no matter how hard he was trying, there was always the chance that she was going to need more help. The advice included information about how an agency nursing assistant might report him to the state authorities because her wounds were not healing. The thought of being accused of neglect worried David and he resolved to get Kate more help by speaking all of her physicians and getting their opinions.

One doctor admitted Kate to a hospital for wound management and from there Kate went to a skilled nursing facility. Once David had his unexpected respite, he realized he could no longer do this type of nursing anymore. It was killing him and possibly hurting her. He would not agree to provide her in-home care upon discharge. He insisted that the discharge planners understand he could not physically do it anymore and that it was incumbent upon the facility planners to understand Kate's needs if he was not able to do it. Now then, what were their options?

ॐ॰ॐ

FACILITY SHOPPING

A well spouse looking for the right facility needs to consider the following:

*1. **Tour the facility.*** Do not schedule a tour. Arrive without warning during business hours and get a "feel" for how you are received. If the staff does not have time to tell you about the facility or take you on a tour, find out why. If the answer seems reasonable, then return later. Again, do not schedule a tour, but ask what time of the day someone could be available.

You should be interested in how the facility handles a disruption in routine. If you find that the staff is hurried, dismissive or abrupt, that may describe the culture of the facility. It could indicate how the staff handles unplanned needs of residents.

During your tour, listen carefully and see if you are invited back "anytime" while you compare facilities. Assisted Living Facilities may have a more open door visitation policy than a nursing home. Those residents sign out more frequently and have more guests coming and going. Nursing home personnel are trained to look for unfamiliar faces and to greet them with a polite "may I help you" because the residents are often vulnerable. They are also attuned to confused residents who may be at risk for "elopement."

Do not bring a camera to take pictures while you tour. Some may think this policy is about "covering up" and not wanting photos circulating depicting the inside of a nursing home. Actually, it is about protecting the privacy of the residents who live in the facility. These buildings are their home; most of us do not like our photos taken by a stranger in our own home.

*2. **Look around.*** Do the residents seem engaged? Do they seem like they are "at home?" While on the tour, do the residents interact with the staff members? Did the tour guide acknowledge and say "Hi" to the residents while you were walking through? Do the living quarters appear to be personalized? If the tour guide shows you a resident's room, did they knock on the door and ask for permission to enter? Some facilities will have an agreement with residents that they may show their rooms on tours. Some residents enjoy being a part of that aspect of their community. Did you see any restraint devices in use? Were catheter bags hanging from wheelchair without a cover? Were the bags dragging the floor? Were the residents' feet covered? Did their hair look combed, or did they have "bed head?" Were the residents smiling? Did they appear engaged with each other?

Did you see residents gathered together talking or participating in activities? Is there a designated smoking area for them to use or are they sharing a smoking space with the staff? Shared smoking areas erode the professionalism of the staff, and residents could overhear the informal chatter from the relaxed staff, often about residents, a violation of privacy.

∾∞

Rhonda once worked for a corporation who managed nursing homes. Her assigned nursing home had a façade designed to be a porch. It had fans, rocking chairs and ashtrays. It was comfortable. The residents gathered in the front to chitchat, get fresh air or visit with their families. The residents would greet visitors and were the unofficial welcoming committee.

The regional director was quite upset every time she arrived to find the residents sitting out front. The director thought it was unappealing and wanted to keep the front "clean, pristine and inviting for prospective families." Rhonda was horrified by the implications and did not respond to the repeated directive in the following months "to find a place to move them." Removing the residents from the front porch of their home was inappropriate. The message from this corporate figure was to "hide" the residents of the facility.

Therefore, the message here is this, if you do not see the residents engaged in meaningful activity out and about, then the residents may not be the primary focus of the staff or ownership.

∾∞

3. Evaluate the Dining Room & Meal Times. Does the dining room look pleasing? Would *you* want to eat in there? Does it smell clean or are whiffs of urine, old food, or mildew? Dining in our society is virtually synonymous with socialization. It is also the most frequent complaint from residents. The "food" is the complaint, but often it is about much more and deserves to be probed and evaluated.

In a nursing home, where do residents eat who have special needs? Are they all intermingled with regular diners or is there a special dining area? Intermingled dining requires special attention to dignity. Your loved one must not be a spectacle and the assistance provided must be attentive and blend in with the other diners.

Some facilities have a special "restorative" (residents requiring intensive help) dining area. It allows for the resident to use special equipment for independent dining while protecting their dignity. In this dining room what type of tables are used? Is it a group-feeding table? How does that appeal to you or your spouse? Can you order a tray for a meal as a guest? Do they have special family events involving barbeques and holiday parties?

4. Do you see their survey results posted? If not, can they be readily produced by the staff readily request? Licensed facilities are evaluated annually at a minimum by various agencies. You may be able to find them on line, depending on your state's system. Many web sites publish that type of information.

5. Is the Resident's Bill of Rights posted? Does it contain information about how to complain, how to contact an Ombudsman, and so forth? This information should be easy to find and read for the families and residents. Do the residents have telephone access and/or internet services available for communication?

৵৽

As a nursing home administrator, Rhonda encouraged the residents to talk openly with the inspectors and visiting Ombudsmen. If the residents had something to say, they need to know they can easily communicate with outside authorities. Transparency is essential to the professional operation of residential living facility. Professionals want to provide the best care and need a culture that supports excellence. So follow your instincts when you visit a facility or go to visit your spouse. If you ever get the impression that someone is hiding information do some research. Medicare, Medicaid, and some insurance companies require nursing homes to make certain operational information available to the public and maintain certain standards for operations.

⁖⁔

If your spouse is admitted to a facility, continuous evaluation as outlined above is still prudent. Continue to be involved and keep your eyes open and get to know the staff. The more familiar they are with the residents' family the more the "faceless" customer disappears. Civility is the key to positive resolutions when something goes wrong. The staff is trained to understand that placements are often fraught with powerful emotions such as extreme guilt. Staff members will understand a certain amount of frustration and anger. However, if every interaction the staff has with you is laced with by accusations and complaints, they will begin to run from you when you come to visit. The informal flow of information from the staff will cease.

Our spouses need the staff to be professionally engaging and friendly. We do not want the staff personnel intimidated by family members. Staff members should enjoy the free flow of informal conversation with family members. This is how families *get the scoop* and know what is happening. This tells them when to have their alarms ring if there is a problem that will affect the care delivered.

DIVORCE AS A LAST OPTION

The authors are not keen on the idea of leaving a caregiving relationship without a great deal of deliberation. Marriage is a serious commitment, and terminating it ought not to be done without a lot of analysis and consideration of other alternatives. This book is full of strategies and tactics designed to allow caregivers to meet their own needs while continuing to care for their ill spouses.

Divorce is, however, the strategy of last resort. When the other approaches outlined in detail in this book have not made it possible for the caregiver to find some measure of joy in life, this is certainly an alternative to consider. Social and religious teachings aside, love is, after all, conditional. We get married for ourselves, not for our spouses. We enter the institution full of hopes and dreams for our own lives, and for no other reason. If no way can be found to achieve these personal goals, divorce can and, for that matter, must be considered.

There are overriding factors that must be taken into consideration, such as safety and financial resources. In the case of a spouse with a form of dementia, violence often accompanies the other symptoms. Spouses with a communicable disease can be a threat to other members of the household. As noted earlier, social agencies often provide little or no financial help, especially when the ill spouse is married to an able-bodied partner who are perceived to be able to supplement medical expenditures. Some chronic illnesses will leave a couple teetering on the edge of bankruptcy. Any of these would constitute grounds for giving divorce serious consideration.

Even with no immediate physical or financial threat, caregiver burnout is itself a threat to the health and longevity of the caregiver. It would seem pointless to live on the verge of total burnout and wait to take action until something collapses or snaps within the caregiver's psychological or physical systems.

Children and other family members might lobby against this seemingly radical strategy, and caregivers probably should explain seeking a divorce. On the other hand, by that time the caregiver has paid his or her dues by trying alternative solutions to no avail, any further explanation is unnecessary. There comes a time when divorce is a win-win solution.

WHEN THE CAREGIVING ENDS, WHAT NEXT?
The caregiving role of the well spouse can end in a variety of ways. Direct caregiving duties may end when the ill spouse requires

nursing home or ALF placement, but there are residual caregiving issues that require attention. This section will focus on what happens when the well spouse dies, or when there is a divorce. Even then, there are responsibilities the well spouse cannot completely sidestep if there are minor children involved.

The first priority for a well spouse suddenly without caregiving duties is to take stock of the damage. By the time the caregiving process has played itself out, there is always a toll on the caregiver, even if some semblance of balance was achieved for the TTC. As suggested at the beginning of this book, once a well spouse, always a well spouse. The recovering TTC will crave interactions with those who have traversed the same ground. Unless someone has been in this situation, they have trouble grasping the importance of the healing process required. This is the great value of the Well Spouse Association, where caregivers assemble and provide ongoing support for each other. Once damage has been assessed, it is time for damage control. It is time to re-assemble the pieces of a broken life, to go through the exercise of creating a new life mission, of setting some personal goals that would have been unattainable in the context of the caregiving mission.

One crucial element of healing is *socializing* in situations that had been impossible; join a bowling group, a night out with friends, walking around flea markets. Neglected social needs probably include intimacy needs as well, so getting into dating situations may be important. Often it is difficult to keep from feeling disloyal, and that is something that all divorced people, widows, and widowers have to go through. It helps to talk this through with a mental health professional, a grief counselor, caregiver coach or confidant. Good friends can also help overcome some of these emotional barriers. As with every other strategy and tactic suggested in this book, the key is *action*. Sitting at home feeling miserable is never the answer. Get up, dust yourself off, do something, take action and resist the urge to mope. Grief is real and necessary, but healing is too.

Chapter 14
WHAT WE LEARNED

The Authors' Stories

ॐ ॐ

DAVID'S STORY

As we embark on a caregiving mission, we do not ask ourselves the right questions. Ten years before Kate entered a nursing home permanently, her physical condition was deteriorating rapidly. She experienced numerous health conditions that required both ongoing therapies and many surgeries.

Much like the boiled frog syndrome, the gradual escalation of these health problems took me unawares until it had become life threatening to both of us. I should have seen the trend coming thirty years earlier when Kate refused to take care of herself. It was our first year of marriage and she was unapproachable about the problem. Only recently has it dawned on me that I married her for all of the wrong reasons. I had my own issues and needed to get my own adult life in order.

Like many spousal caregivers, I found myself in a role that was as unfamiliar as a foreign language. I learned quickly how to cook, clean, and change a hospital bed. I learned to dress wounds, empty a catheter bag and deliver IV medications. Initially, I looked at my new role in life as a temporary detour. However, when the short-term setback became years, over a decade had passed and I was still a nursing assistant. Without warning, I went from a practicing clinical psychologist to nurse's aide. My loss of identity and loss of self-esteem affected the quality of care I was delivering.

Anger turned into "acceptable resignation" and I never stopped doing for my wife long enough to recognize my losses. I essentially gave up my life and could only get through the current 24 hours at a time. Adequate care delivery was enough I was doing my duty. My wife, however, needed more medical attention than I could deliver. Recognizing, via the support group, that I was not the best caregiver for her, sparked my decision to get help. Of course, my wife was not happy, but it was ultimately in her best medical interests.

All intimacy had ceased between us many years before as she became more preoccupied with her health concerns. I assumed, at age 56, that I was a large part of the problem. My wife never seemed to think her limitations were part of our intimacy problems and that suited me because, frankly, it was not worth trying.

However, the physical adjustment accompanying celibacy turned out to be interesting. My body went completely hairless, apparently because it found no use to continue to manufacture much testosterone anymore. With the loss of my male identity, there was apparently a temporary hormonal side effect and I began to feel physically like I was dying. In fact, I was kind of planning for it in subtle ways.

Years before, we moved from mountain regions further south to a one story home where she could navigate the house. We assumed that the sunny weather would lend itself to exercise. In retrospect, it was a ridiculous plan. We cut ourselves off from our support system—friends, professional colleagues and at the time, and our only grandchild. I think we were both so unhappy with life that a permanent move south seemed like an adventure. It occupied some of our otherwise empty days.

The last three years of my caregiving was a whirlwind of hospitalizations, temporary nursing home placements, physical therapy, increasingly sophisticated medical equipment, wound care, building a customized handicap-friendly house, dental problems, handicapped equipped van for transportation and home health agencies. My calendar was full of medical appointments. She was taking almost twenty medications daily, including a great deal of pain medicine.

At home, she slept in an extra-large hospital bed rented by the month. She could not stand up or transfer, and we purchased a hydraulic lift with wheels to move her out of bed, onto the handicap potty, and then onto her electric wheel chair. Of course, she could not bathe herself, clean herself after defecating or tend to her skin ulcers. After her second hip replacement, she developed an enormous abdominal hernia, making her appear pregnant. The hyper-stretching of the skin containing that bulging hernia was extremely fragile, occasionally bursting and requiring trips to the emergency room. Rehabilitation was always complicated by the sores that continuously weakened the hernia.

Worse, she insisted that only I could clean her, bandage her, hoist her, wipe her, and dress her for the trips to doctors that only I could engineer for her. I had no help, no encouragement and no support from my other family members. As we say throughout this book, nobody cares whether the caregiver's needs are met. Everyone is just happy that they do not have to do our job.

Then there was the lack of gratitude. Kate issued orders, made demands, and assumed it was okay to interrupt whatever I was doing for a request. Yet, as always, I was determined to live up to my wedding vows. My survival depended in part on what Freud called sublimation. I busied myself with a few consulting clients and my hobbies, including my classical music collection, my motorcycles and my intermittently entertaining golf game. The main thing that was missing was companionship. I was incredibly lonely. I did some volunteer teaching for a senior citizens organization and rubbed shoulders with some intelligent and interesting people. However, I had no mate. I was despondent. I truly considered injuring myself on the motorcycle to be hospitalized so I would not have to do this anymore.

I got an unexpected break when Kate was hospitalized for about 10 days with a severe urinary tract infection. Months later, her physician told me she nearly died during that time, and if it had not been for my diligent care, she would not have made it. I can honestly say that after ten long years, it was the one and only compliment I had received for taking care of her. At the end of her hospital stay, she could not walk at all and therefore needed more care than I could provide at home. Accordingly, the doctor prescribed placing her in a nursing home for rehabilitation.

All that was routine, in a way, but in retrospect, I took none of the usual precautions we now recommend to insure that the nursing home is professional, clean, with competent caring staff. By that time, I frankly did not really care if she was comfortable. I needed some place for her to go while I continued to rest. It was a welcome coincidence that she was too sick to come home. That sounds crass, but I was truly at my wits end.

I showed up every day to visit during her two-month stay in the nursing home. I kept the refrigerator in her room stocked with her snacks and kept an eye on the care she received. That seems odd in that I did not care much about care quality when I selected the place. In an exercise in self-analysis, which is always suspect for a psychologist, I probably felt guilty for enjoying her absence from the home, and did little extras for her to make myself feel less culpable.

Kate came home for 18 months and her care needs continued to intensify. Her skin broke down even further, and she remained non-compliant with her diet. She sabotaged every move I made to help her regain her independence. I installed a pool lift so she could participate in hydrotherapy, but she rammed her electric wheelchair into the hospital bed in her bedroom the day the lift was installed, severely injuring her shins. This destroyed any chance of therapy in the pool. I know this seemed like an accident, but I cannot help but wonder if the injuries were intentional because there were going to be no further excuses for not exercising.

Exasperation set in at this point and I demanded that Kate allow me some scheduled respite. She reluctantly agreed. Help began with getting a private duty aide a few times a month. She would come over to sit with Kate in the evenings and put her to bed. Bedtime had become a long and complicated process. The demand had been wearing on me. Of course, Kate was not happy about the changes in our routines, but it was ultimately in her best medical interests. The respite evenings were established because I was leading the well spouse group twice a month.

Because of the wheelchair "accident," Kate now required even more wound care management. The home health agency personnel were not much help because they assumed their role was to train me to do the work. One of Kate's doctors warned me again that because of the state of her multiple skin ulcers, someone could easily complain to the authorities that she was being neglected, and I would be considered liable. Shortly thereafter, her wound care doctor referred her to a surgeon. The surgeon refused to treat her because she was not a good candidate for surgery.

At that point, I appealed to her primary care physician for help, and he had her admitted to a hospital with an established inpatient wound care program. After a week in that hospital, they declared they could not help her either. I refused to take her home, arguing that her needs exceeded my abilities. I was a shrink, not an internist. If the hospitals could not effectively treat her wounds, how was I supposed to improve her health status at home?

The hospital was obligated to discharge her to a safe environment, so they cooperated with doctor's orders for nursing home placement for rehabilitation. The discharge planners were having a difficult time finding a skilled nursing facility that would accept her as a new patient. Because of my wife's girth and fragile skin status, it was a complicated medical case. The discharge planners finally appealed to me for some help in locating a nursing home. They believed a personal plea by me would persuade a facility to accept her. After many futile attempts, only one nursing home in a multi-county area would reluctantly accept her. We had to pay extra for a private room so that there was literally enough floor space to handle her size. Still concerned for Kate's ego, I never mentioned the difficulty we were experiencing. It actually could have served as proof she was too much for me to care for at home, but I never used the information. I was still trying to protect her.

Throughout the last year of my caring for Kate at home, Rhonda and I leaned on each other as pals from the Well Spouse Association support group. Kate initially approved of my budding friendship with Rhonda. I had originally avoided telling Kate that my "Well Spouse" friend was a female because I was afraid of Kate's reaction.

She did eventually become angry about my friendship. I suspect now that Kate was aware that my overall outlook on life was changing because of Rhonda's support. She could see, perhaps, that another person mattered to me now—**me.** Kate objected to the relationship continuing and began issuing threats. Nevertheless, I needed a confidant and a friend who understood my pain. For the first time in years, I actually cared about my well-being. Her threats were ignored. Nothing could possibly have been more threatening than losing Rhonda's friendship. I did not consider avoiding Rhonda an option for it was she who threw me a lifeline. In that lifeline, I stopped riding my motorcycle for the next year because I had a new will to survive. I no longer wanted to have an accident. I did not trust myself to be safe and I had to work my way back to safe riding.

Because Kate was in the nursing home toward the end of our marriage and I was living in our house alone, I began to treasure the notion of complete freedom from the marriage. Rhonda had assisted her husband into an ALF and she was finding the separation an overdue parole from her jail sentence. Relatively unencumbered with ill spouses and caregiving, our friendship grew. We began to fantasize about carving out a new life for ourselves. I was consulting divorce attorneys when I discovered Kate had already filed for divorce. I could not have been more relieved.

Of note, I was set for retirement when the divorce was imminent and there was an estate involved. Over my working career as a self-employed professional psychologist and management consultant, I had managed to accumulate enough to retire comfortably. My wife had threatened so many times over the course of our marriage that she would *"clean my clock"* that I cringed at the thought of a divorce. However, I was so frustrated with being a caregiver, the money no longer mattered. I just wanted relief. I knew I could live as a pauper and feel rich with my newfound freedom.

Regarding finances, when I informed my grown children that I was friendly with Rhonda, I fully expected them to say something like, *"Dad, it's about time you found some happiness for yourself. We realize this has been hard on you. We wish you all the joy you have so richly earned as our mother's caregiver."* Alas, they said no such thing. Apparently, as long as I was caring for their mother, it kept them from the bulls-eye of being called upon to help. With the divorce coming, their mother was going to go after them for help. I suspect that they were outraged that I was leaving "mom" in a nursing home, and that I was in the process of establishing my independence. Yet, they were encouraging *her* to file for divorce. I think it is an interesting side-story. After several years, they continue to avoid contact with me, despite my attempts to repair the broken relationships. I miss my grandson very much.

With our divorces finalized, Rhonda and I decided to marry. We started over and so did my new stepchildren. Because of the illness their father had carried into their home, the children needed me to help Rhonda instill stability and demonstrate a healthy father figure. While I miss my children and grandchild, there is no substitute for having peace and being loved by my new family. I know I did the right thing for my former wife and her care she is receiving by professionals will always exceed my capabilities. I understand from mutual friends that Kate has recovered her independence. She makes her own schedule and is no longer dependent on me financially. She always wanted that independence. I now realize there were too many unresolved issues in our marriage prior to the illnesses. We were making each other miserable and had for a very long time. Forty years is a long time to make another person unhappy, but we made the excuses every couple makes as they try to salvage their marriage. This is the precise reason that we believe that the ability to stay a well spouse and be happy is directly related to the quality of the pre-illness relationship. Kate and I did not like each other very much when she became dependent and we took it out on each other in various ways. This was a poor choice for both of us.

RHONDA'S STORY

I was exhausting myself trying to save my husband and find the life I wanted to live. His needs, his wants, and his insatiable appetites for entertainment and food were my primary focus for nearly two decades. Our children suffered emotional scars from his violent nature, from my inability to break bad habits and my misguided attempts to fulfill my ideals of the American Dream. I believed in my faith, but I also believed that my situation was unique. There apparently was not a "one size fits all" doctrine that had accounted for violence, dementia and wedding vow fulfillment. I wondered all the time, *did God bless me with these children to watch them live in fear if I had the power to change their lives? Which fork in the road seems more sinful; stay in a sick, violent marriage or get out of it for safety and the pursuit of happiness?* It was a hard decision and the conclusion was not easy to reach.

Andy was twenty-four when we married and I was twenty-two. Looking back, we were so very young, but we ran immediately into his unexplained illnesses. I had not lived with him before we married. I had never spent an entire night with him. I had no idea he would reveal symptoms of illness literally from our honeymoon forward. It is possible to assume his parents had unintentionally been compensating for him while he still lived with them when we got married. With each decision I made to make my marriage better, ostensibly chasing the ideal marriage, I inadvertently made my life worse, harder for the kids and, sadly, harder for Andy.

Still undiagnosed and clinging to hope, I began showering with him just to get him to be clean. Simply reminding him to shower or telling him to go bathe triggered a bad mood for him, and resulting in his yelling at me about being a "nag" or a "bitch." I felt so bad about myself that I felt like I deserved those words. I was so unhappy. Maybe I was a nag. Maybe I was a bitch to live with. However true that may have been, I also felt quite strongly that Andy's deficiencies became my burden because we were "partners for life." I chose this marriage and I would not give up. I told myself, "This is my lot in life."

His anger and temper kept growing, in magnitude and frequency. I was approaching my wits end. I refused to confide in anyone about what was happening behind our front door. It was our business and all anyone could know is that sometimes Andy smelled bad, but body odor could be explained away. I had excuses for all of his socially inappropriate behaviors.

The isolation I felt living with this chaos was awful. There was no clear way for me to tell anyone that my thirty five year old husband would refuse to bathe, could not remember to brush his teeth, felt sick on a daily basis, hated life, hated me, and was otherwise disinterested in life. I was embarrassed, living in my own hell, and absorbed with giving the children the best possible life I could muster. The "best possible life" turned into no rules, complete indulgence and no stable parent. None of it was turning out the way I had planned; I was angry and unable to look at the bigger picture.

Andy was in and out of the hospital constantly. He had his appendix removed, followed by his gall bladder. He had swallowing tests and a cardiac catheterization. He was diagnosed with h-pylori issues, and subsequently with esophageal dysfunction. He was given medicines for migraines, anxiety disorders, diabetes, extremely low testosterone, psoriasis, and recurrent prostatitis. He would come home with headaches that would put him down for days. He thought he was having a heart attack constantly. We would end up in the ER with oxygen tubes, heart monitors and strange diagnoses.

There were specialists called in for help. I needed to call 911 once because his throat closed up. He could not swallow and he could not breathe. The emergency room staff called in a specialist from another hospital. That doctor performed outpatient surgery in triage because the infection and growth in his throat was so bad they had no idea what else to do to relieve the symptoms. Tissue was sent out for examination, but nothing seemed to be wrong. He had repeated kidney stones and more strange symptomatic trips to the hospital. He developed abscesses in his colon and no test could reveal a problem. From 2001 to 2004, we had no less than two trips a month to the emergency room. We both became highly stressed that there was never a concrete problem addressed and our medical bills were mounting.

Andy was being treated for the symptoms he presented, but never for a larger disease process; nothing made any sense. I surmised that Andy seemed to be aging from the inside out. I wanted to know if we stacked all the ailments together, did it make a syndrome or a disease. Our primary care doctor at the time thought I was crazy and responded to my observation with, *"Well, he is being treated for the problems he has. There is nothing more sinister here, only coincidence."* I supposed that made sense to me at the time, but all of these ailments for a man who is thirty-seven years old?

I tried taking the brave "ethical" view that I would love my husband through this. That all seemed like the right thing to do according to social norms. Of course, I gained weight for all of the many reasons we describe in Chapter 11. I was depressed; which I now recognize as grief. I was never going to be happy in life and I began to fantasize about death. I wanted to survive until our youngest child was grown and then I would go to sleep for eternity. This was not how life was supposed to go and I felt *cheated*. Then I felt *guilty* for feeling cheated. I had tried as hard as I could to make life conform to how I wanted it, and I could never achieve the goal.

Years later, I was still seeking resolution to Andy's problems, listening to screaming and dodging his punches. I was working myself into an early grave. I knew it and I felt it on a daily basis. We had tried marriage counseling, we tried group therapy. We tried everything. My marriage counselor pointed out to me that Andy was not engaged in the therapy sessions. He had a flat affect, but when you spoke to him in the session, he responded with seemingly appropriate answers. The counselor advised me privately that she thought our problems were irrevocable because he was so disinterested. When asked what he thought about something that was said in the session, he would say, "I don't know. What do you want from me?" I decided to get a divorce.

Six weeks later, we got the diagnosis of dementia. Even though our "normal" was so abnormal, it was still a shock to hear the actual diagnosis. That diagnosis destroyed all my plans to leave him. How could I leave a sick spouse? This was my duty. I had taken vows. *I also thought I should have gotten out when I could.* So, I hung on for a few more years telling myself I could handle it. When Andy could no longer recognize us, I would still take care of him. I promised him when we got married to remain with him *"in sickness and in health."*

The diagnosis seemed to suck out of him what was left of the healthy and normal. He seemed to be defeated and I was not offering him support. I was feeling defeated, too. His general health declined to the point where he was on twenty-two different medications in addition to being insulin-dependent. Some days he was not at all oriented and other days we had Andy back to his warmer self. I held on to normal days as if they were a precious gift. I kept hoping that the normal days were back to stay. Then as quickly as the joy set in, he would explode. My children and I now refer to it as trying to stroke a pet viper. You just never knew when you were going to get bitten.

I was frustrated, financially broke, and emotionally beaten. It showed in every element of my daily life. This became Andy's excuse for more outrageous behavior. So profoundly horrible was his behavior that our oldest daughter began to inquire, *"Does Daddy really have problems or does he just hate us?"* She also wanted to know if dad really forgets how he acted or did I (mom) just have on blinders. My child believed that dad knew exactly what he was doing and I kept excusing it. That seeped into excuses for all sorts of behaviors from everyone. Andy only acted badly when he did not get his way. His behavior, a toddler and two young daughters was not working under the same roof, but what was I to do? I was lost.

The nightmare of this time in our lives could fill volumes, but that is not the essence of the book. The point of the book is that Andy's illness is actually only a coincidental footnote. The real story is about me; what I knew about myself and what I did not know. It is a story about how I made the decisions I made, and how my own actions created my life and the hole I dug for myself.

Sometimes we are so buried in our "brick towers" that we cannot see it, but it is clear to others. I was craving a divorce, but I never allowed myself to verbalize it. I kept it secret, or so I thought. Confused about his outward appearance and sometimes normal behavior, I also began to wonder if he was really sick. I figured if he is not sick then why am I living like a caregiver? If he is just lazy then I will not play this game anymore, but I did not act on those feelings. My religion was interfering with my desires to quit. To me, some *"dad"* at home was better than no dad. I believed in the benefits of a two-parent household. What I failed to tell myself in that mantra is that it should have said "a healthy two-parent household." I decided Andy is not always mean or always sick, it is just that those good times are rare. When he punched holes in the wall, I covered them with a picture. When he yelled at me that I was a horrible bitch, I told the kids "Daddy doesn't feel well."

As far as intimacy, it was non-existent. Many years earlier, physical intimacy with my husband became a means to keep him calm and I eventually hated every moment of it. Sex became synonymous with survival. However, even that tactic did not work after awhile. We were all gaining weight, we were angry all the time, and the children were often humiliated. One night when Andy did not get his way, he acted out in a way that was far more aggressive that we had ever seen. He threw food on the walls and threatened to harm to us. He slammed the bedroom door and I called the police. I called his doctor to tell him that Andy was going with the police to the psychiatric hospital.

What took me off guard is that the doctor spent the entire telephone conversation talking to me about how I had done everything a "good" spouse could do. He asked if I was ready to throw in the towel. He asked if I was worried all the time about the safety of the kids and explained that Andy and children should stop living together. He said that dementia is too hard on most caregivers and they usually have to give up for their own health. He said for me to find a way to care for my children and myself first. I am eternally grateful that this man talked to me. I started looking harder at the Well Spouse Association web site because I was not ready to say "uncle" to my marriage. Not one to give up, my marriage was just going to take a different shape.

The episode, however, reinforced my need to stop this caregiver merry-go-round in that Andy *loved* the psychiatric hospital. I realized finally that he needed specialized help and more structure than we could give him at home. The doctor said Andy was still competent enough to make his own decisions, but I was running out of time to make some radical changes. It still took several more months to take any meaningful action. Meanwhile, the psychiatric hospital discharged Andy home with orders for outpatient anger management therapeutic interventions.

I let him come home from the hospital in another attempt to make it all work out. Remember, "bad decisions beget bad decisions." My children had been displaying behaviors that mirrored their biological father's dementia. Any of these issues would have sent alarms off to other "normal" parents. I did not address the children's aggressive behaviors and needs properly. I blindly accepted physical altercations with Andy, his rude remarks, his sexual innuendos, poor hygiene, and mismatched clothes as somehow "normal" and I would verbally attack anyone who looked the wrong way at us when we were out in public. Andy would inevitably make a scene and I would join him. Where better to vent my unhappiness than the poor server who brought the wrong order, or the bill collector on the telephone, or the sales person in the mall, or the person in the car behind me at the fast food restaurant. (*The last person I yelled at turned out to be a deputy who told me I was going to be arrested if I did not calm down; I must have looked insane for not pulling forward to wait for my order.*)

It was only a matter of ninety days before another wild episode occurred. Breaking the van door and swinging a door facing (which he had just ripped from the front door) filled with nails at my head was the grand finale of living together. I calmly called his sister and told her that either Andy was going back to the psychiatric hospital with the police or they should come get him. I was desperately fighting the very strong and real urge to run over him with the car; it scared me as to the rage I was feeling under the surface. They came and got him.

Andy has not been alone with me, nor the children since that night. Meeting David and learning how to make objective, smart decisions helped me place Andy into an assisted living facility. I learned that my paradigms about life were blocking me from making smart decisions. I needed to understand that my marriage was broken and that my "internal ledger" was way out of balance. I felt cheated and I felt owed in a very big way. I had not realized those concepts before David identified them, but the minute I understood them, I felt immediate relief from a blistering anger.

I was riddled with guilt that I had failed my family and my husband. I failed to recognize that I was also living in a constant state of grief; mourning the life I lost and the husband I never had. I was angry at the world and no longer knew how to interact with other women. I had no friends and I thought they were all idiots anyway because they had no idea what a "bad" husband really was. I could not stand being around healthy couples; I was jealous beyond belief.

Understanding that there is no such thing as "feeling guilty" because guilt requires action—you are either guilty or you are not—

was also a relief. I had done nothing for which to feel guilty. I did the best I could do for my family with the wisdom I possessed at the time.

Then David talked to me about my responsibility for the state of my life. Wow! That was a hard admission for me. No one forced me into this misery; I chose to stay this long, my children did not. Where was my loyalty supposed to be? Learning to change my goals and see my world realistically allowed me to make much better choices. I developed a new mission statement and it included a devotion to me so I could take better care of the children and Andy. Living guilt-free is an unbelievable relief. My physical health is better and my heart no longer races under stress. I no longer feel like I am going to die every day.

David's professional philosophy for his therapy clients had been that you have to admit to the problem before you can fix it. I needed a new understanding of what I had been doing wrong and why, in order to take corrective action. Truly understanding that, for me, was revelatory and life changing. I now believe that open honest approaches to life's difficulties is the only way to live. In other words, burying your head in the sand never pays off.

David's wisdom is primarily from his professional expertise, coupled with his time served as a caregiver. My skills come less from my formal education than they do from living in a crucible of dementia laced with domestic abuse. Because of my degree and professional years in gerontology, I thought I knew about dementia. Unfortunately, nothing prepares a person for a spouse with this disease. I strongly believe that living with dementia makes everyone demented by association.

What else dementia brought into our home was that our children thought "letting it fly" (as we called it) was the way people normally spoke to each other in the real world; sharp, sassy mouths without any civility. It truly seemed like Hell in my house. My son thought hitting was acceptable. My daughters began to dislike all men and thought they all acted like dad. I began to realize that no matter what the origin, domestic violence is never acceptable. I have developed a new sense of myself other than spousal caregiver. I am a survivor of domestic violence and it makes me proud. I got out, I saved my kids and I can contribute a lifeline to other women facing similar home lives. The incidence of fronto-temporal dementias and traumatic brain injuries is currently on the rise, increasing the number of families who need this kind of information to help them make decisions. Much of my information came from web sites managed outside of the United States. My resources were limited.

I unknowingly had been setting a standard by excusing "Dad's" behavior as an illness. Even though its roots were in dementia, it was no way to live. My fear was that my son would become an abuser trying to emulate his father. I was afraid my daughters would seek abusive men as boyfriends or companions because that is how their father loved them. David has helped me better educate all three of the children.

After Andy was living in the ALF for a year, he began to improve. His medications were reduced and he was acclimating well. He developed a social group and was free to live his life as he pleased. Andy had a structure and calmness that I could not provide with three young children. He was absolved of adult responsibilities and was thriving. My quest to make him the man I wanted my husband to be had been harming him and I could see it now.

What lingered, though, were the backbreaking financial expenses. I was not getting help from social services or from the ALF administration. I realized as long as I was working, I represented some kind of financial cushion and it kept people from taking our poor financial status seriously. I spoke to Andy about filing for divorce because of it. We divorced and the financial strain disappeared. The facility administration began tending to his finances and his family suddenly found ways to help him. Another year passed and Andy continued on an upward trajectory. He is still doing well, has a girlfriend where he resides and he recently mentioned that he is off the medications that I used to wonder if they were worth the expense. Ironic that when I, the full time caregiver, backed out, he improved. We are pleased for his improvements, but the situation lent itself to wanting to delve into the possibilities via this book that caregivers are actually the problem sometimes.

Finally at ease, my relationship with David blossomed. The children have a father figure in David who is responsible, loving, and who reinforces the home structure they needed. David and I have a marital contract, something we did not negotiate nor enforce in our previous marriages. We are acutely aware of our internal ledgers and we have agreements should we ever become spousal caregivers again. Arrangements have been agreed upon to preserve our friendship should one of us become disabled. The friendship is the most precious part of our relationship; it evolved as we both emerged from our caregiver hell.

As for me, dementia had stolen my self-esteem and will to live. I had low expectations about everything in life. David has helped me find it all again. David took me to a symphony concert years ago and I expressed absolute amazement that he wore dress shoes and clean clothes, and he was amazed that I could get out of the *ca*r under my own power. Our normal expectations were distorted. We laugh now because our needs in a companion were so low that it was easy, and still is, to impress each other. I love the fact he can pump gas, enjoys being clean, has never needed the emergency room in the years I have known him and never comes after me with a knife.

David loves the fact that I can still get up on my own power, I do not need his help in the bathroom and my clothes fit on regular hangers. When we go out nothing has to be prearranged because he no longer worries if the facilities are roomy enough to accommodate his wife. When you are a well spouse, you truly view the world with different eyes. We still freely talk about things we can do now that we could not do in our past life when we cared for a sick spouse, day and night. This is why our interest in well spouses and "former" well spouses needing to interact with each other regularly has become our newest mission. No one but a well spouse seems to understand. The choices I ultimately made were tough. They were unpopular with family at the time I made them and they were painful. However, by saving myself, I saved everyone else I had been trying to save all along.

PUTTING THE TOOLS TO WORK
A CHECKLIST FOR SPOUSAL CAREGIVERS

~~~

_____I understand that I am feeling grief, and it is normal

_____I know indifference is the opposite of love, and it can be harmful

_____I understand my marriage contract is broken and I didn't do it

_____I realize that I now own a majority of the voting stock in the marital corporation

_____I know what I need from a spouse so I know what to ask for

_____I understand the need to invest in a relationship and then send invoices

_____I understand that my Internal Ledger keeps track of what I give and receive

_____I know that what we invest must equal what we receive to achieve Equity

_____I know I feel "Owed" if I my ledger is too far out of balance

_____I know people who say they care about us may not keep their promises

_____I know relationships are governed by a Master Agreement

_____I know my lucid partner must be held accountable for living up to agreements

_____I understand the difference between conflict and simple disagreement

_____I understand confrontation is valuable because it leads to new agreements

_____I know negotiation works better focused on interests, not positions

_____I use politeness and civility at all times in negotiating new agreements

_____I understand the ultimate in agreement enforcement is withholding services

_____I have an in-depth understanding of the Big Club Theory, and use it

_____I know to pick a time when both parties are relaxed to negotiate anything

_____I can now admit I am frustrated and angry, and I am seeking a major change

_____I have read and understood the Deadly Misconceptions about Caregiving

_____I no longer feel guilty about wanting a life of my own

_____I know that nobody else really cares whether I am happy or not, so I must care

_____I understand Enlightened Self Interest; I do for others to get for myself

_____I am obligated to see to it that my needs are met or I cannot be a caregiver

_____I know that Travland's Law allows me to expect only what others can give me

_____I understand that the way my life is turning out is entirely my responsibility

_____I know blaming others for my problems makes it impossible to solve them

_____I understand that my misery is not cosmic punishment for anything I have done

_____I understand boundary errors

_____I am not responsible for my spouse's angry behavior or bad decisions

_____I have a pretty good handle on the nature of my psychological needs

_____I have gone to the trouble to define a 5 year life mission for myself

_____I have used my new life mission to create an action plan for moving forward

_____I understand analysis paralysis, that no decision is a decision

_____I am able to retrace bad decisions back through the chain to original bad decisions

_____I have a new understanding of how to make life decisions slowly and deliberately

_____I am now able to force myself to do what is in my long-term best interests

_____I have found someone to coach and mentor me

_____I now take full responsibility for my decisions; no more blaming my ill spouse

_____I am now able to recognize and fix my worst bad habits

_____I do not confide in relatives or close non-caregiver friends

_____I refuse to be anyone's measuring stick of misery (At least I'm not that bad off!)

_____I understand domestic violence is never acceptable from either well or ill spouse